Language and Culture at Work

Language and Culture at Work provides an overview of the complex role that culture plays in workplace contexts. Eight chapters cover the core aspects of culture at work, comprising:

- Face and politeness
- Decision making
- Leadership
- Identity
- Gender
- Work-life balance

The authors draw on a significant corpus of authentic workplace data collected in numerous professional and medical settings involving participants from a variety of different socio-cultural backgrounds (including Chinese, Filipino, Indian, British, Dutch, Hong Kong, Taiwanese and Australian). Using in-depth analyses of authentic interactions and interviews, the book proposes a new integrated framework for researching culture at work from a sociolinguistic perspective.

This is key reading for researchers and recommended for those working in the areas of sociolinguistics, communication studies, discourse analysis and applied linguistics. It will be of particular interest to students of professional and workplace communication, intercultural communication and intercultural pragmatics.

Stephanie Schnurr is an Associate Professor in Applied Linguistics at the University of Warwick, UK. She is the author of *Exploring Professional Communication: Language in Action* (2013) and *Leadership Discourse at Work: Interactions of Humour, Gender and Workplace Culture* (2009).

Olga Zayts is an Assistant Professor at the School of English, the University of Hong Kong. She is the author of *Doing Discourse Analysis* (in press).

'This is a lucid, highly accessible and timely work on a topic that is justifiably receiving increasing attention both within and beyond academia. A range of data sources are used, allowing the authors to talk confidently and persuasively on topics such as leadership, politeness, gender and work/life balance. The book should be essential reading for students, researchers and anyone else with an interest in the topics of culture and communication in workplaces.'

Michael Handford, *Cardiff University, UK*

Language and Culture at Work

Stephanie Schnurr & Olga Zayts

 **Routledge**
Taylor & Francis Group

LONDON AND NEW YORK

First published 2017
by Routledge
2 Park Square, Milton Park, Abingdon, Oxon OX14 4RN

and by Routledge
711 Third Avenue, New York, NY 10017

Routledge is an imprint of the Taylor & Francis Group, an informa business

British Library Cataloguing in Publication Data
A catalogue record for this book is available from the British Library

Library of Congress Cataloging in Publication Data
A catalog record for this book has been requested

ISBN: 9781138688476 (hbk)
ISBN: 9781138688490 (pbk)
ISBN: 9781315541785 (ebk)

Typeset in Times New Roman
by Apex CoVantage, LLC

To Linus
S.S.

To Timar and Matty
O.Z.

Contents

**5   Moving beyond stereotypes. Constructing and
negotiating identities at work**   87

Introduction 87
Constructing and negotiating identities 88
Mobilising cultural, categories when constructing identities 89
Mobilising company membership as an important
  aspect of professional identity 94
Orienting to the interactional context 97
Discussion 102

6   Gender. The interplay between the 'local' and the 'global'   106

Introduction 106
What is gender and why is it relevant at work? 110
Local practices 112
Discussion 120

7   Work–life balance. Juggling different expectations   124

Introduction 124
Issues of work–life balance in Hong Kong 124
The (perceived) role of culture, 129
Interactional evidence of work–life balance issues 133
Actively negotiating work–life balance. A case study 134
Discussion 140

**8   Understanding language and 'culture' at work.
Taking stock and looking ahead**   144

Introduction 144
Taking stock 144
Looking ahead 153

Tables and figures

Tables

Figures

Acknowledgements

The idea for this book was developed during the conference of the International Association for Languages and Intercultural Communication (IALIC) in Hong Kong in 2013, where we presented the theoretical framework on which the various chapters are based. We are very grateful to everyone who came to our talk at IALIC and who contributed to the very lively and engaging discussions that emerged afterwards and that made us think even more about issues around language and 'culture' at work.

We would also like to express our gratitude to Janet Holmes and Malcolm MacDonald, who have both read and critically commented on earlier drafts of the first chapter. Many thanks for so generously sharing your time with us – not only with regards to this book but also for your constant support and encouragement.

A very big 'thank you' also to Louisa Semlyen at Routledge for her enthusiasm about this project, and to Laura Sandford for swiftly and competently dealing with our endless formatting and editorial questions. And to Angela Chan for her assistance with the Chinese examples, and for always being there and helping out. And to everyone who has helped with putting the manuscript into good shape: to Joelle Loew for helping with the formatting and for fearlessly sorting out the referencing jungle, and to Carina Clark for proofreading the various chapters. All remaining infelicities are, of course, entirely our own.

A massive 'thanks' also to all the people who took part in this project and who allowed us into their workplaces. Many thanks for letting us record and observe you, and for taking the time to answer our many questions and sharing your stories with us.

We would also like to thank Sage Ltd for allowing us to reprint the epigraph in Chapter 4, and to Equinox Publishing Ltd for letting us reprint Example 2.2.

And last but not least, we would like to thank Andi for taking the kids camping so that we could finish the book.

1 Language and culture at work. An introduction

It's a cultural thing.

(Martin, expatriate[1] partner at a large international
financial corporation in Hong Kong)

Introduction

This book aims to explore language and 'culture'[2] at work. More specifically, it takes as a starting point a dilemma that we, as researchers of professional communication, have encountered in many of our previous projects in a range of different workplaces in Hong Kong. When talking to our participants about their experiences at work, most of them mentioned 'culture' in one form or another. Especially those working in so-called 'multicultural' workplaces often stated that they thought 'culture' had a huge impact on their behaviour and, more specifically, on how they interacted with their colleagues and clients. Just as Martin did in the quote above, they used 'culture' as an explanation for their own behaviour and also for their frustration over the behaviour of the people they work with. The following quotes are just two more examples of this:

> *Trying to get the democracy going in the office doesn't work a 100 per cent because I'm working with Chinese people.*

(Janet, expatriate owner and CEO of a
language learning centre in Hong Kong)

> *What takes an hour in the West will take a week in China [. . .]. Hong Kong is similar but to a lesser degree, really frustrating.*

(Roger, expatriate self-employed
entrepreneur in Hong Kong)

These snippets are indicative of a larger pattern we saw in our data: our participants often explained perceived differences in workplace practices as reflections of what they considered to be their colleagues' culturally influenced perceptions, beliefs and assumptions. Among the issues that participants listed as being impacted by what they call 'culture' were misalignments of expectations and practices relating to face and politeness, decision making, leadership, identity, gender and issues regarding work–life balance. We discuss these topics in more detail in subsequent chapters. These claims, however, were often in sharp contrast to participants' actual behaviours at their workplaces. Not only was the picture that emerged from observing their actual practices much more complex (for example, regarding the ways in which decisions were made), but sometimes what people were *actually* doing was at odds with what they *claimed* to be doing. In light of this observation, it is thus perhaps not surprising that 'culture' was much less of an issue than perceived in people's everyday workplace encounters.

This book takes this discrepancy as a starting point and aims to critically analyse language and 'culture' at work by proposing a way of making sense of these differences, and suggesting a possible way of productively combining participants' perspectives with insights gained from analytical inquiry of actual behaviour. Exploring this discrepancy and trying to find ways of bringing both perspectives together, we argue, is analytically rewarding and leads to new insights about the relationship between language and 'culture' at work.

So, what is 'culture'?

'Culture' is an inherently complex concept which has been defined and approached in vastly different ways by researchers from different disciplines across the humanities and social sciences, including for example, anthropology, psychology, history, philosophy, international business studies and applied linguistics. Among the most widely cited conceptualisations are the so-called compositional approaches, which generally view culture as something that is manifested in all aspects of social life – with different levels or layers of 'cultures' capturing more easily observable rituals and practices, as well as hidden values, beliefs and assumptions. The most prominent scholars of these approaches are Geert Hofstede and Edward T. Hall (Hofstede 1980, 1997, 2001; Hall 1959, 1966, 1976), who have proposed the metaphors of culture as an onion and as an iceberg, respectively, to capture this multi-layered nature. Although their works have received much criticism – especially for the relative static and restrictive nature of the dimensions they have developed along which the values and behavioural practices of different cultural groups can be compared (e.g. McSweeny 2002; Cardon 2008) – their frameworks are still frequently used in research and intercultural development.

More recent trends, however, take a critical stance towards these essentialist views of culture and move away from such static conceptualisations of 'culture' as something that people have or belong to. Rather, they understand 'culture' as a dynamic process and something that people *do* (Street 1993). They do not view 'culture' as a given, a priori variable to explain people's behaviour. Instead, scholars have begun to explore how 'culture' is constructed, negotiated and shaped in interaction (e.g. Piller 2007; Ladegaard & Jenks 2015). This more 'dynamic view of culture' (Sarangi 1994: 416) is based on an analysis of the 'use of language by actual people from different cultures doing actual things with language in actual social situations' (Cheng 2003: 10), rather than relying on anecdotal evidence such as that provided in the earlier quotes from our participants. These approaches take a critical look at how 'culture' is actually enacted in an interaction, and question whether 'culture' is relevant and whether we, as analysts, need to refer to this concept to make sense of our observations (Scollon & Scollon 2001).

These differences between earlier essentialist notions of 'culture' and more recent constructivist approaches are also captured in Holliday's (1999) distinction between 'large cultures' and 'small cultures'. Simply put, large cultures refer to ethnic, national or international groups, while small cultures capture 'any cohesive grouping' (Holliday 1999: 237). However, rather than relying on size as a distinguishing criterion, large and small cultures have a different focus. Small cultures are closely related to the activities and practices that take place within a particular group and are not, unlike large cultures, interested in 'the nature of the group itself' (Holliday 1999: 250). Large and small cultures thus present different paradigms: the notion of large culture is primarily concerned with identifying and describing differences 'between ethnic, national and international entities', whereas the notion of small culture is interested in exploring 'social processes as they emerge' (Holliday 1999: 240).

The relationship between small cultures and large cultures is a complex one, with some researchers arguing that large cultures are a reification of small cultures (Holliday 1999). After reification, as Holliday (1999: 242) maintains, 'culture appears large and essentialist, and indicates concrete, separate, behaviour-defining ethnic, national and international groups with material permanence and clear boundaries'. As a consequence, when making claims about culture (e.g. Janet's claim about how 'the Chinese' do not favour a democratic approach to decision making), interlocutors draw on notions of large culture and treat 'culture' as something people *have*, rather than as dynamically and collaboratively constructed. This notion of large culture tends to become relatively fixed in people's minds and runs the risk of leading to over-generalisations and stereotyping (see also Moon 2010). In making such statements about specific cultures, participants simultaneously contribute to constructing 'another culture' and 'their own culture', which are typically placed in opposition to one another (cf. Chapter 5 for further discussion). Thus, statements like the earlier quotes are important sources of information about the processes involved in the production and constant negotia-tion of 'culture' and, we would argue, should thus be considered in research. The subsequent chapters illustrate how these different conceptualisations of 'culture' as relatively static or dynamically constructed might be brought together, and what can be gained from such an endeavour. We show how participants' perspectives on 'culture', cultural characteristics, and cultural differences might be fruitfully combined with discourse analyses of the specific practices that construct and enact 'culture' on the micro-level of interaction.

Researching 'culture' at work

One of the challenges that research on language and culture faces is capturing the complexities of 'culture' and, more specifically, accounting for the differences in the ways researchers and lay people conceptualise and use the term 'culture'.

Although, as we will show in the subsequent chapters, much is to be gained from conceptually and methodologically combining these often different notions of 'culture', researchers have not yet found systematic ways of doing so. Instead, most studies on language and 'culture' have largely engaged in different paradigms, each associated with its advantages and pitfalls.

Three strands of scholarship are particularly relevant to our conceptualisations of 'culture' that we build on and develop in this book. First, because our study is situated in the workplace context, research in the broad field of organisational and management studies should be acknowledged. This research largely builds on lay people's understandings of 'culture', and often describes and compares the (perceived) behaviours of members of specific cultural groups. It typically uses critical incidents, narratives and survey results to explain instances of miscommunication between or differences in the behaviour of members from different cultural groups (e.g. Dekker et al. 2008; Christie et al. 2003; Fink et al. 2006).

A second relevant strand is communication-based studies on intercultural communication. Although not all of these studies deal with workplace communication, their focus on the analysis of real-life interactions in intercultural encounters makes them relevant to our research (for a systematic overview see Sarangi 1994). Within this strand, two specific approaches are particularly noteworthy, namely interactional sociolinguists (e.g. Gumpertz 1982; Gumpertz & Tannen 1979) and cross-cultural pragmatics (e.g. Blum-Kulka et al. 1989). In contrast to organisational and management studies, these approaches provide analyses of data from real-life interactions or use Discourse Completion Tasks (DCTs),[3] and therefore may offer insights into the actual or perceived communicative practices of participants. Many of these communication-based studies, however, have been criticised for overemphasising potential cultural differences as the cause of communicative problems (see e.g. Roberts & Sarangi 1993).

The third strand of research that is relevant for this book is recent work conducted in sociolinguistic, pragmatic and discourse analytic studies, which offer a more dynamic, multifaceted outlook on 'culture' (for an overview see Senft et al. 2009). Although a small number of these studies are situated in workplace contexts, their approach to 'culture' is similar to our own. These studies do not assume that 'culture' is an important contextual variable in an interactional encounter unless participants themselves are orienting to it. This approach to 'culture' does, however, face some difficulties, such as issues regarding the identification of specific linguistic manifestations of participants' orientation to 'culture', as well as difficulties in addressing and systematically incorporating the concerns and experiences of those people who work in intercultural contexts.

A possible way to reconcile these different strands of research and to build on their respective strengths while minimising the effects of their weaknesses is to approach the topic of 'culture' at work by taking a dynamic perspective. This can be done by exploring how 'culture' is constructed and enacted in participants' discourse *and* how they orient themselves to the various cultural issues that they bring up in their daily interactions. Such a combination, we believe, has the potential to lead to new insights and will ultimately contribute to a better understanding of what 'culture' is and how it works – both analytically on the level of interaction, and also as a sense-making tool for lay people. Both aspects of 'culture' are important and should be part of the agenda of anyone researching and working in intercultural contexts. In line with such a conceptualisation, then, 'culture' could be considered a tool, 'not as one thing or another, not as a thing at all, but rather as a heuristic . . . "a tool for thinking"' (Hua 2014: 196; see also Scollon et al. 2012: 3).

As Hua (2014: 199) points out, this struggle with the concept of 'culture', i.e. the very concept that is 'fundamental to the field' itself, is not restricted to inter-cultural communication, but can also be found in other fields of academic inquiry in which lay perceptions of specific concepts sometimes clash with analytical understandings and usages of the same terminology. Among the examples that Hua provides are the discussions around 'politeness' in politeness research, and struggles over 'gender' in gender studies. Since the debates about 'politeness' in politeness research are relatively advanced, in the next section we take a closer look at how politeness research deals with this struggle in its own field of inquiry, and explore what can be learned from these debates and how we might gain new insights from these discussions for our own issues with 'culture'.

Learning from politeness research

Politeness research is experiencing a similar dilemma around lay people's percep-tions of the concept of politeness, or what Watts (2003: 4) calls 'folk interpreta-tions', versus the ways in which politeness is used by researchers as a technical analytical concept. In an attempt to distinguish between these two different kinds or 'orders' of politeness, politeness researchers have proposed different labels and refer to lay people's notion of politeness as 'first-order politeness' (or polite-ness$_1$ to adopt the notation convention proposed by Eelen (2001)) and to the theoretical construct of politeness as 'second-order politeness' (or politeness$_2$) (Watts 2003). The former refers to 'the speaker's assessments of their own linguistic behaviour – the speaker's perspective' – whereas the latter describes 'scientists' assessments of that behaviour – the scientific perspective' (Eelen 2001: 30). In other words, first-order politeness encompasses verbal and non-verbal behaviours that lay people would describe as 'polite', such as saying 'please' and 'thank you', holding the door open for others, etc., while second-order politeness 'means something rather different from our everyday under-standing of it' (Watts 2003: 10) and its epistemological and ontological natures vary across different theories of politeness.

Following this line of argument, we propose to make a conceptual distinction between first-order culture as reflected in the comments of our participants and second-order culture as an analytical term used by researchers to make sense of what is going on in an interaction. This distinction between first- and second-order has proved to be useful by recent politeness research, and we believe it could also be fruitfully applied to the notion of 'culture' in intercultural commu-nication research. As Holliday (2013: 164) points out, 'it is a fact that people everywhere really do use, talk about, explain things in terms of, and present themselves with national culture profiles, despite their lack of scientific basis means.' But, as Baumann (1996) maintains, lay people's use of the term 'culture' does not necessarily coincide with scholars' usage. On the contrary, as Piller (2007: 212) argues, the use of the (same) term 'culture' by researchers and lay people inevitably leads to some difficulties: '[i]f researchers use predefined cultural categories that are salient to them as the basis for their investigations, they can only reproduce the discourses available to them (i.e. those circulating in society at large, rather than analysing those discourses critically).'

A solution to this problem, and also to our dilemma of obvious discrepancies around the notion of 'culture' as described in the previous sections, seems to boil down to the fact that we are using different orders of 'culture': i) a first-order notion of culture (culture$_1$) is used by lay people and the participants in our interviews when they explicitly mention culture to account for specific behaviours or where they actively construct a relatively unified (and often stereotypical) view of 'a culture' to which they then often in problematic ways assign membership based on ethnicity and socio-cultural background, such as when they talk about 'the Chinese' and 'the West' as in Janet's and Roger's comments; and ii) a second-order notion of 'culture' (i.e. culture$_2$) which we understand as discursively constructed rather than pre-existing, and which captures the intricate processes through which people *do* culture throughout an interaction. Culture$_1$ thus typically comes to the fore in how people talk about 'culture' and is often reflected in stereotypical claims and assumptions, while culture$_2$ emerges throughout an interaction.

A crucial difference, thus, between culture$_1$ and culture$_2$ is that while culture$_1$ is conceptualised as relatively static and as something that people *have* (i.e. individuals are either a member of a particular 'culture' or not), culture$_2$ tends to be viewed as more dynamic and as actively constructed by interlocutors as an interaction unfolds. It is important to note, however, that the notions of culture$_1$ and culture$_2$ are not singular, and in fact multiple versions of both exist. This plurality is reflected in the differing images and ideas that lay people have about a specific 'culture' and its members (e.g. about what constitutes 'the Finnish culture' or 'the Russian culture'), as well as in the numerous theories of 'culture' that exist in the academic realm.

The following short example illustrates what we mean by first-order culture.

Example 1.1[4]

Context: Interview with Susan, an expatriate from the UK who is the head of one of the departments in a major international financial corporation in Hong Kong. IR – Interviewer.

1 IR: [..] if you could just tell us a little bit about your leadership style?
2 Susan: Well, it's changed (.). [. . .] Um and-and coming to China what I've
3   realised is that the <u>culture</u> requires you in a way to do this,

4	it actually requires you to act in ways that as a Westerner,
5	I find eh eh surprising eh. I don't think I am
6	gonna have any difficulty when I return to work in- in other cultures
7	or (.) any difficulty returning (.) But it is almost as if you
8	are expected to act in these ways.
9	And if you <u>don't</u>, it <u>confuses</u> people. I think it confuses the Chinese
10	people who work for you.

This excerpt is taken from a longer interview with Susan, one of our expatriate participants, and while we will only briefly comment here on some of her claims, more and longer sections from this interview will occur in later chapters. Here, Susan replies to our question about her leadership style (line 1), which was the focus of the research that we conducted at her workplace. What we found particularly remarkable about Susan's comments, and in fact the responses of others in similar situations, was that she almost immediately mentioned 'culture' as having an impact on her leadership style. More specifically, she claims that when she moved to China (from Australia) she was required to change her leadership style (a point we elaborate in more detail in Chapter 4) and to behave and '*act in ways that as a Westerner, foreigner, you find um, um, (.) surprising*' (line 4). She explicitly attributes this to what she describes as 'culture' in '*the culture requires you in a way to do this*' (line 3). Using 'culture' here as an explanatory variable also makes her criticism of a particular leadership style and the (perceived) behaviour of her subordinates acceptable and puts the blame for her dissatisfaction not on individuals but rather on the abstract concept of 'culture' (see also Gaudio & Bialostok 2005). From Susan's further elaborations we can deduce that she has a relatively static concept of 'culture' which is primarily based on geographical location (i.e. China) and conceptualised as a dichotomy (i.e. China versus the West). Susan's use of the term 'culture' is thus a good illustration of first-order conceptualisations of 'culture' and provides insights into how lay people use the term 'culture' as an explanation when making sense of their own experiences. Although it is important to acknowledge that these notions of 'culture' are, to some extent, co-constructed in these interviews (Roulston 2010) between the participants (i.e. professionals living in Hong Kong) and researchers (i.e. academic expatriates from Germany and Russia living in Hong Kong), comments like these nevertheless nicely illustrate some of the typically restrictive and essentialist assumptions that lay people have about 'culture' and the impact that they perceive it has on their experiences at work. Thus, these views of culture$_1$ expressed by Susan and others in our interviews are important for an understanding of 'culture' at work, even though they are only one aspect of a complex picture.

In contrast to culture$_1$, realisations of culture$_2$ include specific linguistic and behavioural practices which develop or emerge throughout regular interactions among interlocutors. These practices are perceived as normative and appropriate among members of a specific group (such as a project team), though they may not necessarily be interpreted in this way by all members of a particular cultural group (see also Chapter 2). Similar to Holliday's notion of small cultures, our notion of culture$_2$ does not normally refer to 'culture' on the national level, but rather captures the practices of a workplace or a working group.

These smaller 'cultures', which are particularly relevant in workplace contexts, can usefully be captured by the concept of 'community of practice' (henceforth, CofP). Originally proposed by Lave and Wenger (1991) and further developed by Wenger (1998), the concept of CofP describes

> an aggregate of people who come together around mutual engagement in an endeavor. Ways of doing things, ways of talking, beliefs, values, power relations – in short practices – emerge in the course of this mutual endeavor. As a social construct, a CofP is different from the traditional community, primarily because it is defined simultaneously by its membership and by the *practice* in which that membership engages.
>
> (Eckert & McConnell-Ginet 1992: 464; our emphasis)

The CofP concept enables researchers to treat social groups not as static and pre-defined but as dynamically emerging and constantly changing. It is based around the assumption that regularly engaging in specific practices lies at the heart of these groups and creates individuals' membership. This notion of a CofP has received a lot of attention and has frequently been applied to workplace contexts, where it has enabled researchers to account for distinctive communicative practices that members of these groups have developed (e.g. Marra et al. 2006; Holmes & Stubbe 2003; Mullany 2006; Schnurr 2009). These studies demonstrate that there is often considerable variation in the communicative practices that characterise specific CofPs within the same socio-cultural context, and consequently that using the macro-level notion of 'culture' as an explanatory variable to account for these observed patterns is inadequate. Rather, a way forward is to analyse the ways in which members of specific CofPs, such as a department or a project team, negotiate and assign meaning to particular communicative practices, such as regularly using particular kinds of humour or employing specific decision making strategies (e.g. Schnurr & Chan 2009; Holmes et al. 2011; Holmes et al. 2007). These ways of constructing and enacting culture$_2$, in turn, may or may not be in line with partici-pants' views about culture$_1$ norms. Example 1.2 illustrates this.

Example 1.2[5]

Context: This email exchange took place between Robert, an expatriate from the UK who owns a small computer firm, and Carlson, a Chinese subcontractor who has been working for Robert for several years.

Email 1

Carlson,
Do you have time for a site visit on a job on Wednesday 10:00am?
[automated signature line]

Email 2

Sorry, I need to Shenzhen[6] on Wednesday morning, can you change the time to 16:00 or anytime in Tuesday & Thursday,
Carlson

This email exchange is a typical example of the kinds of emails that people send to each other at work when trying to make various arrangements. What is particularly interesting about this example, however, is the informality of these texts, and the relatively explicit and potentially face-threatening ways (see Chapter 2) in which Carlson refuses the request by his boss Robert to do a site visit. Both emails are characterised by minimal greetings and closings (e.g. '*Carlson*' rather than '*Hi/Dear Carlson*' and the official and automatically generated signature line with the company logo rather than a more personal sign-off by Robert) and relative directness (e.g. the question form '*can you*' rather than '*would it be possible/ could you*'). The potentially negative impact of this informality and the explicit refusal, however, are mitigated by several strategies including an apology ('*sorry*'), which can be described as a 'statement of regret' (Beebe et al. 1990), providing some explanations (i.e. that he is busy with another job), and offering an alternative (i.e. to do the visit at a different time or day). Moreover, by referring to some prior engagement (which requires him to be in Shenzhen), Carlson indicates that he does not really have a choice but to refuse Robert's request. He thereby implies that his refusal is not related to Robert personally, which makes it 'impersonal' and hence less face-threatening for Robert (Turnbull & Saxton 1997: 164). In combining these different mitigation strategies, Carlson manages to communicate the face-threatening message while at the same time reinforcing the interpersonal relationship and existing power relations with his boss.

The overall style of these emails is typical for the relatively direct communication style in which these professionals normally interact with each other and can be interpreted as forming part of the shared repertoire that characterises this particular CofP (Wenger 1998). Thus, rather than challenging Robert's face and the asymmetrical power relationship between interlocutors, the style of the email and the ways in which Carlson refuses Robert's initial request are in line with the normal practices that these two have established in their professional relationship. In other words, this direct and explicit email style is one of the practices that contributes to and also reflects and reinforces the culture$_2$ that has developed throughout the regular interactions among these interlocutors.

The ways in which culture$_2$ is enacted on the micro-level of this particular email exchange are not, however, necessarily in line with perceptions of culture$_1$, which tend to describe Hong Kong as a high power distance society in which power relations are generally not questioned and subordinates are expected to be loyal and obedient (Chee & West 2004; Selmer & de Leon 2003). Rather than adhering to the 'indirect, implicit and unassertive communication style' that is often uncritically assigned to 'the Chinese' (Chang 2009: 478; see also Liao & Bresnahan 1996), our culture$_2$ analysis provides a much more nuanced picture. It enables the analyst to identify and observe the processes through which specific discursive practices are actively constructed and negotiated among interlocutors as an interaction unfolds and how these practices become naturalised over time (Fairclough 1989), as well as how they form part of the discursive repertoire that characterises a particular group.

Thus, rather than making a priori assumptions about the role of 'culture' in attempts to understand interlocutors' behaviour (which is typical for claims about culture$_1$), our analysis of Example 1.2 has illustrated that such generalising claims are not always helpful when analysing the discursive processes through which 'culture' is actually produced and enacted on the micro-level of an interaction. But what exactly is the relationship between first-order and second-order culture? How can we usefully draw on this distinction in our research? And how can we utilise it in meaningful ways so that it enables us to move forward with our research agenda in intercultural communication? It is the aim of this book to explore these questions, and we will return to them in the final chapter.

Moving forward

Coming back to the debate in politeness research, it has been proposed that 'investigating first-order politeness is the only valid means of developing a social theory of politeness', and that as a consequence, any theory of politeness (i.e. politeness$_2$) needs to evolve around the lay usage of the term politeness without 'attempting 'to "create" a superordinate, universal term that can then be applied universally' (Watts 2003: 9). By applying this to the term 'culture' in intercultural communication research, it could be suggested that lay people's perceptions and views about 'culture', i.e. first-order perceptions about the ways in which what lay people call 'culture' influences their own behaviour and that of the people they interact with, should not be ignored and simply brushed away by researchers as (useless) stereotypes and over-generalisations, but should rather form an integral aspect of any scientific investigation of 'culture' in intercultural communication.

Watts (2003: 9) states that a 'theory of politeness$_2$ [or in our case, culture$_2$] should concern itself with the discursive struggle over politeness$_1$ [culture$_1$]' and should explore the ways in which first-order uses of the term are being used and evaluated by lay people in attempts to make sense of their experiences, rather than restricting itself to 'the ways in which social scientists lift the term [i.e. "culture"] out of the realm of everyday discourse and elevate it to the status of a theoretical concept' (see also Moon 2010). This is not to say, of course, that researchers should not aim to move beyond these folk perceptions. On the contrary, unlike Watts (2003: 11) we do not want to argue for a 'radical rejection' of the second-order concept. In fact, as we show in the subsequent chapters, we believe that much can be gained by combining both orders of 'culture' in an analysis.

This point is further reiterated by Eelen (2001: 45, emphasis in original), who drawing on Bourdieu (1991) reminds us that

> in *getting involved in* the struggle over reality, one loses sight of reality *as* a struggle. In order to avoid this, one should recognise the 'struggle'

character of reality by making it the object of research, by including representations, or the struggle over representations, in one's conceptualisation
of reality. Only by placing itself above the struggle over reality, can science
get a grasp on the nature of social reality as a struggle.

Similarly, we believe that we should not overlook the struggle over 'culture' in
our own analyses, but should instead explore its very nature, i.e. the discrepancy
between lay or folk perceptions of culture$_1$ and scientific conceptualisations of
culture$_2$. At the same time, as the quote cautions, we as researchers also need to
place our academic endeavours above this struggle by moving beyond 'getting
involved' or entangled in the struggle we seek to elucidate. We should 'instead
incorporate these representations into reality by making the struggle over them
the object of research' (Eelen 2001: 45–6). The subsequent chapters in this book
aim to do precisely this.

There are, of course, also some potential pitfalls with making a distinction
between different orders of 'culture', politeness or any concept in fact. As Eelen
(2001: 31) cautions, if the distinction between the orders is unclear or the orders
are 'simply equated, the epistemological status of the theoretical analysis becomes
blurred' and the analysis will '(possibly randomly) oscillate between both epistemological perspectives' (see also Watts 1992). This poses a potential challenge
to our scientific analyses and in a way addresses directly one of the major criticisms of essentialist approaches to 'culture'. Our analyses in the subsequent
chapters take up this challenge and aim to illustrate some of the ways in which
a scientific and non-essentialist analysis of 'culture' can benefit from a careful
combination of culture$_1$ and culture$_2$.

In spite of these possible limitations, we believe that the conceptual distinction
between different orders of 'culture' is a useful one, which has the potential to
add a new dimension to these debates and to move research forward in our
endeavour to understand what is going on in interactions. In considering both
culture$_1$ and culture$_2$ in our academic endeavours and exploring their complex
relationship, we are attempting to find ways of fusing the different approaches
used to conceptualise 'culture' outlined above. We are in effect attempting to
bring together the different paradigms associated with each. We believe that this
fusion of approaches will enable us to tackle some of the real-life issues that
lay people struggle with when working in diverse (inter)cultural settings (as
suggested by Hua 2014), while utilising scientific tools and methods to further
our understanding of analytic concepts and build theory.

Our corpus

In addressing the issues surrounding 'culture' at work, we draw on a relatively
large corpus that we have compiled over the past decade of research on various
aspects of communication in a wide range of workplaces in Hong Kong. Hong
Kong is an ideal place for an investigation of the different orders of 'culture' at
work because of its ethnically and linguistically diverse landscape. It is famously

described as 'the city where East meets West' (Chan 2005: 75; Cheng 2003; Brooks 2004), and members of the expatriate community are well represented in various commerce and industry sectors.[7] As we have seen in the quotes from some of our participants at the beginning of this chapter, this multicultural and multilingual workforce of expatriates in Hong Kong brings with it not only professional expertise, knowledge and skills but also (often stereotypical) ideas, assumptions and expectations about the most appropriate and effective behaviours and strategies in the workplace, and about how people from other socio-cultural backgrounds work.

During our various projects we have had access to a wide range of workplaces, including hospitals, a multinational corporation, two language learning centres, an NGO, a District Council and an IT consulting company. We have recorded and spoken to people representing a variety of different professions, including CEOs, Heads of Departments, administrative staff, medical professionals, patients, teachers, IT specialists, administrators, members of the District Council and self-employed entrepreneurs. However, rather than being a limitation, we believe that this diversity of workplaces across different professional sectors is an advantage for our undertaking, because it provides a very rich picture of the practices, norms, values, assumptions and expectations that characterise various workplace contexts in Hong Kong. In fact, we hope that our analyses of inter-actional behaviour in different workplaces and the variety of practices that emerge from such an approach are one of the strengths of this study. We believe that our approach is leading us to a nuanced and multifaceted conceptualisation of 'culture', in which we acknowledge diversity and complexity rather than try to generalise or ignore the differing power dynamics, norms and practices across workplaces.

Figure 1.1 provides an overview of the kinds of workplaces where we have collected the interactional data that feed into this book.

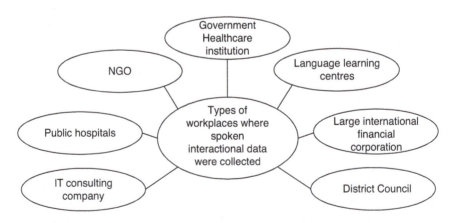

Figure 1.1 Types of workplaces where spoken interactional data were collected

All of these workplaces are located in Hong Kong, and most of them could be described as 'multicultural' in the sense that their members come from different socio-cultural backgrounds (Sarangi 2012). Using the term 'multicultural' to describe the make-up of the workforce of these workplaces is, however, not unproblematic, as the term itself draws heavily on first-order conceptualisations of culture in which members are being assigned – often in quite problematic ways – a 'culture' to which they 'belong'. Although we acknowledge these potential issues with this term and take a more critical stance towards culture, we will continue using the term 'multicultural' to describe these workplaces because this is the term that our participants used themselves and because our analyses aim to bring together lay perceptions of 'culture' (i.e. culture$_1$) and scientific analyses of culture$_2$.

Combining data from different kinds of workplaces in different professional sectors in our analytical endeavours to better understand the complexities of language and 'culture' at work, however, is not without challenges. We acknowledge that each workplace context consists of specific norms and practices which affect the interactions that take place within it and which we discuss in more detail throughout the subsequent chapters. Thus, rather than making grand claims about the representativeness and typicality of our observations, we will conduct in-depth analyses and case studies of the interactional patterns that occur in different teams (or CofPs) in different workplaces. These interactional patterns may be localised and closely linked to the specific characteristics of the professional environment in which they occur. Bringing together insights gained from different workplaces and professions and discussing observations in relation to language and 'culture' at work, however, promise to provide a more holistic picture of the complexities of actual practices and of the ways in which culture$_1$ and culture$_2$ may be relevant at work.

Collecting data

Our corpus consists of various kinds of data, including:

1   Interactional data, in particular:
    - audio- and video-recordings of authentic interactions that participants engaged in during their working days.
2   Rich ethnographic data, such as:
    - interviews with participants before and/or after the collection of these recordings;
    - questionnaires that our participants filled in to report on their experiences (e.g. in medical consultations);
    - researchers' notes from extensive participant observations.
3   Samples of written data:
    - written communication among participating professionals (e.g. internal and external emails); organisational documents (e.g. internal protocols; job descriptions); and

- samples of written communication for and with clients (e.g. information leaflets and brochures about an organisation or the services an organisation provides).

A combination of these diverse data has proved very useful throughout our research, because it has enabled us to construct a complex and multifaceted picture of specific workplaces, which in turn has facilitated and enriched our understanding of what is going on in a particular interaction and how to make sense of participants' behaviour. This section outlines briefly how these different kinds of data were collected and how much data we have obtained overall.

Although the same ethical and methodological principles underlie all our data collection, we have adapted the specific practices involved in obtaining data to the characteristics of the different research sites. In participating business and educational organisations we typically set up our recording equipment before the start of a meeting, and a member of the research team would switch on the recorders before participants started to enter the room for their meetings. However, in order to minimise the potential disruption to the work routine of our participants in the healthcare institutions, the recording equipment was installed on a more permanent basis and the medical professionals switched it on and off before consultations with recruited patients.

Moreover, depending on the specifics of the venue where the recording was conducted and the expected number of participants (which could vary from two to fourteen depending on the kind of interaction), either one or two video-cameras were used. Additional microphones (so-called 'sound-grabbers', which are very sensitive) ensured maximum quality of the audio-recordings. The cameras were positioned in such a way that they captured all participants and provided useful information not only for speaker identification, but also in terms of paralinguistic information (such as participants' facial expressions or gestures). The email samples were collected by asking participants to print out a representative sample of the emails that they have sent and received during the past one or two weeks and to redact, usually with a black marker, any confidential information including names that would identify individuals or companies. Overall, we have collected several hundred emails from eight participants in three different workplaces.

Our data collection process was built on the premise of accommodating our participants' needs and requests, and was designed to be as unobtrusive as possible to ensure that they could focus on their everyday business, which in turn also provided us with as natural and authentic data as possible. While the use of video-cameras and other equipment always runs the danger of impacting on participants' behaviour and may even result in them 'putting on a show', there is very little evidence in our data (and in that of researchers who have taken a similar approach (e.g. Mullany 2007; Baxter 2010; Holmes et al. 2011)) that this was the case beyond the first few minutes of an interaction.

Table 1.1 provides a more detailed overview of the type and amount of interactional data that we recorded in the various workplaces.

Table 1.1 Overview of interactional recordings

Workplace	Type of recorded interactions	Number of participants	Participants	Number of recorded interactions	Overall length of recordings
Public hospital 1	Face-to-face consultations	2–4	Medical professional(s), a client and accompanying family members	120	>4 hours
Public hospital 2	Telephone consultations	2–4	Medical professional(s), a client and accompanying family members	20	>3 hours
IT consulting company	Meetings, one-to-one interactions	2–14	CEO, project managers, administrative staff	15	8 hours
NGO	Meetings, one-to-one interactions, emails	2–8	CEO, project managers, administrative staff, intern	100+	24 hours
Government Healthcare institution	Telephone consultations	2	Nurse and client	50	>2.5 hours
	Inter-professional meetings	6	A team of medical professionals	6	6 hours
Large international financial corporation	Meetings, face-to-face interactions	2–8	Head of Department, team leader, administrative staff	6	6 hours
Language learning centre (Lingsoft Inc.)	Staff meetings	6–8	CEO and owner, team members	6	8 hours
Language learning centre (Sandcastle)	Staff meetings	6	Two co-owners, staff members	2	2.5 hours
District Council	Regular meetings	6–12	Members of the District Council	2	5 hours

Prior to and sometimes during the recordings of the interactional data, a member of the research team would spend several hours at the workplace observing participants' typical everyday business and taking notes of these observations. In addition to the recordings of workplace interactions, we have also conducted interviews with participants, and in some workplaces we issued questionnaires

Table 1.2 Overview of interview and questionnaire data

Profession of interviewees	No. of interviews (questionnaires) of this kind	Overall length of interviews
Nurses	3	2 hours
Patients	>110 (questionnaires)	N/A
Expatriate leaders in different workplaces	10	15 hours
Employees in different workplaces	10	10 hours

and collected written documents. These data provided very useful information about 'the bigger picture' of how people perceived working in Hong Kong in general, and as our analyses in the subsequent chapters will show, this kind of information helps in constructing an understanding of the wider background in which the interactional data (as case studies) are placed. Table 1.2 provides an overview of the interview and questionnaire data that we have collected.

The volume and the different types of collected data, we believe, put us in an excellent position to address the issues around language and 'culture' (both in its first- and second-order meanings) at work. More specifically, these data assist us in combining claims about culture$_1$ (obtained largely through the interviews, organisational documents and participant observations) with insights about culture$_2$ (gained through in-depth analyses of the spoken and written interactional data). However, previous research has often made a distinction between these different data sets and has typically classified interactional data as primary sources on which the analysis and argumentation are mainly based, and has perceived interviews and documents as secondary sources, which are often used to supplement or support the analysis of the primary data. But rather than understanding these different data sources as separate from each other – with each addressing a different set of questions and each providing insights into a particular order of 'culture' – we aim to combine them in ways that acknowledge that they interact with each other in complex ways, and that they both contribute to dynamically constructing 'culture'.

The next section provides a brief overview of the subsequent chapters and outlines which aspects of language and 'culture' at work will be covered in this book.

Brief outline of the book

Having outlined the relevance of different notions of 'culture' in workplace contexts and having introduced the theoretical framework and methodological approach on which this research is built, the subsequent chapters focus on several key themes of 'culture' at work that have emerged from our data. By each exploring a specific topic of professional communication, Chapters 2–4 largely focus on illustrating the discrepancy between culture$_1$ and culture$_2$, while Chapters 5–7 suggest concrete ways of combining these different orders of culture in an analytical endeavour.

Chapter 2 applies the theoretical framework outlined in this chapter to the topic of face and politeness. We take a critical look at some of the ways in which issues of face and politeness are often accounted for by relying on first-order notions of culture. These perceptions and claims, which often run the danger of stereotyping, are then relativised and put into perspective by fine-grained analyses of how people actually *do* politeness and negotiate their own and each other's face needs while constructing, enacting and orienting to second-order notions of culture.

Chapter 3 examines decision making, one of the activities where issues of face and politeness are particularly relevant. This chapter takes as a starting point participants' views and perceptions about the impact of culture$_1$ on the ways in which decisions are being made in their workplaces and by whom. We then critically compare these claims about the role of culture$_1$ with insights gained from our culture$_2$ analyses of the interactional data, and describe some of the diverse discursive processes through which decisions are being negotiated, agreed upon and ratified as an interaction unfolds. A particular focus of our analyses is the ways in which decisions are made collaboratively or unilaterally, and we critically discuss the link between these locally developed decision making practices (which are closely linked to notions of culture$_2$) and participants' often stereotypical assumptions about the role of culture$_1$.

Moving on from the relatively local practice of decision making to the more abstract but closely related concept of leadership, Chapter 4 critically explores the complex relationship between leadership and first- and second-order notions of culture. It challenges the assumption that leadership is a 'cultural activity' (in the sense of culture$_1$) by contrasting participants' views about how their own leadership behaviours are influenced by culture$_1$ with an illustration of the wide diversity of actual leadership practices that can be observed across workplaces. The chapter thereby illustrates that in order to better understand the complexity and diversity of leadership practices that exist in the work domain in Hong Kong, it is most productive to combine different data sources to capture notions of both culture$_1$ and culture$_2$.

Chapter 5 further engages with the notion of stereotypes and explores the topic of identity construction at work. We analyse the processes through which participants make identity claims for themselves and others, and how these identities are enacted and negotiated in their workplace interactions. This chapter brings together first- and second-order notions of culture to illustrate some of the benefits of such an approach. We describe three specific aspects of identity construction that emerged from our data, referring to how interlocutors mobilise and orient to i) cultural$_1$ categories, ii) the specific company they are a member of, and iii) the interactional context in which an encounter takes place.

Following this relatively general account of identity and 'culture', Chapter 6 specifically focuses upon the gender aspect of identity, and combines analyses of local practices with more global issues. Specifically, we begin by examining the contradiction between claims that traditional Chinese values and assumptions (e.g. highly hierarchical and patriarchal family structures in which men are absolute authority figures) are still widespread in Hong Kong workplaces and the general belief among Hong Kong locals that gender issues (particularly gender discrimination) no longer exist. Drawing on a combination of culture$_1$ and culture$_2$ examples we challenge both positions with the aim of producing a more complex picture by identifying and discussing some of the gendered assumptions and practices that characterise many workplaces in Hong Kong – many of which our participants associate with and explain via culture$_1$. These 'global' assumptions about the gender order and the roles of men and women are often closely reflected in participants' first-order notions of culture. We then contrast these culture$_1$ conceptions with two case studies involving a fine-grained analysis of the local practices of two successful women entrepreneurs in their workplace interactions. We examine how they do gender while orienting to, enacting and actively constructing second-order notions of culture.

Chapter 7 deals with another global issue that is closely related to gender: work–life balance. Difficulties around negotiating and maintaining a work–life balance are not only closely linked to gender issues, but are also among the topics that our participants have frequently brought up in the interviews. Work–life balance issues, such as expectations of regularly working overtime and being constantly available for work, are often linked to claims about culture$_1$, and are also reflected in participants' actual workplace interactions, and are thus enacted as part of culture$_2$. In contrast to the previous chapters, wherein we observed often remarkable differences between participants' claims and their actual practices, we find considerable overlap in the ways in which participants talk about work–life balance and the ways these claims are oriented to and enacted in their actual workplace interactions. We argue, however, that these overlaps and similarities do *not* necessarily mean that participants' actual behaviour (as captured in the notion of culture$_2$) is indeed a reflection of first-order notions of culture, but rather that we need to continue taking a critical stance when analysing 'culture' at work.

The final chapter, Chapter 8, brings together the theoretical and analytical insights gained in our analyses of the various aspects of first- and second-order culture discussed in the previous chapters. This chapter is the conceptual continuation of our Introduction (Chapter 1), revisiting central questions about first- and second-order culture and their roles in workplace contexts. We also highlight the various benefits of approaching 'culture' at work by distinguishing between first- and second-order notions of culture, and spell out the implications of our insights for researching language and 'culture' at work both conceptually and methodologically. We end this chapter by pointing to some avenues for future research.

Notes

1 The names of all participants and organisations are pseudonyms. While we acknowledge potential issues with the term 'expatriate' (see e.g. Guilherme et al. 2010), we continue using it, since it is the term that our participants used when describing themselves.
2 We put 'culture' in quotation marks throughout when we use it in its rather general, unspecified meaning as in, for example, conversations by lay people. By using

quotation marks we also signal that in these instances it is a 'so-called' concept and that it can mean different things to different people (see also Berger & Luckmann 1967 in Holliday 1999: 238). In the next sections we specify in more detail our own understanding of this concept.

3 Discourse Completion Tasks are tasks in which a respondent is asked to provide a response to or complete a certain situational prompt provided by a researcher.

4 Example 1.1 is taken from Schnurr & Zayts (2012) and Example 1.2 from Schnurr & Zayts (2013).

5 In all examples spelling and grammar are as in the original.

6 A city in Mainland China on the border with Hong Kong.

7 Information about Hong Kong population, ethnic groups, main occupations and duration of residency can be found at www.censtatd.gov.hk (accessed 29 May 2016).

References

Baumann, Gerd (1996). *Contesting Culture. Discourses of Identity in Multi-Ethnic London.* Cambridge: Cambridge University Press.

Baxter, Judith (2010). *The Language of Female Leadership.* Basingstoke: Palgrave.

Beebe, Leslie, Tomoko Takahashi & Robin Uliss-Weltz (1990). Pragmatic transfer in ESL refusals. In Robin Scarcella, Elaine Andersen & Stephen Krashen (eds), *Developing Communicative Competence in a Second Language.* New York: Newbury House. 55–73.

Berger, Peter & Thomas Luckmann (1967). *The Social Construction of Reality.* Harmondsworth: Pelican.

Blum-Kulka, Shoshana, Julian House & Gabriele Kasper (eds) (1989). *Cross-Cultural Pragmatics: Requests and Apologies*, Norwood, NJ: Ablex.

Bourdieu, Pierre (1991). *Language and Symbolic Power* (ed. J. B. Thompson; trans. G. Raymond & M. Adamson). Cambridge: Polity Press. (Original work published 1982.)

Brooks, Ann (2004). Changing work identities for professional women in Hong Kong. In Leng Leng Thang & Wei Hsin Yu (eds), *Old Challenges, New Strategies: Women, Work, and Family in Contemporary Asia.* Leiden/Boston: Brill. 145–62.

Cardon, Peter (2008). A critique of Hall's Contexting Model: A meta-analysis of literature on intercultural business and technical communication. *Journal of Business and Technical Communication* 22.4: 399–428.

Chan, A. (2005). Managing business meetings in different workplace cultures. Unpublished PhD thesis. Wellington, Victoria, New Zealand: University of Wellington.

Chang, Yuh-Fang (2009). How to say no: An analysis of cross-cultural difference and pragmatic transfer. *Language Sciences* 31: 477–93.

Chee, Harold & Chris West (2004). *Myths about Doing Business in China.* Basingstoke/New York: Palgrave Macmillan.

Cheng, Winnie (2003). *Intercultural Conversation.* Amsterdam: John Benjamins.

Christie, Maria Joseph, Kown Ik-Whan, Philipp Stoeberl & Raymond Baumhart (2003). A cross-cultural comparison of ethical attitudes of business managers: India, Korea and the United States. *Journal of Business Ethics* 46.3: 263–87.

Dekker, Daphne, Christel Ruttle & Peter van den Berg (2008). Cultural differences in the perception of critical interaction behaviours in global virtual teams. *International Journal of Intercultural Relations* 32.5: 441–52.

Eckert, Penelope & Sally McConnell-Ginet (1992). Communities of practice: Where language, gender, and power all live. In Kira Hall, Mary Bucholtz & Birch Moonwomon (eds), *Locating Power. Proceedings of the Second Berkeley Women and Language Conference.* Berkeley: Berkeley Women and Language Group University of California. 89–99.

Eelen, Gino (2001). *A Critique of Politeness Theories.* Manchester: St. Jerome Publishing.

Fairclough, Norma (1989). *Language and Power.* London: Longman.

Fink, Gerhard, Anne-Kathrin Neyer & Marcus Koelling (2006). Understanding cross-cultural management interaction: Research into cultural standards to complement cultural value dimensions and personality traits. *International Studies of Management and Organization* 36.4: 38–60.

Gaudio, Rudolf & Steve Bialostok (2005). The trouble with culture. *Critical Discourse Studies* 2.1: 51–69.

Guilherme, Maria Manuela, Evelyne Glaser & Maria del Carmen Méndez García (eds) (2010). *The Intercultural Dynamics of Multicultural Working.* Bristol: Multilingual Matters.

Gumpertz, John (1982). *Discourse Strategies.* Cambridge: Cambridge University Press.

Gumpertz, John & Deborah Tannen (1979). Individual and social differences in language use. In Charles Fillmore, Daniel Kempler & William S.-Y. Wang (eds), *Individual Differences in Language Ability and Language Behavior.* London: Academic Press. 305–26.

Hall, Edward (1976). *Beyond Culture.* Garden City, NY: Doubleday.

Hall, Edward (1966). *The Hidden Dimension.* Garden City, NY: Doubleday.

Hall, Edward (1959). *The Silent Language.* Garden City, NY: Doubleday.

Hofstede, Geert (2001). *Culture's Consequences: Comparing Values, Behaviors, Institutions, and Organizations across Nations* (2nd edn). Thousand Oaks, CA: SAGE.

Hofstede, Geert (1997). *Cultures and Organisations: Software of the Mind* (2nd edn). New York: McGraw-Hill.

Hofstede, Geert (1980). *Culture's Consequences. International Differences in Work-Related Values.* Beverly Hills and London: SAGE.

Holliday, Adrian (2013). *Understanding Intercultural Communication. Negotiating a Grammar of Culture.* Abingdon: Routledge.

Holliday, Adrian (1999). Small cultures. *Applied Linguistics* 20.2: 237–64.

Holmes, Janet & Maria Stubbe (2003). 'Feminine' workplaces: Stereotypes and reality. In Janet Holmes & Miriam Meyerhoff (eds), *Handbook of Language and Gender.* Oxford: Blackwell. 573–99.

Holmes, Janet, Meredith Marra & Bernadette Vine (2011). *Leadership, Discourse and Ethnicity.* Oxford: Oxford University Press.

Holmes, Janet, Stephanie Schnurr & Meredith Marra (2007). Leadership and communication: Discursive evidence of a workplace culture change. *Discourse and Communication* 1.4: 433–51.

Hua, Zhu (2014). *Exploring Intercultural Communication. Language in Action.* Abingdon: Routledge.

Ladegaard, Hans & Christopher J. Jenks (2015). Language and intercultural communication in the workplace: Critical approaches to theory and practice. *Language and Intercultural Communication* 15.1: 1–12.

Lave, Jean & Etienne Wenger (1991). *Situated Learning: Legitimate Peripheral Participation.* Cambridge: Cambridge University Press.

Liao, Chao-Chih & Mary I. Bresnahan (1996). A contrastive pragmatic study on American English and Mandarin refusal strategies. *Language Sciences* 18.3–4: 703–27.

McSweeney, Brendan (2002). Hofstede's model of national cultural differences and their consequences: A triumph of faith – a failure of analysis. *Human Relations* 55.1: 89–118.

Marra, Meredith, Stephanie Schnurr & Janet Holmes (2006). Effective leadership in New Zealand workplaces: Balancing gender and role. In J. Baxter (ed.), *Speaking Out: The Female Voice in Public Contexts.* Basingstoke: Palgrave Macmillan. 240–60.

Moon, Dreama (2010). Critical reflections on culture and critical intercultural communication. In Thomas Nakayama & Rona Tamiko Halualani (eds), *The Handbook of Critical Intercultural Communication*. Oxford: Blackwell. 34–52.

Mullany, Louise (2007). *Gendered Discourse in the Professional Workplace*. Houndmills: Palgrave.

Mullany, Louise (2006). 'Girls on tour': Politeness, small talk, and gender in managerial business meetings. *Journal of Politeness Research* 2: 55–77.

Piller, Ingrid (2007). Linguistics and intercultural communication. *Language and Linguistic Compass* 1.3: 208–26.

Roberts, Celia & Srikant Sarangi (1993). Culture revisited in intercultural communication. In Tim Boswood, Robert Hoffman & Peter Tung (eds), *Perspectives on English for Professional Communication*. Hong Kong: City University of Hong Kong. 43–54.

Roulston, Kathryn (2010). Considering quality in qualitative interviewing. *Qualitative Research* 10.2: 199–228.

Sarangi, Srikant (2012). The intercultural complex in healthcare encounters: A discourse analytical perspective. *Making Sense in Communication*. IMHSE Publication.

Sarangi, Srikant (1994). Intercultural or not? Beyond celebration of cultural differences in miscommunication analysis. *Pragmatics* 4.3: 409–27.

Schnurr, Stephanie (2009). *Leadership Discourse at Work. Interactions of Humour, Gender and Workplace Culture*. Basingstoke: Palgrave.

Schnurr, Stephanie & Angela Chan (2009). Leadership discourse and politeness at work. A cross cultural case study of New Zealand and Hong Kong. *Journal of Politeness Research* 5.2: 131–57.

Schnurr, Stephanie & Olga Zayts (2013). 'I can't remember them ever not doing what I tell them!' Negotiating face and power relations in 'upward' refusals in multicultural workplaces in Hong Kong. *Intercultural Pragmatics* 10.4: 593–616.

Schnurr, Stephanie & Olga Zayts (2012). 'You have to be adaptable, obviously.' Constructing cultural identities in multicultural workplaces in Hong Kong. *Pragmatics* 22.2: 279–99.

Scollon, Ron & Suzanne Wong Scollon (2001). Discourse and intercultural communication. In Deborah Schiffrin, Deborah Tannen & Heidi Hamilton (eds), *The Handbook of Discourse Analysis*. Malden, MA: Blackwell. 538–47.

Scollon, Ron, Suzanne Wong Scollon & Rodney Jones (2012). *Intercultural Communication: A Discourse Approach* (3rd edn). Chichester: John Wiley.

Selmer, Jan & Corinna de Leon (2003). Culture and management in Hong Kong SAR. In Malcolm Warner (ed.), *Culture and Management in Asia*. London: Routledge Curzon. 48–65.

Senft, Gunter, Jan-Ola Ostman & Jef Verschueren (eds) (2009). *Culture and Language Use. Handbook of Pragmatics Highlights*, vol. 2. Amsterdam: John Benjamins.

Street, Brian (1993). Culture is a verb: Anthropological aspects of language and cultural process. In David Graddol, Linda Thompson & Mike Byram (eds), *Language and Culture*. Clevedon, Bristol: Multilingual Matters. 23–43.

Turnbull, William & Karen Saxton (1997). Modal expressions as facework in refusals to comply with requests: I think I should say 'no' right now. *Journal of Pragmatics* 27: 145–81.

Watts, Richard (2003). *Politeness*. Cambridge: Cambridge University Press.

Watts, Richard (1992). Linguistic politeness and politic verbal behaviour. In Richard J. Watts, Sachiko Ide & Konrad Ehlich (eds), *Politeness in Language: Studies in its History, Theory and Practice*. Berlin and New York: Mouton de Gruyter. 43–69.

Wenger, Etienne (1998) *Communities of Practice. Learning, Meaning, and Identity*. Cambridge: Cambridge University Press.

2 Making it work. Negotiating face and politeness at work

In the UK people are very open with what they want to say. And they will say it.
Hong Kong people not so much because there is the issue of losing face.
(Lily, expatriate co-owner of a language learning centre)

Introduction

In this chapter we apply the first- and second-order culture distinction to the topic of face and politeness – a topic which seems to be of general interest and concern in Asia, not only to the professionals who participated in our research but also to other lay people. As Kádár and Mills (2011: 1) maintain, 'politeness is a stereotypically salient characteristic of the languages and cultures of the East Asian region'. Perceived issues around face and politeness also feature prominently in advice-giving literature and consultancy materials. For example, on the website of *ChinaBiz Consulting*, a company that specialises in providing consulting services for small–medium enterprises who do business in China, we find several 'business tips' presented in the form of a list of do's and don'ts with the aim of informing the readers about the characteristics of 'Chinese cultures'. Among the items they include on their list are:

- *Dress conservatively for business meetings. China is a very conservative country culturally.*
- *Don't immediately put business card in pocket or wallet, which is considered rude in China.*
- *Don't insult or openly criticise someone in front of others; it is very important for Chinese people to 'saving face'.*[1]

A quick search on the Internet reveals countless, similar sources which offer this kind of advice – in the form of books, websites as well as training and coaching courses. Such lists provide summaries of the practices and behaviours that are considered to be appropriate or polite when doing business in a specific 'cultural' context (i.e. nation state). They are targeted at international business people and travellers, and are built on the inherently essentialist assumption that people have or belong to one 'culture', and that members of different 'cultures' (i.e. nation states) do things differently. As a consequence, so the argument goes, when members from different 'cultures' (or nation states) interact or do business with each other, these differences almost inevitably lead to misunderstandings and conflict. This assumption is sometimes directly reflected in the titles of such advice books – for example, *Culture Shock! Hong Kong: A Survival to Customs and Etiquette* (Wei & Li 2008) and *Doing Business in China for Dummies* (Collins & Block 2007). But, as many of the examples in this chapter illustrate, these highly stereotypical claims about culture₁ do not at all capture the interactional dynamics of what is actually going on in real-life encounters at work.

This chapter takes a critical look at the ways in which issues of face and politeness are often accounted for by our participants who largely rely on first-order notions of culture, which cannot capture and are, in fact, often in sharp contrast to their actual behaviour. We analyse and discuss several examples of authentic workplace interactions from our corpus to illustrate some of the complex ways in which people actually *do* politeness and negotiate their own and each other's face needs while constructing, enacting and orienting to second-order notions of culture.

Face and politeness and first-order notions of culture

Perhaps not surprisingly, some of the claims and assumptions about culturally motivated ways of doing things differently alluded to in the list of do's and don'ts mentioned at the beginning of this chapter also came up in the interviews that we conducted with the participants in our studies. For example, many of the expatriates we talked to commented that they – as foreigners to a new company and a new 'culture' – had to learn and adapt to the normative practices and expectations that characterise their new work environment. Susan's comment in Example 2.1 is a good illustration of this.

Example 2.1

Context: During an interview, Susan, an expatriate Head of Department who works in a large multinational financial corporation, provides the following example to illustrate how she had to adapt her behaviour when coming to Hong Kong from Australia in order to meet the expectations of her new Chinese team members.

1	Susan:	say for example this morning, it happens every day,
2		just pick one this morning. So we have to
3		<u>prepare</u> some <u>detailed</u> reports for the global firm.
4		And in-in Australia↑, it's pretty <u>obvious</u> if you think about this
5		that the <u>global</u> firm wants its reports because
6		they are doing a review of learning and development in China.
7		And the automatic thing in over, say in Australia↑ would be,
8		the administration is pretty same-same,
9		they are doing their review, I might lose my job.

10	So what you-, the way you manage it in Australia↑
11	is you explain why they are doing this and
12	you-you <u>allow</u> that question-answer to happen.
13	In <u>China</u>, if you try to do that, it just worries people.
14	They don't <u>actually</u> want to know.

At the beginning of this excerpt Susan describes how she would deliver the negative news of potential job losses to her former team in Australia. According to her, in Australia appropriate ways of managing negative news would be to '*explain why they are doing this*' (line 11), and then to give people the opportunity to ask questions to facilitate their understanding of what is going on (line 12). However, according to Susan, these ways of communicating and dealing with potentially bad news would not work '*in China*' (line 13). Thus, while, according to Susan, sharing and openly discussing information may be perceived as appropriate behaviour in Australia, in China such practice would be interpreted as inappropriate and would have the opposite effect, namely worrying people who '*don't actually want to know*' (line 14).

Comments like these are good examples of what we have described as culture$_1$ in the previous chapter, as they capture participants' views and perceptions rather than actual practice as negotiated and enacted among members of a particular workplace or team. Other areas where our participants have commented on the existence of different expectations, norms and perceived practices are the ways in which their colleagues and subordinates participate in decision making (see Chapter 3), what constitutes appropriate ways of doing leadership (Chapter 4), and difficulties of maintaining a work–life balance (Chapter 7). These comments reflect people's perceptions about what they consider to be appropriate and expected behaviours in the particular socio-cultural context of Hong Kong. However, it is important to note that these comments are precisely this: participants' expectations and perceptions – they are not, by any means, a reflection of what is *actually* going on in an encounter and thus do not provide insights into how participants actually do things on the micro-level of an interaction. Indeed, in spite of the remarks by Susan and Lily, in our corpus of authentic workplace interactions we find very little evidence of any 'cultural' clashes or misunderstandings around what is considered appropriate behaviour that interlocutors were not able to negotiate and solve within the context of the interaction. But, as we have argued in the previous chapter, such comments by participants should not simply be discarded due to their subjectivity but should be considered in an analysis of the role of 'culture' at work, as they provide important insights into first-order conceptualisations of culture.

But what exactly are face and politeness? In the next section we address this question by providing a brief overview of recent research on politeness at work.

Face and politeness at work

In line with much previous research, we understand (linguistic) politeness as discursive behaviour that is intended and perceived as being used to maintain harmonious relations and to avoid conflict with others (cf. Watts 2003; Schnurr et al. 2008). The kinds of behaviours that are considered to meet these criteria are, however, highly context-sensitive and 'emerge [. . .] contextually from instances of socio-communicative verbal interaction' (Watts 2003: 141). There is thus considerable variation of what is considered to be polite behaviour – even within one language and one 'culture' (or nation state) – and no particular linguistic form is inherently polite or impolite (Geyer 2008: 7; see also Kádár & Mills 2011).

Research on politeness in the workplace has demonstrated that there is considerable diversity in the politeness norms that characterise different workplaces as well as different teams within the same workplace (e.g. Holmes & Schnurr 2005). It has been convincingly shown that the specific ways in which individuals use certain discourse strategies when doing politeness are dynamically constructed, enacted and negotiated among members of a particular group or CofP (e.g. Daly et al. 2004).

One theoretical framework that is very useful in this context is *relational work* (originally proposed by Watts 1992, and further developed by Locher & Watts 2005 and Watts 2005), because it allows researchers to capture the potential impact of context on interlocutors' interactional performance without being too rigid or restrictive. According to Locher and Watts (2005: 10), 'relational work refers to the "work" individuals invest in negotiating relationships with others'. It is captured in a continuum representing verbal behaviour ranging from negatively marked non-politic/inappropriate impolite behaviour to negatively marked non-politic/inappropriate over-polite behaviour.

As Figure 2.1 shows, politic/appropriate behaviour can either be unmarked or positively marked, depending on whether it is perceived as non-polite or polite, respectively. So, according to this framework, politeness refers only to those behaviours that are positively marked (bold in the Figure), while most 'normal', everyday behaviour that is not necessarily noticed and judged as being polite or impolite, is referred to as non-polite, politic/appropriate behaviour (the second column from the left). Behaviour captured by this band of the continuum is our focus in this chapter, because, as we have argued, there is very little evidence in our corpus of explicitly polite or impolite behaviour. Moreover, in contrast to some previous research, our interest here is not to focus on, and potentially over-interpret, the relevance and meaning of those relatively rare instances of marked behaviour, which are too often interpreted as being a direct reflection of

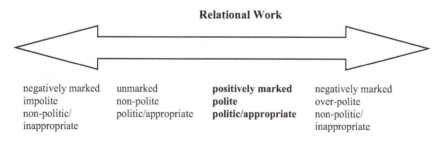

Relational Work

negatively marked	unmarked	**positively marked**	negatively marked
impolite	non-polite	**polite**	over-polite
non-politic/	politic/appropriate	**politic/appropriate**	non-politic/
inappropriate			inappropriate

Figure 2.1 Continuum of relational work (based on Locher & Watts 2005)

cultural norms (in the sense of culture$_1$). Rather, we aim to look at people's everyday normal interactional practices, i.e. at unmarked, politic behaviour, and explore how first- and second-order notions of culture may be relevant for understanding such behaviour.

We believe that the framework of relational work is particularly useful for such an endeavour, because it enables researchers to move beyond static assumptions about culture$_1$ and analyse how some of these often stereotypical claims about culture$_1$ (such as Lily's remark at the very beginning of this chapter) may or may not be relevant at any point in the interaction, and how interlocutors may or may not orient to them while achieving their interactional goals and maintaining their 'equilibri[ous]' (Watts 1989: 135) or balanced and harmonious relationship. In other words, rather than using culture$_1$ as an a priori explanatory variable to account for interlocutors' behaviour, the framework of relational work enables us to move away from potential (over)generalisations associated with first-order notions of culture towards a better understanding of how culture$_2$ is dynamically created and negotiated among participants throughout an interaction.

Central to the framework of relational work is the notion of face (Locher & Watts 2005: 12). Face is a highly debated concept and there is an ongoing controversy about what exactly face means (Haugh & Hinze 2003: 1582). As Spencer-Oatey (2008: 14) notes, '[f]ace is a concept that is intuitively meaningful to people, but one that is difficult to define precisely. It is concerned with people's sense of worth, dignity and identity, and is associated with issues such as respect, honour, status, reputation and competence'. Recent research has begun to question the relative predefined and static nature of face inherent in earlier definitions and instead conceptualises face as discursively constructed and dynamically negotiated among interlocutors (e.g. Locher 2006; Zhu 2014; Haugh 2009). In line with these re-conceptualisations, we understand face as a relational phenomenon that is co-constructed among interlocutors and interactionally accomplished (Arundale, 2006, 2010; Geyer 2008). We view face not as a static and pre-given concept, i.e. as something that people 'have', but rather as dynamically emerging throughout an interaction. Thus, face – just like 'culture' (both in its first- and second-order meanings) – is best described as dynamic and constantly enacted in interactions. As a consequence, what behaviours are considered to be face-threatening or appropriate and politic are dynamically negotiated as an interaction unfolds. This is particularly relevant with regard to our endeavours of exploring the role of first- and second-order culture at work.

In spite of considerable research on politeness and 'culture' at work, there is only very little empirical evidence to support the kind of claims made by Lily, Susan and the *ChinaBiz Consulting* website about frequent clashes and misunderstandings between members of different cultural groups or nation states (for an exception see Du 2015 and Spencer-Oatey & Xing 2000, and see Holliday 2011 for a critique of their approach). Rather than looking for instances of misunderstandings and using first-order notions of culture as a priori explanatory variables, recent research pays more attention to culture$_2$ and explores how what counts as appropriate and normative behaviour in a particular context is dynamically negotiated among interlocutors (Zayts & Schnurr 2013). For example, in their study of a factory in New Zealand, Daly et al. (2004) convincingly argue that the frequent swearing and use of taboo expressions by the members of a particular team are considered to be appropriate ways of expressing solidarity and in-group membership, and are intended to enhance rather than threaten interlocutors' faces. This behaviour, which from an outsider's perspective may be perceived as inappropriate and perhaps even rude, is understood as politic and appropriate in the specific context in which it occurred (see also Schnurr et al. 2008) and could thus be regarded as a reflection of culture$_2$.

In line with this focus on actual practice, in the next section we analyse in detail how norms of what is considered to be appropriate and face-maintaining behaviour are negotiated among interlocutors as an interaction unfolds. We have chosen four examples from different workplaces in Hong Kong to illustrate that these norms vary across workplaces and are thus a reflection of the localised norms and practices developed among members of specific CofPs (as captured in the notion of culture$_2$) rather than an indication of culture$_1$ – in spite of the fact that they may sometimes be in line with claims about first-order culture.

Face and politeness and second-order culture in action

In our analyses of actual workplace interactions in this section we take as a starting point some of the claims made by our participants and some previous (often rather essentialist) literature about (interactional) behaviour that is (allegedly) considered to be appropriate and face-maintaining in the context of Hong Kong or China. We first discuss one example to show how participants' claims about culture$_1$ may sometimes be in line with the interactional behaviour they display. In this instance, what is considered to be appropriate behaviour on the level of culture$_1$ coincides with interlocutors' enactment of culture$_2$. We then discuss several examples of behaviours that contrast general assumptions about culture$_1$ in spite of the fact that these behaviours are considered to be appropriate and politic in the localised culture$_2$ context where the interaction takes place.

Seeking advice and expecting to be told what to do

Kádár and Bargiella-Chiappini (2011: 1) note that in the 'status-sensitive East Asian social context, "polite" – or, technically speaking, "politic" – behaviour is particularly complex in institutional settings'. This sensitivity of Asian participants to existing power relations has also been pointed out in other studies. Gao and Ting-Toomey (1998: 42), for example, describe interactions displaying hierarchical relationships between their Chinese participants as 'listening-centered, asymmetrical, and differential'. These asymmetries among interlocutors are manifested, for example, in the extensive use of directives by those in more powerful positions (e.g. Lee-Wong 2000), while the language of subordinates is said to be characterised by indirectness (e.g. Young 1994; Gao et al. 1995). We discuss one example here in which interlocutors' behaviour could indeed be interpreted as orienting to and reinforcing such norms of appropriate behaviours which are often (stereotypically) associated with institutional contexts in Asia, thereby reflecting first-order notions of culture.

Example 2.2 is taken from the institutional context of prenatal genetic counselling (PGC) at a public hospital in Hong Kong. While we acknowledge that the activity of genetic counselling may not be considered as a prototypical professional activity, in line with recent scholarship (which proposes a rather broad understanding of professional communication as taking place in a context that is broadly related to work, and as including at least one person who is involved in some work-related activities (Schnurr 2013) and who gets paid for their work (e.g. Gunnarsson 2009)), we would describe the interactions involved in the PGC activities as 'professional' since they combine elements of medical consultations, psychosocial counselling and service encounters (Sarangi 2000).

The PGC context in Hong Kong is characterised by relatively hierarchical power relations between the healthcare provider and the clients. Previous research on counselling discourse in Asia has observed that patients of Asian background tend to expect a more directive approach and to be told what to do (e.g. Johnson & Nadirshaw 2002); and a study by Kim et al. (2000), which compared patients in Hong Kong and the USA, found that patients in Hong Kong expressed stronger negative beliefs about patient participation and were generally less assertive in the consultations. In our own research (Zayts et al. 2012; Zayts & Schnurr 2012) we found that during the PGC sessions that we have recorded in a public hospital in Hong Kong, the healthcare providers display various degrees of directiveness, provide advice and routinely engage in the decision making process. These behaviours appear rather marked when compared to the behaviours observed in other socio-cultural contexts. Previous studies in the UK and the US, for example, describe how healthcare providers usually try to avoid giving advice at all costs and aim to maintain a non-directive stance throughout the counselling sessions to enable the clients to reach an autonomous decision (e.g. Benkendorf et al. 2001; Pilnick 1999, 2008; Silverman 1997). The high degree of directiveness in the Hong Kong PGC context might thus be interpreted as reflections and instantiations of first-order notions of what is often described as 'Asian culture' – an assumption which we challenge later in the chapter.

Example 2.2[2]

Context: During a PGC consultation between a healthcare provider (HP), a pregnant woman (client) and her husband, who are all Hong Kong Chinese. This extract occurred during the decision making stage of the consultation after the healthcare provider has introduced the screening test to the couple. Before the consultation the couple has stated their decision to take an amniocentesis.[3] At this stage the clients make a decision whether they would like to pursue screening or testing for Down's syndrome. The exchange was originally conducted in Cantonese.

1   Client: 噉我都可以做羊水㗎嘛:
                I can also do amniocentesis, right?

2	HP:	eh通常我哋係安排一個檢驗:
		uh usually we arrange one test:
3	Husband:	.hhhhhh ((laughs))
4	Client:	一個. 一係羊水一係呢個
		One. Either amniocentesis or this?
5	HP:	係啊
		Yes.
6	Husband:	.hhhhh hehehe
7	HP:	因為既然個報告都話係正常, 其實就真係都係唔
		Since the report came back normal, actually we really do not
8		建議你 .hh唔建議你做:胎水囉.
		recommend you .hh not recommend you to do: an amniocentesis.
		((several lines omitted where HP provides some explanations))
9	Husband:	Mm mm
10	Client:	°嗽點呀?°
		°So what should we do?°
11	Husband:	唔? 羊水.
		Mm? Amniocentesis. ((pointing to the paper))
12	Client:	吓?
		Huh?
13	Husband:	羊水. 抽羊水.
		Amniocentesis. Do an amniocentesis test.
		((Husband and client discuss this for several turns))
14	Husband:	[既然-既然你頭先嗽講啦,你, 你- 即係你做完之後,
		[Since- since just now you said, you- that is after doing the test,
15		你可能最後又擔心剩返嗰可能10零個percent 都有機會
		you may still worry about the remaining ten odd percent opportunity
16		有嘅話呢, 喀, 我就覺得就直頭唔好做依個嘞.
		of having Down syndrome. Yeah. I feel it's better not to do this one.
17		無謂即係攪兩次喇第一樣嘢.
		I mean there's no need to do two tests for the same thing.
18		同埋你就算做咗你-你都擔心嗰10幾個percent嘛:
		And even if you did it, you'd still worry about the ten odd percent right?
19	Client:	Mm mm
20	Husband:	咁意義唔太大。
		So it doesn't make much sense.
21	Client:	°Mm: 嗽[做羊水喇:°
		°Mm: Then [do the amniocentesis.°
22	HP:	[°你點睇呢.°
		[°What do you think.°
		((several turns omitted where husband and client express their preference for amniocentesis))
23	HP:	你嚟之前, 頭先你同我講過
		Before you came in, previously you told me that

24		你想做羊水.=
		you'd like to do an amniocentesis test.=
25	Husband:	=係啊.
		=Yes.
26	HP:	噉喇: 因為依家- 依家到um做羊水
		How about this: because from now- now till um the amniocentesis test
27		都有段時[間喇
		there is still [time.
28	Husband:	[Mm
29	HP:	噉你返去諗吓囉.
		So you go home and think about it.
30		如果真係想改嘅,噉你咪話返俾[我哋聽囉。
		If you really want to change, then you tell [us.
31	Husband:	[Okay。

In this example the healthcare provider takes a very directive stance[4]: she unambiguously tells the couple that usually only one test is arranged, thereby encouraging them to make a choice (lines 2 and 5), and she frames her explanation of why amniocentesis should not be done as a recommendation from an expert, i.e. healthcare professional (lines 7 and 8). She also explicitly expresses her own preference ('*I feel it's better not to do this one*' (line 16)), and suggests the couple take some more time to think about their options before making a final decision (lines 26, 27, 29 and 30). Although prior to this point in the interaction the couple has been very affirmative in pursuing their initial choice of an amniocentesis and resisting the healthcare provider's suggestion about doing a screening test first (not shown in the transcript), at this point in the interaction they do not object to this proposed course of action.

The directiveness of the healthcare provider's discourse in this example is mainly constructed through her active engagement with the couple's decision making by promoting the screening test option, aligning herself with the woman's uncertainties about amniocentesis and delaying the couple's decision until they think it over (for a more detailed discussion of the decision making processes in this example see Zayts et al. 2012). Thus, although the directiveness of the healthcare provider might be perceived as marked and perhaps even as inappropriate from a professional viewpoint, as the main agenda of these encounters is to facilitate clients' autonomous decision making regarding testing and not making recommendations about it, the discursive evidence of this (and other similar) example(s) points to the fact that the healthcare provider's directiveness here is actually considered to be appropriate and politic – and is, in fact, co-constructed among interlocutors.

Moreover, this kind of reliance on those in more powerful positions to give advice and tell them what to do, as here shown by the couple's expectation to be told what testing option to choose, could perhaps be seen as a reflection of what is often considered to be politic behaviour in Chinese institutional contexts more generally. However, while examples like 2.2 seem to provide support for claims about the role of culture₁ in influencing what kinds of behaviours are interpreted as appropriate and politic, more recent politeness research warns against making such prima facie generalisations or stereotyping at this cultural level (e.g. Eelen 2001; Kádár & Mills 2011; Mills 2003, 2004; Watts 2003). In particular, it has been argued that expectations about norms associated with culture₁ may not always be recognised as appropriate and politic by all interactants, i.e. they may not actually be reflected in what is considered to be appropriate behaviour in a particular encounter. Rather, as we have argued, what counts as appropriate or politic behaviour is dynamically negotiated among participants as an interaction unfolds.

Challenging culture₁ claims about appropriate behaviour

In addition to those examples where interlocutors' behaviours could be interpreted as reinforcing general, and often stereotypical, claims about culture₁, such as the strong adherence to hierarchical structures and high level of directiveness in institutional interactions shown in Example 2.2, there are numerous instances in our data where these claims are challenged. To illustrate this, we discuss three examples here – taken from different workplace contexts – which evolve around the potentially face-threatening communicative acts of refusing and disagreeing. Due to their tendency to threaten interlocutors' face needs, refusals and disagreements may challenge 'the personal relationships between the individuals of a social group' (Watts 1989: 135). This is particularly true when they are directed at a superior where they can easily be interpreted as an attempt to challenge existing power relations and the status quo (e.g. Daly et al. 2004; Chan et al. fc). Examples 2.3–2.5 are particularly noteworthy in this respect, as they challenge Kádár and Pan's (2011: 142) claim that in interactions where 'the power difference is obvious to both parties, it is clear that the "powerless" party tends to use politeness markers'.

Lay people's expectations about the occurrence of refusals and disagreements are not only reflected in the list of do's and don'ts quoted at the beginning of the chapter, but are further shown in the remark of one of our participants. Neil, an expatriate from the UK who manages an IT company in Hong Kong, said, 'I can't remember them [his Hong Kong Chinese team members] ever not doing what I tell them! Or at least, not agreeing to it.' Such comments are good examples of participants' views of culture₁. They are, to a large extent, reinforced by the work of Hofstede (1980) who claims that in cultures of high power distance, such as Hong Kong, people tend not to question authority and to maintain and reinforce hierarchical relationships (see also Chee & West 2004; Selmer & de Leon 2003). These claims are in line with the fact that we recorded only a relatively small number of upwards refusals and disagreements in our interactional data. However, these claims are challenged to a certain extent by the relatively high degree of explicitness and directness in which these communicative acts were often performed – thereby increasing their potential face-threat to the addressee.

Refusing a superior

A lot of research has been conducted on refusals, especially from the angle of cross-cultural comparison. Several studies have claimed that refusals 'reflect fundamental cultural values' (Beebe et al. 1990: 68) and that 'while the refusal strategies are universal, the frequency of the refusal strategies used and the content of the strategies are culture specific' (Chang 2009: 479; Allami and Naemi 2011). Of particular interest for our purposes is a study by Chang (2009: 478) which claims that 'the Chinese' prefer an indirect, implicit and unassertive communication style, which is allegedly a reflection of their high-context collectivist society, 'in which in-group interest is considered more important than individual interests and the preservation of harmony among group members is significant'. A similar argument is brought forward by Liao and Bresnahan (1996: 706), who propose that '[t]he omission of the most direct answer of "No, I can't" should result from the politeness theory of *dian-dao-wei-zhi* ("marginally touching the point")', which they consider to be an instantiation of Chinese cultural values and norms. As we discuss in more detail elsewhere (Schnurr & Zayts 2013), however, the problem with much of this research on refusals is that data were often collected by means of Discourse Completion Tasks (DCT), thus capturing participants' views of first-order culture, i.e. their views on what they consider to be appropriate behaviour. These means of data collection do not capture participants' actual behaviour and the processes through which they enact culture$_2$. It is perhaps not surprising, then, that those studies that actually looked at authentic interactions found that naturally occurring refusals are much more complex and conjointly constructed than DCT results suggest. Refusals in authentic and natural interactions involve 'a considerable amount of negotiation among interlocutors and typically unfolded over several turns and involved several refusal strategies' (Schnurr & Zayts 2013: 611; Morrison & Holmes 2003).

We discuss two examples of such upwards refusals here to illustrate that the ways in which these refusals are constructed and negotiated among interlocutors challenge some of the culture$_1$ perceptions in the previous sections. The first example is taken from an email exchange between Neil, an expatriate from the UK who owns a small IT company, and Brad, a local Hong Kong Chinese who is doing a small sub-contracting job for Neil over the weekend.

Example 2.3

Hi Brad,
I'd like to call in a couple of times tomorrow to check on your progress – please can you let me have your mobile number?
Many thanks
Neil

Hi Neil,
You don't have to call but I will email you reporting the progress.
Brad

Brad's refusal of Neil's request about sending him his mobile phone number is skilfully constructed. Although Brad does not provide any reasons for this refusal, which could be perceived as potentially face-threatening – especially if uttered towards a superior – he does provide an alternative, namely to email Neil about his progress. However, Brad's formulation '*you don't have to*' considerably mitigates the potential face-threat of the refusal and makes it look as though Brad is actually doing Neil a favour by relieving him of some of the responsibility of ensuring the work progresses well. He, thus, skilfully manages to do the refusal in ways that at the same time enable him to save Neil's (and his own) face, and to uphold and maintain the asymmetrical power relationship between them: he addresses his boss' request for being informed about any progress while minimising his involvement in (and potential interference in or disruption of) Brad's work. Thus, if we follow Locher and Watts (2005: 17) in arguing that 'appropriateness is determined by the frame or the habitus of the participants [. . .] within which face is attributed by the others in accordance with the lines taken in the interaction', we can explain why such behaviour is not perceived as impolite by interlocutors but merely as unmarked and appropriate and, thus, politic.

We show one more example here before discussing in more detail what these observations mean regarding issues of face and politeness in relation to first- and second-order notions of culture.

Example 2.4

Context: The example comes from a departmental staff meeting at a large financial corporation. The department in which this meeting was recorded oversees staff training in the company. Susan, a UK expatriate, is the Head of the Department. Margaret, a Hong Kong Chinese, is a junior administrator who maintains a spreadsheet for all training courses run by the department. Other participants mentioned in the interaction are Cheryl, a newly promoted team manager, Andy, an IT specialist, and Jenny, another administrator in the team.

1	Susan:	But I think you need to tell them not to change your template=
2	Margaret:	=I [tell them]
3	Susan:	[I think] the solution is to tell them not to do it.
4	Margaret:	Yeah, I tell them many times but I don't know the PRC
5		administrator why always cha::nge.
6	Susan:	Ok, why do you not get Cheryl or myself involved in this matter
7		because we ca:n tell them not to do this.
8	Margaret:	I alr- already told Andy many times, or maybe every week,
9		some of the: maybe I have this problem and Jenny also have this
10		problem for the spreadsheet problem,
11	Susan:	I, OK, if you're not getting a resolution from Andy, if you
12		have told him more than three times,=

13   Margaret: °Hm°
14   Susan: =and you're not getting a solution, than you need to raise this
15   matter with your manager=
16   Margaret: Hm.
17   Susan: =which is Cheryl.
18   Margaret: OK. ((nods))
19   Susan: And if Cheryl is not available you need to raise this matter
20   with me.
21   Margaret: Hm.
22   Susan: Because this is a waste of ti:me and we have a lot of matters
23   that we need to resolve. And they are causing problems and
24   we can tell China to stop doing this.
25   Margaret: OK.

In contrast to Example 2.3, the refusal in Example 2.4 is less explicit and more complex. This exchange is taken from a longer discussion in which team members talk about the various problems they are experiencing with another team in the Mainland China branch of the company. Apparently, the other team keep changing a specific template without informing Susan's team who have devised it. Susan's comment in line 1 directly addresses these issues and reminds the others that their colleagues in the Mainland China branch are not supposed to change their template. She explicitly addresses Margaret, one of the more junior team members, and repeatedly asks her '*to tell them not to change our template*' (lines 1 and 3). After a brief discussion with Margaret about this issue, in lines 6–7 Susan asks her why she did '*not get Cheryl or myself involved in this matter*' to help solve the problem. However, rather than agreeing with Susan or providing explanations for her behaviour, Margaret justifies her own behaviour (e.g. by outlining what actions she did take, such as talking to Andy, the IT specialist), and she indicates that this is not only her problem but that other people in the team (i.e. Jenny) have similar issues (lines 8–10).

Importantly though, Margaret does not explicitly refer back to Susan's request to raise this problem with Cheryl or herself, thereby implicitly refusing it. Thus, by elaborating alternative ways of handling this problem, which could be described as a 'statement of alternative' – one of the refusal strategies proposed by Beebe et al. (1990) and also by Chang (2009) – Margaret skilfully negotiates this refusal and expresses it in very indirect and implicit ways without unnecessarily threatening Susan's, Cheryl's (who also attends the meeting) or her own face. She achieves this by employing several of the refusal strategies mentioned in Beebe et al. (1990: 73), namely 'unspecific and indefinite reply' and 'lack of enthusiasm', which are both different ways of enacting the strategy of 'acceptance that functions as a refusal'. In particular, Margaret's frequent use of minimal feedback (e.g. lines 13, 16 and 21) renders her refusal indirect and almost ambiguous. It also enables her to acknowledge her boss' explanations while at the same time avoiding explicitly disagreeing with her. And due to their ambiguous meanings, minimal acknowledgements seem to be very suitable means to achieve this. Pudlinski (2002) for example, distinguishes between three different functions of minimal acknowledgements, including being a continuer, a minimal agreement to a prior statement or a passive resistance to a prior statement. In this example, Margaret appears to draw on several of these functions including the passive resistance. This interpretation of Margaret's behaviour in Example 2.4 as refusing her superior's request is further supported by her comments in the interview after data collection, where she expressed some discontent with Cheryl's role as the team's manager (see also Schnurr & Zayts 2011), and explicitly told us that she would not ask Cheryl for help if she had a problem but that she would rather seek other people's advice.

Examples 2.3 and 2.4 have thus shown that generalisations about the role of culture$_1$ in terms of how members of a particular socio-cultural group allegedly do refusals and other potentially face-threatening acts are not very useful and are often counterproductive in attempts to explain interlocutors' actual behaviours in a specific interaction. Rather than helping understand interlocutors' behaviour, such claims merely create and reinforce stereotypical perceptions about culture$_1$ and do not provide an adequate picture of the complexities of authentic interactions and the ways in which interlocutors create and enact second-order cultures on the micro-level of an interaction. We discuss one more example here, namely that of a disagreement with a superior, to illustrate this.

Disagreeing with a superior

Like refusals, disagreements are also potentially face-threatening communicative acts which 'jeopardize [. . .] the solidarity between speaker and addressee' (Rees-Miller 2000: 1089). This potential to cause face-threat and to challenge the relationship between interlocutors and perhaps even the status quo is particularly strong in those disagreements that are uttered 'upwards', such as from a subordinate towards their superiors, as in Example 2.5.

Example 2.5

Context: This example is taken from the same team who is involved in Example 2.4 with the exception that Susan, the Head of Department and only non-Chinese-speaking member of the team, is not present. Due to Susan's absence, the meeting was conducted in Cantonese. At this point in the meeting, participants are discussing whether the company provides subsidies for attendance of overseas conferences.

1 Cheryl: 今年冇. 今年(.)今年嘅policy改咗.
                 This year no. this year (.) This year the policy has changed.
2   零八年呢上堂[有㗎
                 In 2008, attending courses [were entitled it.
3 Nancy: [但係以我 (0.2) 所知
                 [but as far as I (0.2) know

4   Cheryl: Mm=

5   Nancy: =淨係presenter先有per diem喫喎
              =Only presenters have per diems

6   Cheryl: 有啊 舊年係有喫, (0.5) 有per diem喫
              Yes. They did have them last year. (0.5) they had per diems.

7   (0.5)

8   Cheryl: 即係::::::: (0.3)
              That means::::::: (0.3)

9   Nancy: 因為係阿Jen- 我問過阿Jenny, 之前我[見到]啲數唔啱吖嘛
              It's because Jen- I asked Jenny, I [found] some figures that weren't
              right.

10 Cheryl: [Mm]

11   (0.4)

12 Nancy: Jenny 阿Jenny話 (0.5) participants一定唔會有per diem.
              Jenny, Jenny said (0.5) definitely participants wouldn't have per
              diems.

13   =淨係presenter先
              =only presenters have them

14 Cheryl: 舊年 (0.3) 個firm policy 係有啊. 因為今:: (0.3) HR-
              Last year (0.3) the firm policy covered them. This:: (0.3) HR-

15   eh即係最近啦. 即係 eh: 零八年年尾呢, HR就出咗
              uh I mean recently, I mean uh: in the end of oh eight, HR issued

16   個policy呢 就係話, .hh今年嘅per diem policy 會改.
              a policy, saying .hh that the per diem policy would change this
              year.

17   就係所有 .hhh淨係:: (0.4) eh: 總之同training 或者同conference
              That means all .hhh only:: (0.4) uh: anyway all training or confer-
              ence related

18   有關嘅per diem就會取消 (0.3) 嘅樣.
              per diems would be cancelled. (0.3) Something like that.

19   .hh嘅所以即係 (.) 如果(.) date back 返去零八年之前
              .hh So therefore I mean (.) if (.) courses dated back to oh eight
              or earlier

20   其實係有per diem喫
              in fact were entitled to per diems.

((Transcript of 18 seconds omitted in which Cheryl further elaborates on the
new company policy))

21 Nancy: Mm

22   (4.5)

23 Cheryl: 嗷::::::: 大家仲有冇問題
              So::::::: does anyone have any questions?

24   (3.1)

25 Cheryl: 冇問題就:: 嗷阿Angela麻煩你. . .
              if no questions, then:: Angela, could you . . .

26 ((Cheryl continues with another topic))

Nancy's comment in line 3 signals her disagreement with her superior, Cheryl. The disagreement can be classified as relatively strong, as it contains 'an evaluation which is directly contrastive with the prior evaluation' (Pomerantz 1984: 74), and it contradicts and challenges Cheryl's previous claim about the non-existence of any subsidies for this year (lines 1 and 2). Although Nancy mitigates her counter-claim to some extent ('*but as far as I know*') and although she does not use any overt disagreement markers (such as *no*), she nevertheless directly opposes what Cheryl said immediately before, which poses a potential threat to Cheryl's face. Moreover, by referring to another person (Jenny, who is further up the organisational hierarchy than Cheryl) as the ultimate source of reliable information, Cheryl's face is further challenged and her authority and knowledge are questioned – especially, since this disagreement takes place in the meeting context in front of the entire team.

In responding to Nancy, Cheryl tries to clarify the situation by referring to last year's practices before outlining this year's changes (lines 14–20). Although there are several hesitation markers in her utterance (e.g. the restarts, interjections and hedges like '*uh I mean*'), she competently conveys this information and stands by her earlier claim. Her comment '*that's all*' in the middle of her utterance gives further weight to her explanation and could be seen as re-establishing her authority. Nancy seems to have understood this message, as she does not challenge Cheryl's claims again but rather produces several tokens of minimal feedback (line 21 and also in omitted part). The noticeable pauses at the end of Cheryl's explanations (lines 22 and 24) and the smooth shift to another topic (line 26) provide further support for this interpretation.

Examples like Nancy's relatively explicit disagreement with her boss, and the ways in which interlocutors in this exchange orient to each other's and their own face, challenge the claims of earlier research in organisational behaviour and cultural studies which suggest that Hong Kong Chinese tend to compromise and avoid direct disagreement (Kirkbride et al. 1991; Pan 2000) and adopt more mitigated and redressive strategies (Cheng & Tsui 2009). In an earlier study on disagreements in co-leadership teams in Hong Kong (Schnurr & Chan 2011; see also Chapter 4), we also observed that most of the linguistic strategies our participants used to do facework when disagreeing with each other could be classified as 'avoidance based' (Goffman 1967). These disagreements were typically characterised by a *yes–but* structure, the use of forewarners to signal disagreement (Kotthoff 1993), and the use of several mitigation strategies. However, we also found several examples of more direct and strong disagreements (Pomerantz 1984) in which explicit disagreement markers (e.g. *no, not*) and other potentially face-threatening strategies were used (e.g. interrupting each other, cutting each other off and negative comments like *I don't care*).

Example 2.5 thus provides further support for our discussions about treating grand claims about the impact of 'culture', as reflected in first-order conceptualisations of culture, with caution. Examples like 2.5 once more highlight the necessity to avoid confusing or equating first- and second-order culture in an analysis of workplace interaction. Not only is there often a considerable difference between what people say they (and others) do and what they (and others) actually do (e.g. Golato 2003), but drawing on cultural stereotypes or relying exclusively on notions of culture$_1$ in an analytic attempt to understand interlocutors' communicative behaviours in a workplace interaction will only reinforce these stereotypes and will not provide an adequate understanding of what is actually going on. Thus, rather than focusing on finding instances of workplace interactions which are in line with and reinforce participants' claims about what is considered to be appropriate and politic behaviour, such as in Example 2.2, it is more productive to try to understand interlocutors' behaviour as constructing, enacting, shaping and negotiating culture$_2$ throughout an interaction, and to explore how this behaviour, in turn, reflects and corresponds to their perceptions and claims about culture$_1$.

Discussion

The examples discussed in this chapter have shown that claims about culture$_1$ as reflected in the comments of our participants and a lot of the popular literature are often not very helpful for an understanding of people's actual behaviour in their workplace interactions – especially regarding issues of face and politeness. Such generalising claims about first-order culture thus need to be treated with caution when trying to understand the complexities of doing face and politeness at work, and what counts as appropriate and politic behaviour in a specific context. Although at first glance it may sometimes appear tempting and perhaps even pervasive to draw on first-order notions of culture in examining the role of 'culture' in how interlocutors negotiate face and politeness issues at work, approaching 'culture' purely on the level of culture$_1$ is analytically not very productive, as such conceptualisations are too general and often too stereotypical to be useful for an analysis of actual behaviour. Thus, in order to account for the ways in which refusals, disagreements and other communicative acts are constructed and negotiated in authentic interactions in ways that are considered to be appropriate and politic among interlocutors, it is crucial to look beyond first-order notions of culture – while still acknowledging their usefulness – and to try to understand the immediate context, as reflected in the notion of culture$_2$, in which the interaction takes place. Analytically and methodologically it is thus important to move beyond finding evidence to support claims about culture$_1$ as expressed by participants or outlined in the literature based on rather essentialist notions of culture, and to consider and accommodate these findings in discussions of the role of 'culture' at work.

As we have briefly discussed in Chapter 1, the concept of the community of practice (CofP) is useful in such an attempt, as it allows researchers to capture normative (and hence appropriate and politic) practices that have developed among the members of a particular, relatively small, group – whether a department, a project team or sometimes even an entire workplace. It is precisely on this level of the CofP that notions of culture$_2$ are constructed, enacted, reinforced and sometimes also challenged by interlocutors. The relatively direct way of refusing displayed in the email (Example 2.3), and the rather implicit and indirect way of refusing in the meeting (Example 2.4) should thus not only be seen as contradictions (Example 2.3) or reflections (Example 2.4) of culture₁ but rather as constructions and enactments of culture₂ since they show normal, unmarked (and politic) ways in which members in these different CofPs regularly interact with each other. In performing these activities interlocutors at the same time actively contribute to creating and shaping second-order notions of culture.

However, as we have argued in the previous chapter, rather than completely discarding participants' claims about first-order notions of culture as merely stereotypical, we would say that they are an important aspect of 'culture' at work since they reflect the kinds of assumptions and expectations that participants hold, and are, thus, potentially relevant in making sense of what is going on during an interaction – at the very least by providing insights into participants' perceptions and interpretations of their own behaviour and that of others. A productive way forward thus seems to be to combine first- and second-order notions of culture and to try to understand and analyse participants' relatively static views of culture₁ in relation to more dynamic enactments of culture₂, as we have done in this chapter. While it is important to analyse how norms of appropriate and politic behaviours are created and negotiated on the micro-level of an interaction (culture₂), it is equally important to acknowledge the potential impact of more macro-level views of culture₁. Both first- and second-orders of culture are thus crucial for an understanding of face and politeness at work.

In the next chapter we continue this line of argument and focus on a specific interactional activity where issues of face and politeness are particularly relevant, namely decision making.

Notes

1 Spelling and grammar are as on the website (www.chinabizconsulting.com/china-business-etiquette-dos-donts.htm) (accessed 29 May 2016).
2 Example 2.2 is discussed from a different angle in Zayts et al. (2012), and Examples 2.3 and 2.4 also occur in Schnurr & Zayts (2013).
3 The clients who come for PGC services are offered three options: 1) non-invasive tests that are performed on the mother (blood tests and the measurement of nuchal translucency, the thickness of the foetus's neck); 2) invasive tests that are performed on the foetus (amniocentesis or CVS; both procedures involve puncturing the placenta to extract samples for testing); 3) women can also choose not to pursue testing. While the non-invasive tests are safer than the invasive ones, they have a lower detection rate of identifying an abnormality in a foetus.
4 This point is further discussed in the next chapter where we analyse in more detail the decision making practices typically displayed in these PGC encounters.

References

Allami, Hamid & Amin Naeimi (2011). A cross-cultural study of refusals: An analysis of pragmatic competence development in Iranian EFL learners. *Journal of Pragmatics* 43: 385–406.

Arundale, Robert B. (2010). Constituting face in conversation: Face, facework, and interactional achievement. *Journal of Pragmatics* 42, 2078–105.

Arundale, Robert B. (2006). Face as relational and interactional: A communication framework for research on face, facework, and politeness. *Journal of Politeness Research* 2, 193–216.

Beebe, Leslie, Tomoko Takahashi & Robin Uliss-Weltz (1990). Pragmatic transfer in ESL refusals. In Robin Scarcella, Elaine Andersen & Stephen Krashen (eds), *Developing Communicative Competence in a Second Language.* New York: Newbury House. 55–73.

Benkendorf, Judith L., Michele B. Prince, Mary A. Rose, Anna De Fina & Heidi E. Hamilton (2001). Does indirect speech promote nondirective genetic counselling? *American Journal of Medical Genetics* 106: 199–207.

Chan, Angela, Stephanie Schnurr & Olga Zayts (fc). Exploring face, identity and relational work in disagreements in business meetings in Hong Kong. *Submitted to Journal of Politeness Research.*

Chang, Yuh-Fang (2009). How to say no: An analysis of cross-cultural difference and pragmatic transfer. *Language Sciences* 31: 477–93.

Chee, Harold & Chris West (2004). *Myths about Doing Business in China.* Basingstoke/ New York: Palgrave Macmillan.

Cheng, Winnie & Amy Tsui (2009). 'Ahh ((laugh)) well there is no comparison between the two I think': How do Hong Kong Chinese and native speakers of English disagree with each other? *Journal of Pragmatics* 41: 2365–80.

Collins, Robert & Carson Block (2007). *Doing Business in China for Dummies.* Hoboken: Wiley.

Daly, Nicola, Janet Holmes, Jonathan Newton & Maria Stubbe (2004). Expletives as solidarity signals in FTAs on the factory floor. *Journal of Pragmatics* 36: 945–64.

Du, Ping (2015). *Intercultural Communication in the Chinese Workplace.* Basingstoke: Palgrave Macmillan.

Eelen, Gino (2001). *A Critique of Politeness Theories.* Manchester: St. Jerome Publishing.

Gao, Ge & Stella Ting-Toomey (1998). *Communicating Effectively with the Chinese.* Thousand Oaks, CA: SAGE.

Gao, Ge, Stella Ting-Toomey & William B. Gudykunst (1995). Chinese communication process. In M. H. Bond (ed.), *The Handbook of Chinese Psychology.* Hong Kong: Oxford University Press. 280–93.

Geyer, Naomi (2008). *Discourse and Politeness: Ambivalent Face in Japanese.* London: Continuum.

Goffman, Erving (1967). *Interaction Ritual: Essays on Face-to-Face Behaviour.* New York: Random House.

Golato, Andrea (2003). Studying compliment responses: A comparison of DCTs and recordings of naturally occurring talk. *Applied Linguistics* 42.1: 90–121.

Gunnarsson, Britt-Louise (2009). *Professional Discourse.* London: Continuum.

Haugh, Michael (2009). Face and interaction. In Francesca Bargiela-Chiappini & Michael Haugh (eds), *Face, Communication and Social Interaction.* London: Equinox. 1–30.

Haugh, Michael & Carl Hinze (2003). A metalinguistic approach to deconstructing the concepts of 'face' and 'politeness' in Chinese, English and Japanese. *Journal of Pragmatics* 35: 1581–611.

Hofstede, Geert (1980). *Culture's Consequences. International Differences in Work-Related Values.* Beverly Hills and London: SAGE.

Holliday, Adrian (2011). *Intercultural Communication and Ideology.* London: SAGE.

Holmes, Janet & Stephanie Schnurr (2005). Politeness, humour and gender in the workplace: Negotiating norms and identifying contestation. *Journal of Politeness Research: Language, Behaviour, Culture* 1: 121–49.

Hua, Zhu (2014). *Exploring Intercultural Communication. Language in Action.* Abingdon: Routledge.

Johnson, Amanda Webb & Zenobia Nadirshaw (2002). Good practice in transcultural counseling: An Asian perspective. In Stephen Palmer (ed.), *Multicultural Counselling: A Reader.* London: SAGE. 119–28.

Kádár, Daniel Z. & Francesca Bargiella-Chiappini (2011). Institutional politeness in (South) East Asia: An introduction. *Journal of Asia Pacific Communication* 21.1: 1–9.

Kádár, Daniel & Sara Mills (2011). Introduction. In Daniel Kádár & Sara Mills (eds), *Politeness in East Asia.* Cambridge: Cambridge University Press. 1–19.

Kádár, Daniel & Yuling Pan (2011). Politeness in China. In Daniel Kádár & Sara Mills (eds), *Politeness in East Asia.* Cambridge: Cambridge University Press. 125–46.

Kim, Min-Sun, Renee Storm Klingle, William F. Sharkey, HeeSun Park, David H. Smith & Deborah Cai (2000). A test of a cultural model of patients' motivation for verbal communication in patient–doctor interactions. *Communication Monographs* 67: 262–83.

Kirkbride, Paul, Sara Tang & Robert Westwood (1991). Chinese conflict style and negotiating behaviour: Cultural and psychological influences. *Organization Studies* 12.3: 365–86.

Kotthoff, Helga (1993). Disagreement and concession in disputes: On the context sensitivity of preference structures. *Language in Society* 22: 193–216.

Lee-Wong, Song Mei (2000). *Politeness and Face in Chinese Culture.* Frankfurt: Peter Lang.

Liao, Chao-Chih & Mary I. Bresnahan (1996). A contrastive pragmatic study on American English and Mandarin refusal strategies. *Language Sciences* 18.3–4: 703–27.

Locher, Miriam (2006). Polite behaviour within relational work: The discursive approach to politeness. *Multilingua* 25.3: 249–67.

Locher, Miriam & Richard Watts (2005). Politeness theory and relational work. *Journal of Politeness Research: Language, Behaviour, Culture* 1: 9–33.

Mills, Sara (2004). Class, gender and politeness. *Multilingua* 23.1/2: 171–91.

Mills, Sara (2003). *Gender and Politeness.* Cambridge: Cambridge University Press.

Morrison, Anthea & Janet Holmes (2003). Eliciting refusals. A methodological challenge. *Te Reo* 46: 47–66.

Pan, Yuling (2000). *Politeness in Chinese Face-to-Face Interaction.* Stamford, CT: Ablex Publishing.

Pilnick, Alison (2008). 'It's something for you both to think about': Choice and decision making in nuchal translucency screening for Down's syndrome. *Sociology of Health and Illness* 30.4: 511–30.

Pilnick, Alison (1999). 'Patient counseling' by pharmacists: Advice, information, or instruction? *Sociological Quarterly* 40: 613–22.

Pomerantz, Anita (1984). Agreeing and disagreeing with assessments: Some features of preferred/dispreferred turn shapes. In J. Maxwell Atkinson & John Heritage (eds), *Structures of Social Action: Studies in Conversation Analysis.* Cambridge: Cambridge University Press. 225–46.

Pudlinski, Christopher (2002). Accepting and rejecting advice as competent peers: Caller dilemmas on a warm line. *Discourse Studies* 4.4: 481–500.

Rees-Miller, Janie (2000). Power, severity, and context in disagreement. *Journal of Pragmatics* 32:1087–111.

Sarangi, Srikant (2000). Activity types, discourse types and interactional hybridity: The case of genetic counseling. In Srikant Sarangi & Malcolm Coulthard (eds), *Discourse and Social Life.* London: Pearson. 1–27.

Schnurr, Stephanie (2013). *Exploring Professional Communication. Language in Action.* Abingdon: Routledge.

Schnurr, Stephanie & Angela Chan (2011). Exploring another side of co-leadership: Negotiating professional identities through face-work in disagreements. *Language in Society* 40.2: 187–210.

Schnurr, Stephanie, Meredith Marra & Janet Holmes (2008). Impoliteness as a means of contesting power relations in the workplace. In Derek Bousfield & Miriam Locher (eds), *Impoliteness in Language: Studies on its Interplay with Power in Theory and Practice*. Berlin: Walter de Gruyter. 211–30.

Schnurr, Stephanie & Olga Zayts (2013). 'I can't remember them ever not doing what I tell them!' Negotiating face and power relations in 'upward' refusals in multicultural workplaces in Hong Kong. *Intercultural Pragmatics* 10.4: 593–616.

Schnurr, Stephanie & Olga Zayts (2011). Constructing and contesting leaders. An analysis of identity construction at work. In Jo Angouri & Meredith Marra (eds), *Constructing Identities at Work*. Houndmills: Palgrave. 40–60.

Selmer, Jan & Corinna de Leon (2003). Culture and management in Hong Kong SAR. In Malcolm Warner (ed.), *Culture and Management in Asia*. London: Routledge Curzon. 48–65.

Silverman, David (1997). *Discourses of Counselling: HIV Counselling as Social Interaction*. London: SAGE.

Spencer-Oatey, Helen (2008). Face, (im)politeness and rapport. In Helen Spencer-Oatey (ed.), *Culturally Speaking: Culture, Communication and Politeness Theory*. London: Continuum. 11–47.

Spencer-Oatey, Helen & Jianyu Xing (2000). A problematic Chinese business visit to Britain: Issues of face. In Helen Spencer-Oatey (ed.), *Culturally Speaking. Managing Rapport Across Cultures*. 1st ed. London: Continuum. 272–88.

Watts, Richard (2005). Linguistic politeness research: *Quo vadis?* In Richard Watts, Sachiko Ide & Konrad Ehlich (eds), *Politeness in Language* (2nd edn). Berlin: Mouton de Gruyter, xi–xlvii.

Watts, Richard (2003). *Politeness*. Cambridge: Cambridge University Press.

Watts, Richard (1992). Linguistic politeness and politic verbal behaviour. In Richard J. Watts, Sachiko Ide & Konrad Ehlich (eds), *Politeness in Language: Studies in its History, Theory and Practice*. Berlin and New York: Mouton de Gruyter. 43–69.

Watts, Richard (1989). Relevance and relational work: Linguistic politeness as politic behaviour. *Multilingua* 8.2–3: 131–66.

Wei, Betty & Elizabeth Li (2008). *Culture Shock! Hong Kong. A Survival Guide to Customs and Etiquette*. Singapore: Marshall Cavendish.

Young, Linda W. L. (1994). *Crosstalk and Culture in Sino-American Communication*. New York: Cambridge University Press.

Zayts, Olga & Stephanie Schnurr (2013). '[She] said: "take the test" and I took the test.' Relational work as a framework to approach directiveness in prenatal screening of Chinese clients in Hong Kong, *Journal of Politeness Research* 9.2: 187–210.

Zayts, Olga & Stephanie Schnurr (2012). 'You may know better than I do'. Advice giving in Down's syndrome screening in a Hong Kong hospital. In Miriam Locher & Holger Limberg (eds), *Advice in Discourse*. Amsterdam: Benjamins. 195–212.

Zayts, Olga, V. Yelei Wake & Stephanie Schnurr (2012). Chinese prenatal genetic counseling discourse in Hong Kong: Health care providers' (non)directive stance, or who is making the decision? In Yulin Pan & Daniel Kádár (eds), *Chinese Discourse and Interaction: Theory and Practice*. London: Equinox. 228–47.

Zhu, Weihua (2014). Managing relationships in everyday practice: The case of strong disagreement in Mandarin. *Journal of Pragmatics* 64: 85–101.

3   The complexities of decision making. A question of culture₁?

People won't make decisions here [in Hong Kong].
> (Susan, expatriate Head of Department in a large financial corporation)

Introduction

In the previous chapter we have identified and discussed remarkable differences in how people talk about and perceive issues of face and politeness, on the one hand, and the ways in which they orient to and negotiate these issues throughout an interaction, on the other. We continue illustrating this discrepancy between participants' perceptions and actual practice in this chapter, and explore the topic of decision making. As in the previous chapter, we take as a starting point some of the comments made by our participants in the interviews, before analysing in more detail several instances of authentic decision making episodes. We thereby provide further evidence for our claims that i) solely relying on participants' perceptions is often problematic, and ii) a wide diversity of decision making practices exists. Empirical evidence of both i) and ii) supports our argument about the necessity to distinguish between different orders of culture, and to move away from exclusively focusing on claims about culture₁ towards paying more attention to local practices (as reflected in the notion of culture₂).

Decision making has been described as 'an important and complex aspect of workplace interaction' (Holmes & Stubbe 2003: 75), and it is one of the activities that have been linked to cultural₁ practices and beliefs – by some of our participants, as well as previous literature. The following quote by Janet, an expatriate from the UK who owns a language learning centre in Hong Kong, is a good example of this.

Example 3.1[1]

| 1 Janet: | Trying to get the democracy (.) going in the office, doesn't work a |
| 2 | hundred percent because I'm working with Chinese people, |

```
3          um but that (.) that would be my ultimate goal is that
4          they work fully as a team and they they're fully
5          democratic in the decision making hmm but having said that um (.) that
6          doesn't work, so that I get quite (frustrated).
```

In the interview Janet makes it clear that she is not satisfied with the current decision making practices in her team, and she laments in particular the passive role of the '*Chinese people*' (line 2) she is working with. She states that her '*ultimate goal*' (line 3) is to implement democratic processes, to get her subordinates to '*work fully as a team*' (line 3) and to more actively engage in democratic or collaborative decision making. By explicitly mentioning the socio-cultural background of her team members (i.e. '*Chinese*'), she makes culture$_1$ an issue and uses it as an explanatory variable to account for her frustration that arises out of what she perceives to be an incompatibility of her own expectations and those of her subordinates. A relatively similar picture emerged in the interview with Susan, an expatriate from the UK who holds a senior position in a large financial corporation.

Example 3.2

```
1 Susan:   The style taken here is that you are the ultimate decision maker.
2          You are expected to take the shots. It is definitely not collective
3          decision making which can be very, very frustrating.
4          But people, people won't make decisions here because they, (.)
5          if you make a decision, then you would be the one who
6          can get shot.
```

Like Janet, Susan also criticises the passive role of her local Hong Kong Chinese team members in decision making. She explicitly claims that '*you* [i.e. herself] *are the ultimate decision maker*' (line 1) and '*you are expected to take the shots*' (lines 1 and 2). Throughout the quote she frequently uses the deictic marker '*here*' to refer to what she perceives to be local practices in Hong Kong. She thereby creates an 'us' versus 'them' dichotomy in which she sets up distinct and opposing subject positions for the Hong Kong locals ('*people [. . .] here*' (lines 3 and 4)) and herself and others in her position (cf. her use of the generic '*you*'). She thereby not only generalises her, potentially relatively local and specific experiences, but also makes culture (in its first-order notion) an issue. Like Janet, she also describes this experience as '*very, very frustrating*' (line 3).

These views are also reflected and reinforced in some of the literature on decision making and 'culture', as briefly outlined in the next section.

Decision making and 'culture' – a brief look at the literature

As our quotes show, among lay people and in informal conversations, reference to 'culture' as an explanation to account for perceived differences is not uncommon (Gaenslen 1986). Indeed, among many of our participants there seemed to be a sense that decision making is heavily influenced by cultural norms, and that – almost as a consequence – their Chinese team members shy away from participating in this activity. This impression about the role of culture₁ in decision making is also reflected and reinforced in some of the earlier, often relatively essentialist, literature on decision making and 'culture'.

The line of argument that this literature proposes is largely based on the assumption that '[c]ulture affects decision making based on the nation's traditional culture which generates collective patterns of decision making, and through culture based value systems affect each individual decision maker's perception or interpretation of a situation' (Khairullah & Khairullah 2013: 4). For example, based on the assumption that Hong Kong has measured relatively high in power distance (Hofstede et al. 2010), many subsequent authors have claimed that 'the Chinese management situation in Hong Kong is characterized by "followership" (Redding 1990; Redding and Wong 1986), where subordinates habitually submit and defer to the superior wisdom of their manager for decisions' (Yeung 2004: 121). Similarly, based on the claim that Hong Kong has been described as a relatively collectivist culture (e.g. Hofstede, 1991, 2001), it has been argued that people follow a high-context communication style, in which interlocutors prefer 'an indirect verbal mode and interpreter-sensitive values, in which the receiver or interpreter of the message assumes the responsibility of inferring the hidden or contextual meanings of the message' (Du-Babcock & Tanaka 2013: 266).

These studies maintain that culture (in its first-order meaning) has an impact on people's decision making (and other communicative behaviour), and that in Hong Kong there is a clear tendency for those in lower organisational positions to expect decision making to be mainly an activity performed by those in more senior positions. In line with the emphasis that members of collectivist cultures are said to put on group harmony, studies also assert that these lower-level professionals tend not to disagree with those in more powerful positions or utter their opinion if it is in contrast to group consensus. However, as we have seen in the previous chapter and in our other research (e.g. Schnurr et al. fc), these are clearly stereotypes, and there is, in fact, ample evidence in our data of subordinates disagreeing with their superiors (cf. Chapter 2).

Nevertheless, these stereotypes seem to persist among lay people as well as academics, where the kind of group-oriented decision making described above has been attested to be the norm and has often been described negatively as 'buck-passing', 'procrastinating' and 'hyper-vigilant' (e.g. Mann et al. 1998; Lewis 2000). According to this line of argument, these allegedly culture-specific ways of making decisions among (Hong Kong and other) Chinese are a reflection of socio-cultural practice, beliefs and norms. These 'Chinese' decision making styles have been explained, for example, with reference to the Chinese education system, in which students are encouraged 'to follow traditions and precedents rather than to criticise them' (Weber & Hsee 2000), as well as the cyclical or spiral (rather than linear) thought and decision patterns typically preferred by members of a particular 'culture' (i.e. nation state) (e.g. Du-Babcock 1999, 2006).

In recent communication and discourse analytical research the topic of decision making has also received some attention, and research is conducted on authentic (or quasi-authentic) interactional data rather than with interviews and other kinds of self-reports. As a consequence, often a more nuanced picture of the activity of decision making emerged in these studies than in the literature discussed above.

For example, in a study of participative decision making in three banks in Hong Kong, Yeung (2004) found that although managers employed various discourse strategies to encourage their subordinates to participate and, for example, to 'articulate problems and supply information' (Yeung 2004: 142), they also limited subordinates' choices. Thus, the team's decision making was not 'purely egalitarian' and overall, maintained a 'directive fame' with (the managers') control still being visible. However, rather than interpreting these observations as being direct reflections of the socio-cultural context, Yeung emphasises that participants' 'sociocultural knowledge' plays a more indirect role in that they draw on it throughout an interaction – for example, in order to decide what behaviour may be considered appropriate or inappropriate in a specific communicative event (cf. Chapter 2).

In a study of simulated business interactions with Hong Kong bilingual Chinese (Cantonese/English), Du-Babcock (2006: 28) found different patterns regarding topic management in decision making meetings that were held in Cantonese and English: while 'a spiral or circular topic management pattern occurred in Cantonese meetings [. . .] a linear or sequential pattern occurred in English meetings'. She explained these findings – at least partly – with participants' different levels of English language proficiency and the fact that decisions in one group may have been made outside the meeting and that the recorded meetings served different purposes. However, in a more recent study, which compared simulated business interactions with Japanese and Chinese professionals in inter- and intra-cultural contexts, Du-Babcock and Tanaka (2013) argue – in line with the rather essentialist literature – that 'both groups generally reflected their high-context communication orientations, [and] exhibited some deviations from the general discourse patterns' (Du-Babcock & Tanaka 2013: 264). But rather than purely using culture (in its first-order meaning) as an explanation for their observations, they pointed to the crucial role of the power relationship among interlocutors, which they claim is 'the most relevant factor in accounting for unequal turn distribution' (Handford 2010). A similar point is made by Holmes and Stubbe (2003: 77) who maintain that

> [p]articipants in a workplace where authority relationships and relative statuses are emphasised and regarded as paramount will more readily accept a unilateral decision on a contentious issue, while workplaces with a more

egalitarian work ethic and an emphasis on participation will be more likely to engage in negotiation in such circumstances.

Moreover, in one of our own studies on prenatal genetic counselling (PGC) in Hong Kong (Zayts et al. 2012), we found that the healthcare providers played a crucial role and often influenced their clients' decision making. We argue that this relatively directive approach by the healthcare providers (which we also briefly discussed in the previous chapter), which is in contrast to the relatively neutral stance that is typically associated with the professional practice of genetic counselling (Benkendorf et al. 2001; Pilnick 2008), needs to be understood in the specific institutional and socio-cultural context in which these encounters are situated. Rather than explaining the healthcare providers' relative directiveness as an expression or a reflection of cultural values, however, we maintain that it is more productive to analyse how interlocutors construct and negotiate this particular behaviour as appropriate and politic in this particular context in ways that take into account the clients' unfamiliarity with this particular activity type (Levinson 1992; see also Chapter 5) and the (often different) expectations of clients and healthcare providers about the purpose of these encounters (see also Zayts & Schnurr 2013).

In the next section we explore several examples of authentic decision making episodes recorded in different workplaces in Hong Kong. Our analyses illustrate that decision making is a complex activity which is often conjointly performed by interlocutors, and we show how different ways of negotiating, reaching and ratifying a decision can be linked to second-order notions of culture.

Decision making in action

Decision making plays a central role in many workplace contexts, and has thus received considerable attention from research in social sciences, as well as management and organisational studies (for a brief overview, see Halvorsen 2010). While many earlier studies have primarily taken a descriptive approach and have focused on investigating the rationality behind decision making, in the literature from the 1970s onwards, issues of power and decision making, and variations and patterns in decision making processes, have become more prominent. Many of these studies have been relatively large-scale and have employed quantitative research methods (based on data obtained from surveys and interviews) in which participants reported their *perceptions* of the processes and the outcomes of decision making. Two qualitative studies on decision making in the workplace from a sociolinguistic/discourse analytical perspective are Marra (2003) and Holmes and Stubbe (2003).

In their studies, which draw on the relatively large corpus of the Language in the Workplace Project (www.victoria.ac.nz/lals/centres-and-institutes/language-in-the-workplace), they also observed the occurrence of spiral or cyclical patterns in the New Zealand workplaces where they collected data. Thus, in spite of the fact that New Zealand has been classified as a rather individualist society

unilateral   collaborative

Figure 3.1 Continuum of decision making styles

(Hofstede et al. 2010), they observed behaviours often described as typical for collectivist cultures (e.g. Du-Babcock 1999, 2006). These observations further problematise any claims that suggest a direct relationship between different kinds of first-order culture and specific interactional practices.

Moreover, the authors identified two strategies that were frequently used in relation to more problematic decisions, namely unilateral decision making where 'one person made a unilateral declaration' and collaborative decision making where 'the decision was negotiated, often at great length' (Holmes & Stubbe 2003: 76). We take up this distinction between different decision making styles and suggest a continuum ranging from unilateral to collaborative decision making, as displayed in Figure 3.1. However, while such a continuum is useful for visualising the different ways in which decisions are made in a team context, it is important to emphasise that even within the same decision making episodes interlocutors may display different styles and move along the continuum. For example, a particular instance of decision making may start off at the collaborative end (as may be reflected in participants' contributions and active engagement in the discussion) and may then move towards the unilateral end when the actual decision is stated (or ratified) by one person who may, or may not, take into consideration the contributions of others when formulating the actual decision.

We now analyse six examples of decision making which can be placed along this continuum – starting with relatively unilateral decisions and then moving on to more collaboratively made decisions. In analysing these instances of authentic workplace discourse we move away from the generalising and often stereotypical claims about the potential role of culture$_1$ with the aim of developing a more complex and nuanced picture of actual practices illustrating culture$_2$ at work.

Unilateral decision making

In spite of the fact that many of our expatriate participants suggested (and lamented) that unilateral decision making is the norm in their team, in our corpus of authentic workplace interactions we only found a relatively small number of decisions that were made more or less unilaterally by those in positions of (institutional) power and authority. The following two examples illustrate this. Example 3.3 is taken from a weekly meeting at an NGO and Example 3.4 occurred during a PGC session in one of the public hospitals in Hong Kong.

Example 3.3

Context: Weekly meeting at an NGO. Sabitha, the CEO and founder of the organisation, is chairing the meeting. At this point in the meeting participants are discussing the length of their lease agreement. Beth is the Business Development Manager. Beth is Hong Kong Chinese and Sabitha is ethnically Indian.

```
 1  Beth:   The other issue (.) so I approved of this recently [because er (.)]
 2  Sab.:   [Okay my] er I know but you're (.) for five years that's my issue
 3          you're committing for FIVE years (0.2) that's a HUGE
 4          commitment, and that's why I was saying
 5          can do something for a two year period, or three year period.
 6  Beth:   Even if it's (.) cause the thing is (.) even if you spend a few hundred,
 7          I don't think (.)=
 8  ??:     Yeah.
 9  Beth:   =and that includes the paint [and deco]ration.
10  Sab.:   [Okay, fine], made the decision let's move on. I don't want to
11          think about this anymore. I've spend talked about this with Betty
12          so many time.
13  Beth:   Okay
14  ((Participants move on to discuss a different topic))
```

This example is typical for the ways in which many decisions are being made by this particular team (Schnurr 2010). It shows how Sabitha, the most senior member of the team, almost unilaterally makes the decision. She thereby cuts off Beth, the Business Development Manager, and brings the discussion about the lease agreement to an end. With her comment '*okay fine made the decision let's move on*' (line 10) she ratifies a decision that has apparently been made previously (see Sabitha's reference to previous discussions with another team member, Betty, in line 11). By re-stating the decision, the decision gets made and literally talked into being – in line with previous research which observed that a decision was often only considered to be made after it had been ratified by the Chair (Holmes & Stubbe 2003: 77). After Sabitha ratifies the decision here, which is very briefly acknowledged by Beth ('*okay*' in line 13), participants move on with the agenda and discuss another topic.

This relatively unilateral way of making a decision (and deciding when to move on with the agenda) is typical for Sabitha's behaviour in the weekly meetings of her team (Schnurr & Mak 2010). These established practices leave little doubt about the fact that Sabitha is the one in charge (see also Chapter 4, where we discuss more examples of Sabitha and her team). They are largely in line with the claims by earlier (often relatively essentialist) studies in Chinese professional contexts, which suggest that managers mainly favour autocratic decision making styles (e.g. Khairullah & Khairullah 2013) and that subordinates tend to rely on their managers or more senior people to make decisions (e.g. Redding 1990). However, in contrast to these claims, Sabitha's decision making style (and in fact her behaviour displayed in all the meetings that we recorded at this NGO) does not show or reflect a preference for indirect communication (which is allegedly typical for high-context communities like Hong Kong). On the contrary, her very direct and potentially face-threatening communication style challenges earlier studies which observed that in simulated business interactions, Hong Kong participants preferred more indirect communication styles (e.g. Du-Babcock & Tanaka 2013). Thus, rather than drawing on culture$_1$ perceptions, assumptions and stereotypes to explain Sabitha's behaviour in Example 3.3, it is analytically more productive to understand it in the specific context in which this interaction occurs. Taking into account other examples where she displays similar interactional behaviours, we would argue that the relatively unilateral decision making displayed here and her overall rather direct communication style are a reflection of, as well as an active contribution towards, the locally developed interactional practices and norms that characterise this relatively close-knit community of practice (CofP). Thus, in line with the argument presented in Chapter 2, rather than perceiving this relatively direct behaviour as face-threatening, the other team members consider it to be normal and appropriate practice. This interpretation is supported, for example, by Beth's immediate reaction (line 8) and her supportive and active behaviour in the rest of the meeting without any indication of being upset or interpreting this as anything but appropriate, normative and hence politic (see also our analysis and discussion of Example 4.5 in the next chapter for further support).

The next example occurred in another professional context, namely a PGC consultation. This interaction takes place between a doctor, a pregnant woman (client) and her husband. The woman has just received the results of her antenatal screening test, which indicate a higher risk for a chromosomal abnormality (i.e. the so-called Edwards' syndrome).

<u>Example 3.4</u>

The woman in this consultation took a screening test for chromosomal abnormalities that came back with a high-risk result for Edwards' syndrome (1:40). The woman already has two healthy children. The participants are discussing what further tests could be performed to confirm if the abnormality is indeed there. All participants are Hong Kong Chinese and the consultation was conducted in Cantonese.

1 Doctor: 不過我哋就話呢四十分之一. (0.3) 嘅呢個我諗我哋
             But we say the chance is one in forty. (0.3) For this, I think we
2   暫時嚟講都(.)就(0.6) .hh em::: (0.4) 我諗要
             for the time being say then (.) also (0.6) .hh em::: (0.4) I think
             we need to

3		照一照超音波囉.
		have an ultrasound test.
4		(0.4)
5	Client:	Mm [hmm]
6	Doctor:	[因為]有陣時(.)我哋 (0.2)睇咗之後呢, .hh(0.4)因為
		[as] sometimes (.) after we (0.2) have seen it, .hh (0.4) because
7		超音波, (.) 因為呢個 (0.3) 呢個condition
		ultrasounds, (.) because this (0.3) this condition,
8		同唐氏綜合症唔係好同嘅.
		is different from Down syndrome.
9	Client:	[Mm hmm]
10	Husband:	[Mm hmm]
11	Doctor:	因為超音波係有明顯嘅結構問題係可以睇到囉.
		Because ultrasounds can show it if there's a clear structural problem.
12		(0.2)
13	Husband:	好.
		Okay.
14	Doctor:	係因為睇到先繼續, 就可以好D囉.
		So (.) it would be better if we proceed after we have seen it.
15	Client:	[Mm hmm.] ((while nodding))
16	Husband:	[Mm hmm.] ((while nodding))

At the beginning of this excerpt the doctor explicitly states the decision for the woman to undergo an ultrasound scan in order to obtain more information about the suspected abnormality. This decision is framed as a recommendation (*'we need'* (line 2)) and its imperative character is mitigated by the repeated use of the softener *'I think'* before and after the decision is uttered, as well as invoking temporal factors (*'for the time being'*) (lines 1 and 2). This statement is followed by a brief pause and minimal acknowledgement by the pregnant woman (line 5). The doctor then continues with providing a rationale for the decision to undertake more tests (lines 6–8 and 11), which is accompanied by minimal responses from the husband (lines 10 and 13). In line 11 the doctor explicitly states the main reason for the decision (*'Because, the ultrasound can show it if there's a clear structural problem'*), which he rephrases with an emphasis on the benefits of the proposed additional ultrasound – to which both the woman and the husband seem to agree (as signalled by their affirmative minimal responses (*'mm hmm'*) and nodding (lines 15 and 16)).

This relatively short excerpt is a very interesting case of a decision, as it is constructed as a (strongly advocated) proposal by the doctor, for which he seeks the pregnant woman's consent in spite of not eliciting her views. Although the doctor leaves some interactional space for the woman (and/or her husband) to utter their views (e.g. the pauses in lines 4 and 12), he does not explicitly ask them for their preferences. Thus, since he presents only one treatment option (i.e. an ultrasound scan) and does not provide any alternative scenarios to the patients (Pilnick & Zayts 2016; see also Toerien et al. 2013), it is perhaps not really surprising that the clients agree to his initial decision to have an ultrasound.

The interactional behaviour displayed by the doctor in this example is in line with previous research by Collins et al. (2005), who maintain that unilateral decision making is characterised by the emphatic presentation of test results or a diagnosis, pointing to the necessity of doing something and perhaps of acting quickly, while omitting to mention the option of doing nothing. This option would be a viable alternative in the case of the pregnant woman here since there is no treatment for the suspected condition, should it be confirmed. The doctor's behaviour in this excerpt can thus be described as a unilateral approach (Collins et al. 2005) in which he more or less autonomously, and without explicitly consulting with the pregnant woman and her husband, makes a decision.

Upon a first glance, the relatively unilateral decision making displayed in this example seems to be in line with expected behaviour based on first-order notions of culture, and also confirms previous research (on counselling discourse in Asia) which noted that patients of Asian background tend to expect a more directive treatment and to be told what to do (Johnson & Nadirshaw 2002). However, this kind of unilateral decision making behaviour is relatively untypical for these antenatal consultations; and although healthcare providers often play an important role in the decision making (see also Zayts et al. 2012), in most cases decisions are made much more collaboratively and involve the pregnant women and their partners more actively (see also our discussion of Example 2.2 in the previous chapter and Example 5.5 in Chapter 5).

Collaborative decision making

In the vast majority of examples in our data, decision making is done more or less collaboratively with the input of various people – although often the most senior person has the last word or ratifies a decision by explicitly formulating it (this point is further discussed in the next chapter). We would thus place most of the decision making episodes in our corpus towards the 'collaborative' end of the continuum, as the following four examples illustrate.

The first two examples we discuss here are taken from Janet's and Susan's teams, respectively, and they directly contradict and, thus, considerably relativise the implications of the claims made by these women about the perceived lack of participation of their Chinese team members in decision making. The examples show that in both cases, the actual practice of decision making displayed in regular meetings of their teams is much more collaborative and participative than stated in the interviews. Example 3.5 is taken from a regular meeting at Lingsoft Inc., Janet's language learning centre, and it is representative of the ways in which she and her team members typically reach decisions in these meetings (see also Example 6.8 in Chapter 6 and Schnurr & Zayts 2013 for another example).

Example 3.5

Context: During the weekly meeting of the administrative team of Lingsoft Inc., a language learning centre. Participants in the conversation include Janet, the owner of the company and Chair of the meeting, and Valerie and Ivan, two employees. Janet is an expatriate from the UK, while the other participants are Hong Kong Chinese. Lingsoft Inc. offers English tutoring in some public schools in Hong Kong, and at this point in the meeting participants are discussing timetabling issues.

1	Janet:	Can we do two lessons on a Tuesday and, can we do?=
2	Ivan:	=You mean the time change?
3	Janet:	No, not time change 'cause we can't do earlier than fo:ur.
4		Or could we do, four to five thirty and five thirty to seven?
5		Are the only ones five thirty to seven?

((2 lines are omitted in which Ivan asks another clarifying question which Janet answers))

6	Ivan:	Mm hmm. You want to put the medium writing and the higher
7		writing? Like, for example today it might be have twelve to
8		fourteen student will show up.

((several lines are omitted))

9	Janet:	So I think then we, if we, if we got more people you have to save
10		four o'clock to five thirty for the smaller ones.
11	Ivan:	So, for the, yeah, for the lower writing group I put it in four to
12		five thirty, and then five thirty to u:h seven o'clock.
13	Valerie:	Ah! So you can (.) move Melanie and Celia.
14	Ivan:	Melanie already, Celia already moved to the Tuesday.
15	Janet:	They are already moved to Tuesday.
16	Ivan:	Yeah. Mm hmm.
17	Valerie:	Because they just have (.) two=
18	Ivan:	=because Friday is only two and then uh, mm hmm.
19	Valerie:	Yeah, Friday just two student.
20	Janet:	So, can we move them then five thirty to seven? Mm, or=
21	Ivan:	=I working on it and working on it with the uh, medium, medium
22		student and when they come back on the September and
23		then uh probably will your class is more than sixteen student.
24	Janet:	Okay.
25	Ivan:	Mm-hmm.
26	Janet:	Okay.

In contrast to Janet's claim (in Example 3.1) that the decision making in her team of Chinese subordinates is not '*fully democratic*' and that, by implication, she perceives them as not being as active as she would have liked, Example

3.5 shows a rather different picture. In this short excerpt (as in other examples of decision making in this team (see Schnurr & Zayts 2013)), two of her subordinates, Ivan and Valerie, contribute actively to the discussion and the decision making. For example, Ivan asks a clarifying question (line 2), provides explanations (lines 11 and 12, 18) and makes various suggestions throughout (lines 6 and 7, 21–23). One of his suggestions (lines 21–23) is eventually taken up as the team's decision, which is ratified by Janet in lines 24 and 26. More specifically, Ivan's suggestion to move the '*medium student*' to Janet's class (lines 21–23) is prefaced by his confirmation that he is '*working on it*' (line 21), which indicates that he is taking responsibility for these timetabling issues and is actively trying to find a solution. Moreover, although Valerie plays a less crucial role in this discussion, she also contributes and makes a suggestion as to how to solve the problem (line 13), and provides some explanations (lines 17 and 19).

A similar picture of equally engaged and participative team members emerges when we look in more detail at how decisions are actually being made in Susan's team. As in Janet's team, there is ample evidence of collaborative decision making, as the next example illustrates.

Example 3.6

Context: In the weekly meeting of the administrative team at Company K, a financial corporation, members discuss technical problems they have experienced with some of their equipment. The meeting is chaired by Cheryl (the team leader), Susan is the Head of the Department, and Angela, Pauline and Margaret are ordinary team members. Susan is an expatriate from the UK and all other participants are Hong Kong Chinese. Participants are discussing problems with video-cameras which Cheryl's team is providing to other people in the company.

```
 1 Cheryl:    ((clears throat)) So is the technical problem of the video
 2            camera solved already?
 3 Margaret:  Sometimes we uhm have a presentation skills foundation
 4            together with the presentation skills advanced coming together (.)
 5            on the same day. Uhm we can not only have one AV connecting
 6            cable for two video cams
 7 Susan:     Why don't we just buy another one?
 8 Cheryl:    Yah ((nods))
```

((7 turns are omitted in which participants discuss whether their department has enough cables))

```
 9 Angela:    Is it the mean the AV cable?
10 Margaret:  AV cable because th- when they- Laura and Eva er have to use
11            the connecting cable
```

12 Susan: Yeah OK [so we've] put an order in right?
13 Angela: [But I alr-] yes I already (already)
14 Susan: GREAT
15 Angela: Arrange (one) last year, December (.) but no stock, but not [in stock]
16 Cheryl: [The cable], you mean the three colour cable?=
17 Angela: =Right.
18 Susan: So it's still not in stock from December?
19 Angela: Yeah.
20 Susan: Would it be better buying it on the internet?=
21 Angela: °hmm° [(I)]
22 Susan: =[You] know, and getting it shipped here?
23 Angela: Ha-hah-hah
24 Susan: I mean you know we've been waiting since December
25   it's- it's al(h)most April.
26 Angela: Ri:::ght
27 Susan: I mean it can't be that's it's going to be that expensive.
28 Cheryl: Yah, I don't think so.
29 Pauline: So we can buy it first and then ca::n=
30 Susan: =We just claim it back on petty- p(h)etty ex(h)penses I mean,
31   you know probably the shipping will cost more.
32 Pauline: He-heh

((6 turns are omitted in which participants discuss Susan's suggestion of buying a cable on the internet))

33 Susan: I-I can't believe we've been putting up with this situation for
34   t(h)ree and a(h) h(h)alf month, you poor thing. Okay.
35 Cheryl: So the equipment problem is solved

((participants move to the next agenda item))

At the beginning of the excerpt, Cheryl, the Chair of the meeting, enquires whether the problem that her team has experienced with their video-cameras has been solved (lines 1 and 2). After Margaret's account of the problem (lines 3–6), Susan, the Head of Department and most senior person in the room, makes a concrete suggestion as to how to deal with the problem: '*Why don't we just buy another one?*' (line 7), which is supported verbally and non-verbally by Cheryl (line 8). This decision then leads on to another related issue about cables (omitted part and also lines 10–11). While various team members contribute to this discussion, it is again Susan who moves the discussion towards a solution (and hence decision) when she clarifies the prior decision on ordering some more cameras (which would at the same time solve the cable issue). Particularly noteworthy here is her utterance-initial agreement marker '*Yeah*' and her use of '*OK*' (line 12), which can be interpreted as introducing the next step in the decision making (Fung & Carter 2007).

Angela's response to Susan's suggestion (and her explanation that she has put in an order previously) (line 13) is briefly interrupted by Susan's expression of appreciation ('*GREAT*' spoken with emphasis (line 14)) before Cheryl follows up by asking further clarifying questions (about the cable's colour (line 16)). After another clarifying question – this time by Susan (line 18) – which gets responded to by Angela, Susan makes another suggestion, in the form of a question, on how to solve the issue: '*Would it be better buying it on the internet?*' (line 20). Her use of the relatively tentatively phrased question here is interesting, as it enables her to make a concrete suggestion while still keeping the floor open for alternative suggestions. Moreover, by using the relatively neutral formulation '*would it be better*' she manages to convey her proposition without explicitly assigning the task (or the blame for not having done it yet) to anyone specifically. After another brief exchange with Angela, Susan provides further reasons for her suggestion (lines 24, 25, 27). Interestingly, she uses the inclusive pronoun '*we*' here to signal her co-ownership of the issue. At this point Cheryl joins the conversation again and explicitly agrees with Susan (line 28), although it is Pauline, in the subsequent line, who has a first go at formulating the team's decision that emerges from this discussion: '*So we can buy it first and then ca::n*' (line 29). She gets more support from Susan, who makes some concrete suggestions on how to finance this (using petty cash), again by using the inclusive pronoun '*we*' (line 30).

After more discussion about the details (omitted here), Susan expresses her sympathy with Cheryl for having to deal with this situation. Her utterance is accompanied by some laughter throughout and the affectionate address form '*you poor thing*' (lines 33 and 34), which are an expression of Susan's empathy with the situation (rather than her disapproval for taking so long to solve the problem). Her utterance-final '*Okay*' indicates that she considers the decision to be made, which is then picked up by Cheryl (in line 35) who explicitly states '*So the equipment problem is solved*', thereby ratifying it and declaring the decision to be made. Thus, although Susan seems to be the driving force behind this decision and the one to initiate the solution to the problem, various team members contribute to the discussion, and in the end it is Cheryl who makes the decision visible (by stating that a solution has been found and by moving on with the agenda).

These observations are partly in line with Susan's own accounts shown in Example 3.2, where she maintains that she is the main decision maker. Yet, in contrast to her claims that there is no collective decision making in her team, Example 3.6 portrays a rather different, and more complex, picture in which the different team members do contribute to the decision making. For example, Angela's provision of important information, Cheryl's agreeing and Pauline's initial attempt at formulating a decision are all important aspects in the decision making process, and show that the decision is reached collaboratively (rather than unilaterally as claimed in Example 3.2). Thus, while Susan's generalising claims about '*people here*' not wanting to make decisions (Example 3.2) are largely in line with the earlier literature on (allegedly) preferred decision making practices in 'the Chinese culture', they are in sharp contrast to the actual practice displayed by her team of Hong Kong Chinese. The same also applied to Janet's claims (Example 3.1), which were contrasted considerably by the actual decision making behaviour of her team in Example 3.5.

In addition to these examples, which specifically challenge the claims made by some of the participants regarding the perceived role of culture$_1$ in decision making, we analyse two more examples of collaborative decision making here. In all instances, the decision making takes slightly different forms and demonstrates different kinds of collaboration. The next example, which could be placed towards the very end of the collaborative side of the continuum displayed in Figure 3.1, is taken from a meeting of a team of geneticists at a specialist clinic in Hong Kong (see also Example 4.8 in the next chapter). In these meetings, members discussed the patients they were going to see during the coming week.

Example 3.7

Context: The patient that the geneticists are discussing in this extract is a 2-year-old boy who was referred to the specialist clinic due to suspected dwarfism (short stature). There are three geneticists who participate in the interaction: Drs Lee, Chau, and Ho. Dr Ho saw the child at his previous visit to the clinic and conducted the examination (which involved taking measurements of different parts of the child's body) that appeared to support the diagnosis. Dr Ho is presenting the case to the rest of the team. Dr Lee chairs the meeting. The team members are discussing the measurements that were used to confirm the diagnosis. Although all participants are Hong Kong Chinese, these team meetings were typically conducted in English (to help members practise their English for conference presentations and other public speaking events as they told us in the interviews).

  1 Ho: One point one something, less than one point two. (.)
  2 Lee: One year old with one point one something is a problem.
  3 Chau: °One year old.°
  4 Ho: Ehh one point six for a new born. One point three when he is three
  5   year old.
  6 Lee: °Three year old is one point one.°
  7 Ho: I remember six years old is one degree.

((3 turns are omitted in which the participants are trying to recollect what the exact measurements should be))

  8 Lee: You measured it? [You measured it?] ((in a laughing voice))
  9 Chau: [((laughs))]
10 Ho: [((laughs))]
11 Lee: You measured it yourself and you didn't even know if it was normal.
12 Chau: Just reassess.
13 Ho: No, there is no reassessment.
14 Chau: °Right.° You have taken my measurement.

((4 turns are omitted in which C and H talk about what the measurement should be))

15 Lee: How about the patient's (xxx). Is it normal?

16 Chau: If it is normal, it should be one point something.
17 Lee: One point something. It shouldn't be one point one. It should be one
18   point three, one point five, one point seven.
19   °It's really not reliable.°
20 Ho: One point three, three years old, one point three, I remember.
21   ((laughs))
22 Lee: °What was it when we studied it in school?° ((laughs))
23 Ho: Your, the book you studied is different from mine. ((laughs))
24 Lee: One point one something, one point one something. One year old,
25   one point three. °One point three.° ((murmurs to himself)) .hh
26   Okay. It means nothing is found after ((inaudible))?
27 Ho: Just measure it one more time.
28 Lee: Okay, let's measure it one more time.

((Lee makes a note in a client's file and moves on to the discussion of the next client case)).

In this excerpt the team discuss and come to a decision about the best way of confirming the diagnosis of one of their patients, a boy with suspected dwarfism. In order to achieve this, participants need to agree on what measurement is '*normal*', as repeatedly mentioned. As becomes clear early in the extract, the question of what is considered to be the '*normal*' or age-appropriate measurement is not straightforward and there is a relatively high degree of uncertainty among the geneticists – as is reflected, for example, in their use of approximate descriptions (e.g. '*one point one something*' (e.g. lines 1 and 2), hesitations markers ('*ehh*' (line 4)) and lower voice volume (e.g. lines 3 and 6)).

This uncertainty among the geneticists, however, presents a problem, as the exact measurements are necessary clinical evidence to confirm the diagnosis of the patient. The geneticists are thus confronted with a relatively serious problem, and, perhaps not surprisingly, various team members actively contribute to finding a solution and reaching a decision. Throughout the excerpt, different members participate in the discussion and decision making processes. For example, after Dr Lee states the problem in line 2, '*One year old with one point one something is a problem*', Dr Ho responds by offering his own recollection of what the measurement should be: '*Ehh one point six for a new born*' (line 4). This is followed by Dr Lee's own recollection of information about the measurements for 3 year olds (line 6). When participants seem to realise that this discussion is not leading to the expected results (namely, a specific number which would give them certainty about their diagnosis), Dr Lee enquires whether Dr Ho, who is responsible for this patient, has actually measured his height (line 8). This potential critical and hence face-threatening question is mitigated considerably by Dr Lee's friendly and laughing tone of voice, which soon turns into joint laughter between the interlocutors (lines 9 and 10). Dr Chau then suggests repeating the measurement (line 12), which is opposed by Dr Ho (line 13). This leads to a discussion (omitted here) between Drs Ho and Chau about what the measurement should be, and which is brought to an end by Dr Lee who brings up another topic by asking about whether another measurement was normal (line 15). Just like the previous topic, this also generates considerable discussion among the geneticists about normal measurement results, and again, no conclusion is drawn – largely because people do not seem to be certain about measurements and seem to recall different numbers (e.g. *'one point three, I remember'* (Dr Ho in line 20) versus *'One point something. It shouldn't be one point one. It should be one point three, one point five, one point seven'* (Dr Lee in lines 17–20)). However, what is of particular interest to us here is how in spite of these disagreements, in the end participants reach a decision, namely to *'measure it one more time'* (as suggested by Dr Ho (line 27)), which is then further ratified by Dr Lee: *'Okay, let's measure it one more time'* (line 28).

This excerpt is thus a good illustration of how team members work collaboratively towards making a decision. By drawing on their own expertise (i.e. their knowledge about normal measurements) they can build up a collective 'expert opinion' which then helps them manage and eventually resolve their uncertainty (see also Zayts et al. fc). This highly collaborative decision making style which characterises this particular team (and which could thus be understood as a reflection and at the same time an active contribution to the team's negotiated shared norms and practices (as captured in second-order notions of culture)), largely challenges the rather essentialist claims about preferred decision making styles in Hong Kong made in some of the earlier literature. In contrast to these claims about the role of culture₁, there is only very little evidence in this example (and all the interactions that we recorded among the members of this team) of traces of high power distance among team members (we elaborate this aspect in more detail in the next chapter).

Similar points can be made about the last example we briefly want to illustrate here, in which an equally collaborative decision making style is displayed. This example occurred during a meeting among team members at Sandcastle, another language learning centre in Hong Kong.

Example 3.8

Context: Jenny and Lily are the managers and co-founders of the company, and Penny is the Office Manager. Lily is an expatriate from the UK, and Jenny and Penny are Hong Kong Chinese. The meeting occurred during their lunch break and participants are eating throughout the meeting. At this point in the interaction they are discussing timetabling issues and when to schedule a particularly small class.

1 Jenny: Can they not do the half hour? Two times a week option.
2 Lily: Could they come at five? (.)

((participants are eating))

3 Lily: Five to six.
4 Penny: I can check. But what is matter? Five to six or two half an hour?

5   (.) Because I just think if start the half an hour, is hard to add the
6   other students.
7   Jenny: Huh hmm.
8   Lily: Yeah. I think probably an hour is better.
9   Jenny: We've got nothing now. We can do it. I'm just concerned there're
10   only two students, that's really, (.)
11 Lily: °maybe maybe we'll just go for it.°

((A student comes to the centre with her parent. The staff greets them. Penny
leaves her seat to arrange a classroom for the student.))

12 Jenny: Yeah. Let's go ahead.

This excerpt involves making a relatively routine decision about when to schedule
a class with only a small number of students. At the beginning, Jenny, one of
the co-owners of the language learning centre and Chair of the meeting, makes
a concrete suggestion about possible schedules for this class. This suggestion is
then further elaborated by Lily, the other co-owner, who proposes a concrete
time for the class. This is followed by Penny's initial agreement and some further
clarifying questions regarding the proposed timing of the class. After a short
pause (due to participants eating their lunch), Penny continues her turn and
provides further explanations to her earlier questions, which signal her reluctance
to Jenny and Lily's suggestions. Penny's explanations and concerns are agreed
to by Jenny (who produces minimal agreeing feedback in line 7) and by Lily,
who after uttering the agreement marker '*Yeah*' (line 8) repeats (albeit in slightly
different words) Penny's suggestion to schedule the class at the hour rather than
half hour. This is then further supported by Jenny, who initially agrees before
bringing up another concern about relatively low student numbers (lines 9–10).
After another brief pause (caused by participants eating their lunch), Lily repeats
the earlier consensus without explicitly orienting to or commenting on Jenny's
concern. She thereby makes the team's decision explicit. After another brief
interruption (due to clients arriving), Jenny agrees ('*Yeah*' (line 12)) and ratifies
the decision.

What is particularly noteworthy about this example is not only the fact
that it is reached very collaboratively with different team members (almost
regardless of their organisational position) making contributions, but also the
observation that the actual decision making (rather than only the prior discussion) is a collaborative accomplishment: while Lily initially formulates the
decision (line 8), thereby literally talking it into existence, it is Penny, the
most junior person, who eventually ratifies the decision and who has the last
word on this matter.

As we elaborate in more detail in Chapters 4 and 6 (where we discuss further
examples of this team at Sandcastle), this collaborative and relatively inclusive
interactional style is very typical for the meetings of this team. Most of the
decision making is collaborative and various team members regularly contribute
to and play an active role in this interactional activity. These behaviours, as we

explain further in Chapter 6, are a crucial aspect of the shared practices that have developed among the members of this particular CofP and they are, in fact, an important element of the workplace culture of Sandcastle as Lily and Jenny explained in the interview after data collection. The decision making behaviours displayed in this excerpt thus challenge the claims about the alleged importance of organisational rank and positions in terms of decision making, and provide further empirical illustration of how decisions are actually made in authentic workplace interactions. As with the previous examples, first-order notions of culture do not appear relevant in analysing the observed behaviour. On the contrary, there is considerable variation in the ways in which decisions are being made by the members of a specific team in any workplace, and attempts at trying to identify patters and making generalisations – especially with regard to the alleged role of 'culture' – are highly problematic and are likely to result in stereotyping rather than adding analytical value.

Discussion

In this chapter we have been guided by the claims made by some of our partici-pants (which are to some extent reinforced and supported by the findings of earlier studies) about the potential impact that first-order culture may have on how people make decisions at work. Our analyses, which mainly focused on the extent to which decisions were made more or less unilaterally or collabora-tively, have shown that a wide variety exists in terms of actual practices of decision making displayed by members of different teams and in different workplaces. While some of these practices seem to reinforce claims about the role of culture$_1$ (as uttered by some of our participants in the interviews), the majority of examples in our corpus challenge such generalising comments and illustrate that most decisions are reached after some input and collaboration from colleagues and subordinates. These observations, based on our in-depth analysis of several examples of authentic workplace interaction, largely reject generalising grand claims about the alleged role of 'culture' and rather point to the crucial role of localised practices and norms that are emerging and negoti-ated among members of a specific team (as captured in notions of culture$_2$). In other words, where exactly on the continuum (Figure 3.1) a particular episode of decision making is to be placed, is primarily a question of culture$_2$ rather than culture$_1$.

Moving away from making claims about the role of culture$_1$ in people's decision-making activities, and looking for other explanations, the observed diversity in practice could perhaps be related to the different kinds of workplaces where we collected data – including an NGO, two language learning centres, a large interna-tional financial corporation as well as different public hospitals. These different workplaces, and the professional industries they represent, as well as the specific professions they house (e.g. language teachers, administrators, healthcare profes-sionals) may have developed their own practices and norms regarding appropriate ways of making decisions.

For instance, based on Examples 3.5 and 3.8, which were both recorded at staff meetings in companies that provide language teaching, it could perhaps be suggested that relatively collaborative ways of decision making are typical for these kinds of professional contexts. However, while the professional context may, of course, have an impact on the interactional behaviour displayed by participants, we are cautious not to overstate this influence and would rather focus on the local context in which specific practices are enacted and constantly negotiated. Support for this caution can also be found in our data, where, in addition to similarities in decision making practices across different workplaces in the same sector, we also found considerable differences (cf. the different decision making styles displayed by the healthcare providers in Examples 3.4 and 3.7). Moreover, as Examples 3.5, 3.6 and 3.7 show, collaborative decision making is not specific to a particular professional context but does regularly occur in very different teams across a wide range of workplaces.

Further empirical evidence to question the assumption of a direct link between actual decision making practices and a specific profession is provided by the examples of PGC discussed in this and the previous chapter. The profession of PGC has developed the ethos of non-directiveness (see also Chapter 5), according to which healthcare providers are expected to provide information in an unbiased and non-imposing way in order to ensure that their clients (i.e. pregnant women) are in a position to make a decision (about available testing options) that reflect their own values and judgements (e.g. White 1997; Marteau & Dormandy 2001). As a consequence of this professional ethos, it could be expected that the counsellors take a very passive role in the decision making process and leave it to their clients to decide. However, as Examples 3.4 and 2.2 (in the previous chapter) have shown, considerable variation exists in the ways in which this ethos is actually oriented to and put into practice in an interaction. In both instances, rather than upholding this ethos by taking a passive and supportive role, the healthcare providers play a very active and guiding part in the decision making. In Example 2.2 they try to influence and perhaps even steer their clients' decision making, and in Example 3.4 they make the decision unilaterally without leaving much room for their clients to participate in and take ownership of the decision.[2]

These observations, once more, point to the crucial importance of looking at local practices (as reflected in the notion of culture₂) and moving away from exclusively focusing on claims about culture₁. Similarly, rather than making grand claims about how a specific profession or professional sector may influence decision making practices, it is important (and very much in line with the proposed focus on culture₂) to analyse actual behaviour and to understand that the specific ways in which decisions are actually made are negotiated among interlocutors throughout an encounter.

In the next chapter we explore a topic that is closely related to decision making, namely leadership, and we return to some of the observations that were made in this chapter – especially regarding questions of who contributes to the decision making and who has the last word. We address these issues by analysing more examples of authentic workplace interactions taken from different teams in a wide range of professional contexts.

Notes

1 Examples 3.1 and 3.2 are also used in Schnurr & Zayts (2013), Example 3.3 in Schnurr (2010), Example 3.4 in Pilnick & Zayts (2016), and Example 3.6 in Schnurr & Zayts (2011).
2 This diversity in actual practice is also discussed in the literature on PGC, where it is argued that although the ethos of nondirectiveness is generally accepted among professionals, several studies have questioned its attainability in practice (see, for example, Anderson 1999; Gervais 1993; Shiloh 1996). It has been shown that upholding the ethos of nondirectiveness may not always be in the best interest of the client – for example when they explicitly ask for advice (e.g. Zayts & Schnurr 2012; Burke and Kolker 1994; Brunger and Lippman 1995).

References

Anderson, Gwen (1999). Nondirectiveness in prenatal genetics: Patients read between the lines. *Nursing Ethics* 6.2: 126–36.

Benkendorf, Judith L., Michele B. Prince, Mary A. Rose, Anna De Fina & Heidi E. Hamilton (2001). Does indirect speech promote nondirective genetic counselling? *American Journal of Medical Genetics* 106: 199–207.

Brunger, Fern & Abby Lippman (1995). Resistance and adherence to the norms of genetic counseling. *Journal of Genetic Counseling* 4: 151–67.

Burke, B. Meredith & Aliza Kolker (1994). Directiveness in prenatal genetic counseling. *Woman Health* 22: 31–53.

Collins, Sarah, Paul Drew, Ian Watt & Vikki Entwistle (2005). 'Unilateral' and 'bilateral' practitioner approaches in decision-making about treatment. *Social Science and Medicine* 61: 2611–27.

Du-Babcock, Bertha (2006). An analysis of topic management strategies and turn-taking behavior in the Hong Kong bilingual environment: The impact of culture and language use. *Journal of Business Communication* 43: 21–42.

Du-Babcock, Bertha (1999). Topic management and turn-taking in professional communication: First versus second-language strategies. *Management Communication Quarterly* 12: 544–74.

Du-Babcock, Bertha & Hiromasa Tanaka (2013). A comparison of the communication behaviors of Hong Kong Chinese and Japanese business professionals in intracultural and intercultural decision-making meetings. *Journal of Business and Technical Communication* 27.3: 263–87.

Fung, Loretta & Ron Carter (2007). Discourse markers and spoken English: Native and learner use in pedagogic settings. *Applied Linguistics* 28.3: 410–39.

Gaenslen, Fritz (1986). Culture and decision making in China, Japan, Russia, and the United States. *World Politics* 39.1: 78–103.

Gervais, K. G. (1993). Objectivity, value neutrality, and nondirectiveness in genetic counseling. In Dianne M. Bartels, Bonnie S. LeRoy & Arthur L. Caplan (eds), *Prescribing Our Future: Ethical Challenges in Genetic Counseling*. New York: Aldine de Gruyter. 119–30.

Halvorsen, Kristin (2010). Team decision-making in the workplace: A systematic review of discourse analytic studies. *Journal of Applied Linguistics and Professional Practice* 7.3: 273–96.

Handford, Michael (2010). *The Language of Business Meetings*. Cambridge, UK: Cambridge University Press.

Hofstede, Geert (2001). *Culture's Consequences: Comparing Values, Behaviors, Institutions, and Organizations across Nations* (2nd ed.). Thousand Oaks, CA: SAGE.

Hofstede, Geert (1991). *Cultures and Organization: Software of the Mind—Intercultural Cooperation and its Importance for Survival*. Maidenhead, UK: McGraw-Hill.

Hofstede, Geert, Gert Jan Hofstede & Michael Minkov (2010). *Cultures and Organizations. Software of the Mind. Intercultural Cooperation and its Importance for Survival*. New York: McGraw Hill.

Holmes, Janet & Maria Stubbe (2003). *Power and Politeness in the Workplace: A Sociolinguistic Analysis of Talk at Work*. London: Longman.

Johnson, Amanda Webb & Zenobia Nadirshaw (2002). Good practice in transcultural counseling: An Asian perspective. In Stephen Palmer (ed.), *Multicultural Counselling: A Reader*. London: SAGE. 119–28.

Khairullah, Durriya & Zahid Khairullah (2013). Cultural values and decision-making in China. *International Journal of Business, Humanities and Technology* 3.2: 1–12.

Levinson, Stephen C. (1992). Activity types and language. In Paul Drew & John Heritage (eds), *Talk at Work: Interaction in Institutional Settings*. Cambridge, UK: Cambridge University Press. 66–100.

Lewis, Richard D. (2000). *When Cultures Collide: Managing Successfully Across Cultures*. London: Nicholas Brealey.

Mann Leon, Mark Radford, Paul Burnett, Steve Ford, Michael Bond, Kwok Leung, Hiyoshi Nakamura, Graham Vaughan & Kuo-Shu Yang (1998). Cross-cultural differences in self-reported decision-making style and confidence. *International Journal of Psychology* 33.5: 325–35.

Marra, Meredith (2003). Decisions in New Zealand business meetings. Unpublished PhD thesis, Victoria University of Wellington, Wellington, New Zealand.

Marteau, Theresa M. & Elizabeth Dormandy (2001). Facilitating informed choice in prenatal testing: How well are we doing? *American Journal of Medical Genetics* 106.3: 185–90.

Pilnick, Alison (2008). 'It's something for you both to think about': Choice and decision making in nuchal translucency screening for Down's syndrome. *Sociology of Health and Illness* 30.4: 511–30.

Pilnick, Alison & Olga Zayts (2016). Advice, authority and autonomy in shared decision-making in antenatal screening: The importance of context. *Sociology of Health & Illness* 38.3: 343–59.

Redding, Gordon & Gilbert Y. Y. Wong (1986). The psychology of Chinese organizational behaviour. In Michael H. Bond (ed.), *The Psychology of the Chinese People*. Hong Kong: Oxford University Press. 267–95.

Redding, S. Gordon (1990). *The Spirit of Chinese Capitalism*. Berlin/New York: Walter de Gruyter.

Schnurr, Stephanie (2010). 'Decision made – let's move on'. Negotiating gender and professional identity in Hong Kong workplaces. In Markus Bieswanger, Heiko Motschenbacher & Susanne Mühleisen (eds), *Language in its Socio-cultural Context: New Explorations in Global, Medial and Gendered Uses*. Berlin: Peter Lang. 111–36.

Schnurr, Stephanie, Angela Chan, Joelle Loew & Olga Zayts (fc). Leadership and culture: When stereotypes meet actual workplace practice. To appear in Cornelia Ilie & Stephanie

Schnurr (eds), *Challenging Leadership Stereotypes through Discourse: Power, Management and Gender*. Delhi: Springer.

Schnurr, Stephanie & Bernie Mak (2010). Leadership and workplace realities in Hong Kong. Is gender really *not* an issue? *Gender and Language. Special Issue on Gender and Language in the Workplace.* 5.2: 337–64.

Schnurr, Stephanie & Olga Zayts (2013). 'I can't remember them ever not doing what I tell them!' Negotiating face and power relations in 'upwards' refusals in multicultural workplaces in Hong Kong. *Intercultural Pragmatics* 10.4: 593–616.

Schnurr, Stephanie & Olga Zayts (2011). Constructing and contesting leaders. An analysis of identity construction at work. In Jo Angouri and Meredith Marra (eds), *Constructing Identities at Work*. Houndmills: Palgrave. 40–60.

Shiloh, Shoshana (1996). Decision-making in the context of genetic risk. In Theresa Marteau & Martin Richards (eds), *The Troubled Helix: Social and Psychological Implications of the New Human Genetics*. Cambridge, UK: Cambridge University Press. 82–103.

Toerien, Merran, Rebecca Shaw & Markus Reuber (2013). Initiating decision-making in neurology consultations: 'Recommending' versus 'option-listing' and the implications for medical authority. *Sociology of Health & Illness* 35.6: 873–90.

Weber, Elke & Christopher Hsee (2000). Culture and individual judgement and decision making. *Applied Psychology. An International Review* 49.1: 32–61.

White, Mary Terrell (1997). 'Respect for autonomy' in genetic counseling: An analysis and a proposal. *Journal of Genetic Counseling* 6.3: 297–313.

Yeung, Lorrita (2004). The paradox of control in participative decision-making: Facilitative discourse in banks. *Text & Talk* 24.1: 113–46.

Zayts, Olga & Stephanie Schnurr (2013). '[She] said: "take the test" and I took the test'. Relational work as a framework to approach directiveness in prenatal screening of Chinese clients in Hong Kong. *Journal of Politeness Research* 9.2: 187–210.

Zayts, Olga & Stephanie Schnurr (2012). 'You may know better than I do'. Advice giving in Down's syndrome screening in a Hong Kong hospital. In Miriam Locher & Holger Limberg (eds), *Advice in Discourse*. Amsterdam: Benjamins. 195–212.

Zayts, Olga, Stephanie Schnurr & Srikant Sarangi (fc). Shared expertise in negotiating future actions in the genetics case conferences. To appear in Srikant Sarangi and Per Linell (eds), *Team Talk: Decision Making Across Boundaries in Health and Social Care Professions*. London: Equinox.

Zayts, Olga, V. Yelei Wake & Stephanie Schnurr (2012). Chinese prenatal genetic counseling discourse in Hong Kong: Health care providers' (non)directive stance, or who is making the decision? In Yulin Pan and Daniel Kádár (eds), *Chinese Discourse and Interaction: Theory and Practice*. London: Equinox. 228–47.

4 Leadership. A 'cultural' activity?

In bringing culture and leadership together we are effectively asking for trouble as culture has been defined, debated and disputed to an even greater extent than leadership.

(Jackson & Parry 2008: 63)

Introduction

In spite of this note of caution, in this chapter we explore one particularly interesting aspect of 'culture' at work, namely leadership. Leadership is a fascinating topic which, we believe, should not be overlooked in any research monograph on language and 'culture' at work. Perhaps more importantly, the topic of leadership and its relationship to 'culture' was frequently brought up by the participants in our research. Susan, an expatriate from the UK, who also featured in some of the previous chapters, puts forward a view that many of our more senior expatriate participants share:

Example 4.1[1]

Context: During the interview after data collection we asked Susan to tell us a little bit about her leadership style.

```
 1 Susan:  Well, it's changed (.). I swore that I'd never let this happen
 2         because when I arrived, I, I saw people, I saw managers and senior
 3         managers and partners doing things that I thought were really
 4         atrocious, and really not, not appropriate and quite a dictatorial
 5         style and [. . .] I don't think it's effective.
 6         Um and- and coming to China what I've realised is that the
 7         culture requires you in a way to do this, it actually requires you
 8         to act in ways that as a Westerner, I find eh eh surprising eh. I
 9         don't think I am gonna have any difficulty when I return to work
10         in- in other cultures or (.) any difficulty
```

11   returning. (.) But it is almost as if you are expected to act in these
12   ways. And if you <u>don't</u>, it <u>confuses</u> people. I think it confuses
13   the Chinese people who work for you. [. . .]
14   So, so you are <u>forced</u> in a way to <u>change</u> your
15   management[2] style and I find that surprising, I find it <u>odd</u>.
16   But then, you know, you have to do what you have to do.
17   I am just hoping that everything will just,
18   just flip back and I try to do it as little as I can.

Although there is clearly a lot to say about this extract, we focus here on what it reveals about Susan's perception of leadership and first-order notions of culture. Two points are particularly worth mentioning: first, her claim that she (and other '*Westerner[s]*' (lines 6 and 7) in similar positions) had to change leadership styles when moving to Hong Kong. According to Susan, she had to adapt her ways of doing leadership according to what she considers to be the expectations of the Chinese people she works with – '*if you don't, it confuses people*' (line 10). The second point that she makes refers to what she perceives to be distinct ways of doing leadership that are preferred (and exercised) by different 'cultural' groups, namely '*the Chinese people*' (line 11) and '*Westerner[s]*' (line 7). Both of these claims are expressions of Susan's views of first-order notions of culture, and they are shared by many of the people we interviewed.

This impression that people are '*forced*' (line 11) to change or adapt their 'normal' and often preferred ways of doing leadership was one of the themes that came through in many of the interviews that we conducted with several expatriates in Hong Kong. The reasons for these perceived changes in leadership were often explicitly linked to first-order notions of culture – for example, when Susan comments that '*the culture requires you in a way to do this*' (lines 5 and 6). These points were raised by many of our interviewees regardless of the industry in which they work and the amount of time they have spent in Hong Kong.

Another theme frequently mentioned in the interviews was that this change was perceived as involving a move towards more autocratic, directive leadership styles which required the expatriates with whom we spoke to become more '*dictatorial*' (line 4), and to change their ways of exercising power – for example by explicitly telling their subordinates what to do and by making decisions unilaterally (cf. Chapter 3).

<u>Example 4.2</u>

1 Susan: The longer I am in China, I think, the more I- the more I realise
2   that- that for a lot of employees here it's better <u>not</u> to know
3   because if you know, it actually gives you responsibilities
4   that may be difficult to deal with. [..]
5   So this morning it was just simply, please do this, do it by

6   eleven am, please drop it on my desk, we are having a discussion.
7   by eleven thirty It's just <u>not</u> the approach taken in Australia. [. . .]
8   But I can give you thousands of examples. [..]
9   You just <u>tell</u> people, you just <u>tell</u> people to do things.

Example 4.3

Context: Interview with Lily, an expatriate from the UK who is the co-owner of a language learning centre in Hong Kong.

1 Lily: I think people <u>do</u> become a lot more accepting and therefore they do
2   what they are <u>told</u> to do, rather than what they want to do. [. . .]
3   They want to do what they <u>should</u> do.

In these quotes, the interviewees describe their leadership styles as very directive and autocratic. They position themselves as being solely in charge of and
responsible for getting things done, while their subordinates are portrayed as
having no interest in participating in various leadership activities, such as
contributing to decision making and discussions around what needs to be done.
Although our analyses in the previous chapters relativise these claims – especially
with regard to decision making practice – it is noteworthy that in the interviews
our participants typically conceptualised leadership as a 'one (wo)man show'
characterised by a relatively rigid top–down, hierarchical command structure
with a clearly identifiable leader who is in charge and the team below waiting
to be told what to do. Such views, as expressed by our participants, are reminiscent of the earlier, often relatively essentialist literature which described
Hong Kong as a Confucian society in which leaders are absolute authority
figures who, similar to a parent, expect complete obedience in return for caring
and parental guidance (e.g. House et al. 2004; Lowe 1998). These claims about
'cultural' leadership expectations also come through in some of the culture$_1$
comments of our participants discussed in previous chapters, which, as we have
argued throughout, provide important insights into participants' perceptions and
sense-making processes.

However, as we will illustrate in more detail below, when we look at the
interactional data that we collected for our corpus, and the ways in which leadership is actually enacted on the local level of a particular workplace – as captured
by second-order notions of culture – a very different and much more diverse
picture emerges which relativises these claims about leadership and culture$_1$. As
we elaborated in the previous chapter, there is often a considerable discrepancy
between what our participants say in the interviews and their actual behaviour
reflected in the interactional data that we collected in their workplaces with
regard to decision making. For example, in the previous chapter we contrasted
Janet's comments about her team members not participating in the decision-
making process with some examples of decisions that were reached conjointly
among the members of her team. Perhaps unsurprisingly, a similar picture emerges

in Susan's and Lily's teams where we find very little evidence of Susan displaying what she herself refers to as a '*dictatorial*' leadership style (Example 4.1). Equally, there is abundant evidence in the data that we collected in Lily's workplace of her team members playing a much more active role in the meetings than she suggests in the interviews (Example 4.3).

Example 4.4 illustrates this. It is taken from a meeting that we recorded at Susan's workplace. We have included it here to show that contrary to Susan's claims in the interviews, her team members are actually much more proactive and do not need to be explicitly told 'to do things' – quite the opposite: in this case, the decisions are being made among team members without Susan's explicit input.

Example 4.4

Context: At the opening stages of the meeting. Cheryl, the newly appointed team leader, is chairing the meeting. Julia is an administrator. Susan, the Head of Department, is also present at the meeting but does not contribute to this discussion.

1	Cheryl:	Ok. Then we start our meeting.
2	??:	Hmmm.
3	Cheryl:	Uhmmm the (interaction) item (s-s-s-ays) that Jamie (need) to
4		prepare the guidelines from ((name)).
5	Julia:	Yeah, u[hhh].
6	Cheryl:	[Yeah], so how is the update?
7	Julia:	Uhm heh (we) already review, and I'm ah changing the [course
8		uhm].
9	Cheryl:	[Uhhum], ok.
10	Julia:	We have to revise and the other point- I already sent the [sister
11		company] the update staff list and they checking.
12	Cheryl:	The [sister company] staff list is fo:::r=
13	Julia:	=Yeah, the training li- [database]
14	Cheryl:	[Database].
15	Julia:	So they can update the ahm[m in]formation.
16	Cheryl:	[Ahum] Ok. So that- that means they are updating the: [sister
17		company] staff list and then when they send back to you
18		you can send it to IT or=
19	Julia:	=No just the training database cause ahmm we want- we hope the
20		training database is update if they leave we can take the current
21		staff if they leave.

What is particularly interesting about this example is how team members, in particular Julia and Cheryl, negotiate among themselves what actions need to be undertaken. After Cheryl, the Chair of the meeting, asks for updates on the preparation of some guidelines (line 6), Julia provides this information (line 7) and also proactively outlines planned future activities (lines 10–11). Cheryl and Julia then conjointly construct and negotiate the meaning and implications of this, as the frequent overlaps and latching onto each other's utterances indicate (lines 12–19). As displayed in this short example, the conjoint negotiation of meaning and the proactive and collaborative approach to getting things done sharply contrast with Susan's claims in her interview (Example 4.1). These behaviours paint a very different picture of how things are actually done in this particular team.

In fact, contrary to what many of our participants said in the interviews when we asked them about their leadership styles, we found only a relatively small number of instances in our corpus of the kinds of top–down ways of doing leadership described in the examples above, which emphasise and uphold hierarchical structures and which are based on and reinforce direct, clear, unidirectional lines of power. In other words, we have very little evidence in the spoken interactions that we recorded of the kind of directive and unmitigated ways of telling people what to do that Susan and Lily described in their interviews. Instead, we observed a wide diversity of leadership styles (as we will illustrate in more detail), which makes it impossible to attempt generalising about leadership in Hong Kong and its relationship with first-order culture. There is clearly no 'one-size-fits all' method of doing leadership in Hong Kong (or any other socio-cultural context for that matter) (see also Schnurr et al. fc). This chapter aims to capture and illustrate some of these complexities of leadership in different workplaces in Hong Kong, and to critically discuss the potential role of culture (in both its first- and second-order meanings).

Conceptualising leadership

Before going into more detail, we should take a step back and explicate what we actually mean by 'leadership'. This is crucial since there exist 'almost as many different definitions of leadership as there are people who have attempted to define the concept' (Bass 1981: 7). It is an ongoing debate among researchers – often from different disciplines – as to what exactly leadership is (e.g. Alvesson & Spicer 2012; Grint 2005). While earlier research tended to conceptualise leadership in terms of 'traits, behaviours, influence, interaction patterns, role relationships, and occupation of an administrative position' (Yukl 2002: 3), more recently researchers have started to acknowledge the dynamic nature of leadership and understand it as a process or an activity rather than a relatively static attribute or position that individuals occupy in their organisation's hierarchy (Heifertz 1998: 347; see also Hosking 1997; Northouse 1997).

This more dynamic conceptualisation of leadership is also at the heart of recent discourse analytic studies of leadership (e.g. Schnurr fc). Located in the tradition of discursive leadership (Fairhurst 2007), these studies explore the specific processes through which leadership is performed in and through discourse. In line with this research, we base our definition of leadership around the observation that discourse plays a crucial role in the enactment of leadership, and we view leadership as (often discursive) behaviours that may be performed by an individual or a group, and that typically, but not necessarily always, combine transactional and relational behaviours. These behaviours are in line with and aim at advancing the goals and vision of a group. For leadership to be successful it needs to be supported by others. Transactional behaviours refer to those activities that primarily aim at getting things done (such as decision making (cf. Chapter 3) and giving instructions), while relational behaviours describe those activities which contribute towards creating team harmony and a productive working atmosphere. As we illustrate in the subsequent sections, both transactional and relational behaviours are integral aspects of leadership and often occur simultaneously (e.g. Ferch & Mitchell 2001). This definition of leadership discourse is particularly useful for our endeavour here, because it takes into account that leadership may take different forms in different contexts. Moreover, by acknowledging the dynamic nature of leadership, researchers are able to focus on leader*ship* rather than being restricted to a focus on individual leaders (see also Schnurr fc; Gronn 2002: 423; Choi & Schnurr 2014).

Our analyses of leadership and culture in its first- and second-order meanings take this dynamic definition of leadership as a starting point and explore several examples of authentic leadership behaviour in various workplaces in Hong Kong. Rather than focusing on the behaviour of individuals in particular hierarchical positions (i.e. designated leaders), this involves the analysis of specific behaviours which have been identified by previous research as being indexed for leadership, such as making decisions, getting things done, solving problems and managing conflict, moving a discussion along, creating meaning and making sense, reaching consensus, etc. (e.g. Choi & Schnurr 2014; Schnurr & Zayts 2011; Marra et al. 2006; Clifton 2006; Holmes & Marra 2004; Schnurr & Chan 2011; Wodak et al. 2011).

Leadership and 'culture'

A substantial body of literature exists within leadership studies which claims that what people generally refer to as 'culture' is among the most prominent factors that have an impact on defining 'the array of preferred and acceptable leader behaviours' (Cullen 1999: 527; see also Guirdham 2005; Chee & West 2004; House et al. 2004). The main argument of proponents of this assumption is that people's different expectations about what constitute appropriate ways of doing leadership are often linked to what they perceive to be culture-specific values; consequently, notions of what are considered to be 'effective' leadership vary considerably across cultures. Such claims draw heavily on first-order notions of culture and almost completely ignore more locally enacted notions of culture$_2$.

Following this line of argument about the relevance of culture$_1$, it has been claimed that, borrowing Hofstede's dimensions (cf. Chapter 1), in so-called high power distance 'cultures', such as Hong Kong, a superior is typically seen as a 'benevolent autocrat' or a 'good father'. In these 'cultures' (i.e. nation states), more senior people are expected to be faithful and caring, while more junior staff are expected to be loyal and obedient (Redding 1990; Westwood 1992; Selmer & de Leon 2003). In low power distance 'cultures' such as the UK and Australia, on the other hand, a leader is often viewed as a 'resourceful democrat' (Hofstede 1995: 151) who accounts for the views of her subordinates, for example when making decisions. According to the Confucian mindset, which, as Ladegaard (2012: 1674) argues, is 'believed to be the predominant ideology for Chinese organisations', the ideal leader 'may be an autocrat who can expect complete obedience, but s/he is, in turn, expected to behave responsibly towards his/her employees, almost like a father'.

Research within this paradigm almost exclusively utilises first-order notions of culture and is largely based on data obtained via questionnaires and interviews. For example, in the seminal GLOBE (Global Leadership and Organizational Behavior Effectiveness) study (House et al. 2004), which aimed at understanding the impact of (national) 'culture' on leadership effectiveness, 170 researchers across the globe collected questionnaires, conducted interviews and focus groups and performed content analysis of printed media, gathering data involving 17,000 managers in more than 950 organisations in 62 countries. Their relatively static conceptualisation of 'culture' (as something that people have) falls under what we would describe as the first-order notion of culture, and their ways of capturing it were heavily based on Hofstede's dimensions and other earlier essentialist studies. Within these parameters the GLOBE study identified 21 attributes and behaviors that are universally viewed as contributing to leadership effectiveness (e.g. being participative, autonomous and team-oriented), and 35 specific characteristics that are considered to be contributors to effective leadership in some countries and impediments in others.

Such large-scale studies and their generalising claims are highly problematic from our point of view – mainly because they focus exclusively on first-order notions of culture (as reflected in participants' views) and run the danger of over-generalising and producing new stereotypes as well as reinforcing old stereotypes. It is perhaps unsurprising, then, that the GLOBE study has received considerable criticism in the past, for example for not providing an adequate theory of how exactly 'culture' impacts leadership, and for the potentially problematic way of conceptualising leadership (i.e. by exclusively taking the perspective of followers). Other points of criticism relate to various issues regarding the study's measurements and levels of analysis (i.e. do their findings really allow them to make claims about leadership preferences on the societal level or are they restricted to the individuals who took part in the study?), and the etic approach to 'culture' that the study has taken. Other, more methodological problems with GLOBE relate to issues around sampling (e.g. highly diverse nations such as India, China and the US were treated as one 'culture'), potential problems with the translation of the questions and the fact that some of the questions were said to be culturally biased (like the mostly Western researchers who interpreted the answers) (for an overview of these criticisms see Guthey & Jackson 2011).

Moreover, recently the findings and 'grand claims' about leadership made by studies like GLOBE have been challenged by several smaller-scale studies, which conducted in-depth case-studies of how leadership is actually performed in specific contexts. For example, Wong et al. (2007) found that differences in how leadership and power relations are perceived by participants are considerably less pronounced in so-called multicultural workplaces. In our own research on leadership discourse in a range of different workplaces in Hong Kong and New Zealand, we observed a wide variation in the ways in which people in each context do leadership, and we found evidence of behaviours that reinforce as well as challenge stereotypes about leadership expectations and practices (e.g. Schnurr et al. fc; Schnurr & Chan 2009; Schnurr & Zayts 2012, 2013).

In light of these findings from largely qualitative studies, it is thus perhaps not surprising that more recent research on leadership and 'culture' distances itself from these grand claims (which often do not go beyond stereotypes) made by earlier, mainly quantitative, studies. There is a move among more recent research, away from an exclusive focus on participants' views (as captured in notions of culture$_1$) and towards conducting in-depth analyses of leadership performance in situ (e.g. Ilie & Schnurr fc) which focus on the largely overlooked aspect of culture$_2$. This chapter also falls within this second strand of research, as it aims to consider localised practices and norms. But – just like in the previous chapters – we aim to go one step further than most previous research, and explore possible ways of combining participants' views (on leadership and culture$_1$) as reflected, for example, in Examples 4.1–4.3, with an in-depth analysis of the discursive practice through which leadership is actually accomplished on the micro-level of an interaction, and discuss our observations in relation to culture$_2$.

Leadership in action

This section looks in more detail at the interactional data in our corpus and provides in-depth analyses of four examples[3] of leadership in action in order to provide a snapshot of actual leadership practice that can be found in different Hong Kong workplaces. A particular focus is on critically discussing the role of 'culture' – both in its first- and second-order meanings – in relation to leadership. Our analyses are data driven and based on the assumption that leadership is an emergent phenomenon (e.g. Clifton 2012) rather than a static attribute or a behaviour displayed by an a priori assigned individual. We have selected five examples to illustrate this. These examples were chosen because they represent different leadership constellations, namely relatively traditional top–down leadership, co-leadership and team leadership.

In relatively traditional top–down constellations of leadership, there is typically a clearly identified person 'in charge' (i.e. the leader), who is often one of the more senior people on the team. In such constellations, ways of exercising power are largely top–down, as reflected, for example, in the leader's central role in decision making processes and when giving instructions. In co-leadership and team leadership constellations, in contrast, leadership responsibilities are shared among several people, and transactional as well as relational leadership activities (such as making decisions, getting things done as well as creating and maintaining group harmony) are usually conjointly performed. Co-leadership refers to those constellations where typically two people in hierarchically contiguous positions share the leadership role and collaboratively perform the various leadership activities (e.g. Heenan & Bennis 1999), while in team leadership constellations this sharing involves (more or less) the whole team (e.g. Day et al. 2004; Burke et al. 2011). We illustrate each of these constellations in turn with a particular focus on the role of first- and second-order culture.

Top–down leadership

The first example we discuss here is taken from a weekly team meeting at an NGO in Hong Kong. It is a good example of a relatively traditional top–down leadership constellation in which Sabitha, the CEO and founder of the organisation, not only acts as the Chair of the meeting but is also clearly the one in charge and the one who drives the meeting. This central role of Sabitha is further reflected in other areas of the organisation's business of both strategic and representative nature.

Example 4.5

Context: Internal weekly staff meeting at an NGO in Hong Kong. Sabitha is the Chair and Betty is the office manager. Participants are discussing the new layout of the office and in particular which furniture items to move where. Sabitha is ethnically Indian and Betty is ethnically Chinese.

1 Sabitha:	So the first thing Betty is
2 ??:	(it will have to be)
3 Sabitha:	Print yeah I I'll do that today, and then we'll set. You arrange for-
4	I think what we should do m- move the stuff out of the door, cause
5	then we know, we have an idea (2.0). And so what we should do, is
6	get um a (.) booking for just one or two days and just use them to to
7	move um. And then everything's out the door. And then we use a
8	(xxx) to move the pantry. And then we can we can talk again next
9	Monday. But if you can do both of those by this week, and this will
10	give us a better idea. And then the other thing you do if you can
11	do, is book the contractor [name], um [name], and anything else
12	you can find. And we can have a meeting with them this week,
13	before I go
14 Betty:	(And the rest of the stuff?)

((Sabitha then moves on to tell them about new cupboards she has had installed in her house recently))

This example leaves little doubt about the fact that Sabitha is the one in charge. At this stage in the meeting she mainly focuses on transactional objectives and on making sure that things are getting done and, more specifically, that Betty, the office manager, knows exactly what to do. Sabitha utters several directives (e.g. *'you arrange for'* (line 3), *'but if you can do both of those by this week'* (line 9), *'the other thing you do if you can do is book the contractor'* (lines 10 and 11)), which are relatively direct and explicit, as she provides concrete timeframes (e.g. *'next Monday'* (lines 8 and 9), *'this week before I go'* (lines 12 and 13)) and the names of people to be involved (line 11). These directives are primarily transactionally oriented and aim at getting things done. They are, however, to some extent counter-balanced by more relationally oriented behaviours, such as her frequent use of the inclusive pronoun *'we'* when outlining what needs to be done (e.g. lines 3, 4, 5, 7 and 8). Nevertheless, in spite of using these (and other) mitigating strategies, there is very little doubt about the fact that Betty is the one who is expected to perform most of these tasks. In this example, then, and throughout the meeting (see Schnurr & Mak 2011) Sabitha displays a relatively decisive and authoritarian leadership style when delegating her subordinates and assigning them work.

Sabitha's relatively autocratic way of doing leadership is further reflected in the observations that there is generally very little negotiation regarding decision making in the meetings, and that she does most of the talking and often explicitly and unambiguously tells her team what they are expected to do and within what timeframe. This relatively unidirectional, top–down leadership is further reflected in the primarily transactionally oriented emails that Sabitha sent to her subordinates in which she tends to give very brief instructions – often without greeting or closing or any other mitigation strategies to down-tone the potential face-threat of these directives. Examples include the following:

- *'Can you work on this?'*
- *'What are you doing about this?'*
- *'Bonnie [C]An you pls write a blurb about this in Other events for our website'*[4]

These ways of giving directives are thus another good reflection of the relatively hierarchical top–down chain of command that characterises this particular team, where it is mainly Sabitha who emerges as the leader and who performs leadership behaviours. She is the one in charge of the day-to-day business of this NGO and the one to ensure that the team's objectives are met. She also plays a central role in developing the vision and strategy of the organisation. Sabitha's directive, decisive, authoritarian and sometimes autocratic leadership style as displayed in Example 4.5 and the emails seems to reinforce claims about first-order notions of culture in relation to leadership as expressed by our participants and much of the earlier literature on leadership and 'culture' in the previous section.

However, Sabitha's leadership behaviours also need to be understood in the specific context in which they appear, and based on our knowledge of Sabitha's workplace and her team, we would classify these kinds of to-the-point, relatively unmitigated and direct ways of giving directives as appropriate and unmarked behaviour that is characteristic of interactions among the members of this particular community of practice (CofP). Based on our analysis of several hours of spoken (in addition to written) workplace interactions at this organisation involving Sabitha and her team members, we are confident in describing these kinds of behaviours as politic (cf. Chapter 2), and interpret them as forming part of the discursive norms and behavioural practices that have been developed among members of this relatively close-knit CofP over the course of their professional relationships. In this sense, Sabitha's way of doing leadership can also be understood as actively contributing to constructing, shaping and reinforcing these locally developed shared interactional practices and norms. In other words, these behaviours, which are indicative of Sabitha's leadership style, have emerged and can be seen as responses to the discursive repertoire and behavioural norms that members of this CofP have developed during their regular interactions and mutual engagements (cf. Wenger 1998). Through being used regularly, these behaviours at the same time actively contribute to constructing and shaping these norms. According to this interpretation, Sabitha's leadership behaviour is not primarily a reflection and indication of first-order notions of culture, but rather part and parcel of creating and enacting culture$_2$ (see also Chapter 3).

This distinction between locally created, enacted and negotiated practices which can be linked to culture$_2$ – as opposed to the generalising and often stereotypical claims that are typical for culture$_1$ – becomes even more relevant in those instances where practices associated with the two notions of culture contradict each other, as in the next two examples.

Co-leadership

In addition to the relatively traditional, hierarchical leadership constellation displayed by Sabitha's team in Example 4.5, we found abundant evidence in our data of other, more collaborative leadership constellations. For example, in several workplaces where we recorded data, the leadership role was shared among two members of the team (e.g. Schnurr & Chan 2011). In some cases this sharing involved the most senior person and a more junior person, or, as in Example 4.6, it took place between two individuals of similar organisational standing. In all cases, both team members displayed behaviours indexed for leadership, which was often particularly evident in relation to meeting management, as the next example illustrates.

Example 4.6

Context: During a meeting of the staff at Sandcastle, a language learning centre in Hong Kong. Jenny and Lily are the managers and co-founders of the company and, as the example illustrates, they share the chairing and leadership responsibilities. Jenny is an expatriate from the UK and Lily is Hong Kong Chinese.

1 Jenny: Good. Thank you.
2 Lily: We've only got ten minutes. Should we:?
3   (.)
4 Jenny: °Quickly.°
5 Lily: I was thinking to talk about the curriculum, but it's pretty much okay
6   [We'll start]
7 Jenny: [Yeah, it's] pretty much okay. Emm please I'll look at this.
8 Lily: Yeah.

This short excerpt occurred after an item on the agenda had been discussed. Throughout the meetings that we recorded at this workplace, Jenny and Lily are sharing leadership responsibilities – especially with regard to chairing meetings, inviting people to contribute, having the last word in decisions (see also Chapter 3) and moving on with the agenda. This particular extract displayed here occurred towards the end of the meeting where participants have discussed which students are going to attend a particular trial session. During the previous discussion, both Lily and Jenny took turns giving feedback to Paula who reported on the trial sessions. At this point in the meeting, Jenny, one of the most senior people and co-owner of the language learning centre, takes the floor and thanks the previous speakers for their contributions (line 1). She brings the previous discussions to a close and signals her readiness to move on. She thereby claims a leadership role. However, in line 2, Lily, the other co-owner of the language learning centre, joins in and reminds everyone (including Jenny) of the time, which could also be interpreted as claiming a leadership role. She uses the inclusive pronoun '*we*' and follows up her rather factual statement ('*we've only got ten minutes*') with a more explicit expression of her intentions to bring up and briefly discuss another topic. However, interestingly, and perhaps because her attempt to claim a leadership role overlaps with Jenny's attempt, this new topic initiation is considerably mitigated: it is formulated as a question ('*should we*') and it does not explicitly mention the new topic but Lily rather leaves a pause at the end of her utterance, which then allows Jenny to come back in and take over the chairing (and hence leadership) role. But rather than taking over the leadership role here, Jenny's brief contribution in line 4 invites Lily to initiate the new topic – albeit '*quickly*' – and, thereby, legitimises Lily's attempt at doing leadership. Lily then brings up the new topic 'curriculum' but downplays its relevance and the need for further discussion at this point ('*but it's pretty much okay*' (line 5)). Interestingly, at this point Jenny takes over the lead again by over-lapping with Lily and then taking over the floor (lines 6 and 7). By agreeing with Lily's assessment, Jenny swiftly brings this topic to an end, and by stating '*I'll look at this*' takes over the responsibility of dealing with it. Lily's short agreement '*yeah*' (line 8) brings this episode to an end, and Jenny introduces a new topic.

    This example is a good illustration of co-leadership in action, and shows how the leadership responsibilities may be shared among interlocutors. We analyse one more example here, taken from another team at a different workplace, before discussing these observations in relation to first- and second-order notions of culture. Example 4.7 occurred in a team meeting at an IT consulting company, ABC

Consulting, where the two most senior people in the company have been working together for several years and consequently have established a very close working relationship. In this team, QS, the CEO of the company, and Danny, the Managing Director, effectively share the leadership role, each of them performing activities associated with leadership at different times and relating to different aspects of the company's performance. As Danny explained in an interview, '*whenever business strategy arise, it's always [QS] has come to question. When it's from the business operations, it's always me. Then he steps sort of step aside a little bit. I can have to step in, that doesn't stop him from his interest or whatever he's doing.*'

The example we have chosen illustrates this division of responsibilities between QS and Danny. This division results in clearly defined areas in which each of them is doing leadership. Part of Danny's leadership responsibility over the operational side of the company includes chairing the regular staff meetings, such as the one from which the following extract is taken. As the example illustrates, he performs this transactional leadership activity very conscientiously – even if it means reprimanding the more senior QS.

Example 4.7

Context: Participants are discussing a particularly complex project. At this stage in the discussion they have already agreed to talk about this project in more detail in an extra meeting when QS, the CEO and most senior member of the team, brings up this item again. Danny is the Managing Director and Chair of the meeting. Miles is one of the people working on the project. All participants are ethnically Chinese, and QS is from Taiwan.

```
 1 QS:      Yeah, other than the- the other idea is that er part of the (project
 2          launch) promote with some more [(confidence)].
 3 Danny:   [(I under]stand) but right now we're discussing this [item].
 4 QS:      [Yeah, right,] right. You can start from there er (1.0).
 5 Danny:   (In another xxx) I don't want those (xxx) at this stage still just have
 6          (worth it).
 7 Miles:   Yeah.
 8 Danny:   I want to do some presen[tations]. What to do they actually?
 9 Miles:   [Mm mm]. (0.3) Yeah.
10 Danny:   The problems they're solving, [how] do they=
11 Miles:   [Yeah.]
12 Danny:   =thinking?
13 QS:      But that's- that's- that's not your, so schedule is not part of the
14          meeting.
15 Danny:   Not in here.
16 QS:      Not in here.
((several lines are omitted))
17 Danny:   So let's get back to business.
```

((participants continue with the next item on the agenda))

This example shows how Danny, who is responsible for the operational side of ABC Consulting and chairing this meeting (a behaviour which is often associated with leadership (e.g. Marra et al. 2006)), makes sure people (here in particular: QS) stick to the topic and do not digress into discussing another item. When QS, the CEO and most senior person in the meeting, continues with a discussion which they had just decided to postpone to another meeting (lines 1 and 2), Danny interrupts and reminds him that they have moved on to discuss another item (line 3). Although Danny's interruption of the more senior QS is mitigated to some extent by his acknowledgement '*I understand*' (line 3), his reminder to stick to the other topic is relatively direct and potentially face-threatening (cf. Chapter 2). However, QS does not seem to feel threatened in any way, as becomes clear from the ways in which the interaction proceeds. Rather, he and Danny agree that his comment should be discussed elsewhere (lines 13–16), and Danny brings the discussion to an end by reminding participants '*so let's get back to business*' (line 17), which is a behaviour that is indexed for power and associated with leadership (Holmes 2000; Marra et al. 2006; Wodak et al. 2011).

This example, thus, shows co-leadership in action and illustrates how one of the co-leaders does leadership without upsetting the other and without interrupting the flow of the meeting. Danny skilfully achieves the team's transactional objectives, namely to continue with the agenda set for the meeting, while also orienting to relational concerns, making sure that team harmony is maintained and that QS does not feel offended.

The point worth reiterating about these two examples of co-leadership is that the particular ways of doing leadership and of sharing (Example 4.6) and distributing (Example 4.7) leadership responsibilities and activities are typical for these teams. Their practices are reflective of the close working relationship between the co-leaders, and have emerged as a consequence of the long-standing collaboration between them. They have become an integral part of the discursive norms that characterise the particular teams or CofPs in which the co-leaders are members.

These ways of doing leadership are thus prime examples of culture$_2$ in action, but are not, we would argue, a reflection of first-order notions of culture. In fact, if we try to relate these collaborative and participative ways of sharing power and responsibility to culture$_1$ claims about leadership in Hong Kong, we would encounter several difficulties. We would probably have to classify examples of non-traditional non-top–down leadership constellations, like the ones displayed here, as marked exceptions. However, the data we collected at these two (and other) companies in Hong Kong indicate that these kinds of non-traditional ways of exercising leadership frequently occur and do not constitute outliers (see also Schnurr & Chan 2011). Instead, such examples are good illustrations of the role of second-order culture and of how a team's locally constructed, enacted and negotiated repertoire and practices give rise to various forms of leadership, which may not be in line with culture$_1$ expectations but which are a reflection (and at the same time a reinforcement) of culture$_2$. The next example illustrates this further.

Team leadership

Of the examples discussed in this chapter, Example 4.8 is the most collaborative, because it shows how leadership is conjointly performed by various team members. It sits in stark contrast to the relatively hierarchical top–down constellation displayed by Sabitha in Example 4.5. Example 4.8 is taken from one of the regular meetings of a team of geneticists at a specialist clinic in Hong Kong. This team is particularly interesting from the perspective of leadership, because members assured us in the interviews that they are all '*equals*' and that status differences do not exist. All participants are qualified paediatric doctors with additional training in clinical genetics. They all hold similar institutional positions (senior medical officers). In spite of these similarities of rank and the alleged absence of status differences, one participant, Dr Lee, performs the responsibilities of a deputy head of the specialist clinic, meaning he is accountable to the head of the clinic for any decision that the team makes.

The meeting during which Example 4.8 was recorded mainly consists of so-called case conferences involving the geneticists going through and discussing the clients they are going to see during the week case by case (see also Chapter 3, where we discussed another example to demonstrate this team's collaborative decision making style).

Example 4.8

Context: The team is dealing with a specific patient case wherein a number of tests have been performed in the clinic, and only the MLPA test has shown a pathological abnormality – duplication within chromosome band 3p. Participants are discussing whether this is a case of a genuine abnormality that can only be detected by newer technologies like MLPA, or whether this is an 'artefact', i.e. a false positive result. The extract occurs after the presentation of the medical history of 'the case'. All participants are Hong Kong Chinese but the meeting was conducted in English.

```
1 Chan:   For the midline hand movement, it didn't- didn't mention. It is
2         ((inaudible)) (3p duplication) ((looking through the report))
3 Lee:    It means,=
4 Chan:   =For the karyotype, (.) it is (.) ((searching his notes)) we did (.) the
5         normal, we have counted seventeen, seventeen cells.
```

((passing the report to Lee))

```
6 Lee:    But (.) how about FISH?
7 Chan:   For FISH, emm it's normal. FISH for 3p ((passing the report to Lee)) (.)
8         (I couldn't find any=)
9 Lee:    =3p duplication.
10        (8.0) ((Lee is reading the report))
```

((6 turns are omitted; the team examines the client's report))

```
11 Lee:   (There is nothing special in the features.)
12        (3.0) ((Lee is reading the report))
```

13 Ma: The features are quite obvious.
14   (4.0) ((Ma is reading the report))
15 Ho: We can refer to the document ((laughs))
16 Lee: It's like (.) it's like, what the book mentions. There're a few similarities.

((15 turns are omitted; the team talks about the specialist literature))

17 Ho: See if you have the MLPA report underneath.
18 Lee: Do you have it? We should check. (.) We should use another MLPA to
19   confirm.
20 Ma: [Mhm.] ((nods))
21 Ho: [Mmm.]
22   (3.0) ((Lee is looking through the report))
23 Lee: When did the patient do the scan?
24 Chan: The scan, (.) umm (.) ((looking at the report)) in 2005.
25 ((the team moves to the discussion of the next client case))

In this extract, as well as in other recorded meetings of this particular team or CofP, members are collaboratively doing leadership by collectively performing transactional and relational behaviours. Dr Chan is in charge of presenting the particular client case that the geneticists are discussing at this point in the meeting (e.g. lines 1 and 2, 4 and 5, 7 and 8), which could be interpreted as a leadership activity. However, Dr Chan's leadership gets interrupted by Dr Lee in line 3 when he starts to clarify what the facts actually mean. All of these behaviours are transactionally oriented, because they aim at making sure the team achieves its objectives. Interestingly, rather than letting his colleague finish his explanations, Dr Chan quickly regains the floor and briefly continues with the information delivery before providing further support and explanations for his interpretations (lines 4 and 5). In doing so, he uses the inclusive pronoun 'we', thereby indicating that these previous tests and assessments were a team-work exercise and involved various people. With his choice of pronouns he also at the same time creates and reinforces solidarity and harmony among the team (which are relational behaviours).

Dr Lee continues asking questions, thereby further probing into this partic-ular case (e.g. line 6). Again, what is noteworthy throughout these turns is the high degree of collaboration between Drs Lee and Chan, reflected in the fact that they frequently latch onto each other's utterances and even finish each other's sentences (thereby complementing each other's knowledge). This kind of behaviour, which skilfully combines transactional and relational aspects, could be interpreted as a conjoint construction of meaning and is indicative of the team's collaborative approach to dealing with these cases. This collaboration is further reflected in the fact that none of the doctors 'owns' a case, but that responsibilities for all patients are collaboratively shared among them and that the cases are randomly allocated to a team member during the meeting.

These collaborative methods of decision making and getting things done (which are both leadership activities) are further demonstrated by the fact that everyone actively contributes (e.g. different people make suggestions (e.g. Dr Ho in lines 15 and 17, and Dr Lee in lines 16, 18 and 19)), and that decision making among this team is generally very implicit (cf. Example 3.7 in the previous chapter). As shown in line 25, team members seem to almost intuitively know when a case has been closed and when it is time to move on to the next one. There is no verbal or non-verbal clue that gives this away to outsiders, yet there is abundant evidence in the data that we collected of this team that this kind of 'invisible' decision making is typical for this CofP.

So, although at some points during the meeting Dr Lee seems to take on a more active or 'leadership role' (e.g. when asking clarifying questions, prompting the presenter to provide more information and issuing various possible assessment strategies), other team members play equally crucial roles and perform the same functions. The leadership in this group is, thus, a team effort (e.g. Day et al. 2004; Burke et al. 2011).

However, these observations provide a challenge to the comments of our participants and to the claims made by earlier research about leadership in Hong Kong, which are typically built upon first-order notions of culture. Examples 4.6–4.8 question the validity and usefulness of such conceptualisations, and it is more productive to analyse them with reference to culture$_2$. The sharing of leadership responsibilities by our participants is best understood as part of the locally negotiated practice among members of these CofPs, which have emerged over time, and which are constantly shaped and modified as team members continue to work closely with one another. In other words, the leadership practices displayed in the various examples contribute to enacting, constructing, shaping and negotiating second-order notions of culture. We discuss this point in more detail in the next section.

Discussion

This chapter has further explored the analytical dilemma that researchers often face when trying to better understand the complex relationship between leadership and 'culture'. Our examples have shown that any analytical endeavour that exclusively focuses on first-order notions of culture (as reflected, for example, in the quotes of some of our participants at the beginning of the chapter) is too limiting and runs the risk of stereotyping. As our examples of authentic leadership discourse have demonstrated, there clearly exists a wide diversity of leadership constellations and leadership styles in Hong Kong (even beyond the three constellations that we have briefly discussed here). Thus, any exclusive focus on culture$_1$ and its alleged relationship with leadership can only ever be unnecessarily limiting, as it only shows part of a very complex picture while ignoring diversity in leadership practice.

In this chapter we have tried to overcome these limitations by providing insights into both participants' views and perceptions about leadership *and* actual leadership practices in situ. We have shown that in contrast to the perceptions of many of our expatriate participants regarding the crucial role that they consider first-order notions of culture to play in their own leadership experiences, there was very little evidence in our interactional data of the kinds of leadership styles described in the interviews (e.g. wherein Chinese subordinates were portrayed as preferring and, to some extent, expecting autocratic and dictatorial ways of doing leadership). However, as our in-depth analyses of actual workplace interactions have illustrated, the leadership performance that we find in actual workplaces was much more complex, and participants displayed a wide range of leadership styles, including both autocratic and participative behaviours (see also Schnurr et al. fc for further examples).

We have argued that explaining this wide variation in leadership practice that we find in workplaces in Hong Kong by reference to first-order notions of culture would almost inevitably lead to over-generalisations and stereotyping. As demonstrated in our analyses, it is more productive to link the observed practices in leadership behaviour to second-order notions of culture, and to view them as enacting and shaping the specific discursive and behavioural norms and practices that are developed locally by the members of the specific teams or CofPs in which the leadership occurred. Given this variation on the local level, then, it is perhaps unsurprising that in the four CofPs that we have discussed here, very different and distinct ways of doing leadership have emerged – each constituting appropriate, and (presumably) the most effective, behaviours in the specific context in which they occurred.

According to this line of argument and largely rejecting generalising claims about culture$_1$ in favour of a fine-grained in-depth analysis of interactional data to understand the workings of culture$_2$ in relation to leadership practice, we would interpret Sabitha's relatively direct and autocratic way of getting things done (Example 4.5) not as a reflection of the allegedly 'Confucian' or 'high-power distance culture' of Hong Kong, but rather as a reflection and reinforcement of the specific practices that members of this particular team or CofP have developed as part of their negotiated repertoire. Sabitha's ways of doing leadership are, thus, illustrations of culture$_2$ in action. In a similar vein, the sharing of leadership responsibilities of Jenny and Lily (Example 4.6) and QS and Danny (Example 4.7), as well as the collaborative decision making and co-construction of knowledge as shown in Example 4.8 by the team of geneticists, are further examples of how second-order notions of culture are created and enacted in interactions. All these ways of doing and sharing leadership, while largely contradicting stereotypical assumptions about leadership in Hong Kong (such as leaders being (and expected to be) autocratic and paternalistic (e.g. Chee & West 2004; Cullen 1999)), emphasise the importance of looking beyond culture in its first-order meaning and of paying more attention to the localised practices that have developed among the members of a particular team or CofP.

By focusing on the particularly interesting and incredibly complex concept of leadership, then, this chapter has provided further support for taking a critical stance towards research that exclusively focuses on first-order notions of cultures, like the seminal GLOBE study described at the beginning of this chapter. Rather, it is important to relativise participants' own views and perceptions with fine-grained analyses of leadership discourse as it is used in actual workplace encounters. Such an approach, we believe, not only contributes to a better understanding of leadership and its relationship with 'culture' (in both its first- and second-order meanings) while at the same time avoiding unnecessary stereotyping and being caught in over-generalisations, but it is also in line with recent trends in leadership research, which aim to move away from grand claims about leadership towards carefully conducted case studies of leadership performance in situ (e.g. Clifton 2012; Choi & Schnurr 2014).

In the next chapter we continue illustrating the crucial importance of considering the localised interactional context. In the previous chapters we have demonstrated some of the problems of an exclusive focus on first-order notions of culture and the importance of contrasting participants' views and assumptions with analyses of their actual practices, and in the remaining chapters we show how culture$_1$ and culture$_2$ can be usefully combined in an analysis. The next chapter deals with the topic of identity construction, and we analyse some of the processes through which participants make identity claims for themselves and each other – thereby setting up and orienting to specific subject positions that provide insights into the complexities of first- and second-order culture.

Notes

1 Parts of this example also appeared in Chapter 1 to illustrate the concept of first-order culture.
2 Although there is an ongoing debate in the literature as to whether 'leadership' and 'management' are different or similar terms and what exactly the relationship between these concepts is (e.g. Kotter 2001; Rost 1998), we use mainly the term 'leadership' here in the sense as defined in the next section, although our participants, like Susan here, used the terms leadership and management interchangeably.
3 Further examples of leadership can be found in other chapters throughout this book – for example where we discuss some of the behaviours associated with leadership, such as decision making (Chapter 3) and getting things done (Chapter 2). Example 4.5 and Sabitha's leadership style are discussed in more detail in Schnurr & Mak (2011), and Example 4.8 also appears in Zayts et al. (fc) where it is analysed from a different angle.
4 Spellings in all emails are left as in the originals.

References

Alvesson, Mats & André Spicer (2012). *Critical Leadership Studies: The Case for Critical Performativity and Organizations across Nations* (2nd edn). Thousand Oaks, CA: SAGE.

Bass, Bernard (1981). *Stogdill's Handbook of Leadership. A Survey of Theory and Research*. New York: Free Press.

Burke, C. Shawn, Deborah Diaz Granados & Eduardo Salas (2011). Team leadership. A review and looking ahead. In Alan Bryman, David Collinson, Keith Grint, Brad Jackson & Mary Uhl-Biehl (eds), *The SAGE Handbook of Leadership*. London: SAGE. 338–51.

Chee, Harold & Chris West (2004). *Myths about Doing Business in China*. Basingstoke/New York: Palgrave Macmillan.

Choi, Seongsook & Stephanie Schnurr (2014). Exploring distributed leadership. Solving disagreements and negotiating consensus in a 'leaderless' team. *Discourse Studies* 16.1: 3–24.

Clifton, Jonathan (2012). A discursive approach to leadership. Doing assessments and managing organizational meanings. *Journal of Business Communication* 49.2: 148–68.

Clifton, Jonathan (2006). A conversation analytical approach to business communication. *Journal of Business Communication* 43: 202–19.

Cullen, John (1999). *Multinational Management. A Strategic Approach.* Cincinnati, OH: South-Western Publishing.

Day, David, Peter Gronn & Eduardo Salas (2004). Leadership capacity in teams. *Leadership Quarterly* 15: 857–80.

Fairhurst, Gail (2007). *Discursive Leadership: In Conversation with Leadership Psychology.* London: SAGE.

Ferch, Shann & Matthew Mitchell (2001). Intentional forgiveness in relational leadership: A technique for enhancing effective leadership. *Journal of Leadership & Organizational Studies* 7.4: 70–83.

Grint, Keith (2005). *Leadership: Limits and Possibilities (Management, Work and Organisation).* Basingstoke: Palgrave Macmillan.

Gronn, Peter (2002). Distributed leadership as a unit of analysis. *Leadership Quarterly* 13: 423–51.

Guirdham, Maureen (2005). *Communicating across Cultures at Work.* Basingstoke: Palgrave Macmillan.

Guthey, Eric & Brad Jackson (2011). Cross-cultural leadership re-visited. In Alan Bryman, David Collinson, Keith Grint, Brad Jackson & Mary Uhl-Biehl (eds), *The SAGE Handbook of Leadership.* London: SAGE. 165–78.

Heenan, David & Warren Bennis (1999). *Co-Leaders: The Power of Great Partnerships.* New York: John Wiley & Sons.

Heifertz, Ronald (1998). Values in leadership. In Gill Robinson Hickman (ed.), *Leading Organizations: Perspectives for a New Era.* London: SAGE. 343–56.

Hofstede, Geert (1995). The business of international business is culture. In Terence Jackson (ed.), *Cross-Cultural Management.* Oxford: Butterworth-Heinemann. 150–65.

Holmes, Janet (2000). Women at work: Analysing women's talk in New Zealand workplaces. *Australian Review of Applied Linguistics* 22.2: 1–17.

Holmes, Janet & Meredith Marra (2004). Leadership and managing conflict in meetings. *Pragmatics* 14.4: 439–62.

Hosking, Dian Marie (1997). Organizing, leadership, and skilful process. In Keith Grint (ed.), *Leadership. Classical, Contemporary, and Critical Approaches.* Oxford: Oxford University Press. 293–318.

House, Robert, Paul Hanges, Mansour Javidan, Peter Dorfman & Vipin Gupta (2004). *Culture, Leadership, and Organizations: The GLOBE study of 62 Societies.* Thousand Oaks, CA: SAGE.

Ilie, Cornelia & Stephanie Schnurr (eds) (fc). *Challenging Leadership Stereotypes. Discourse and Power Management.* Delhi: Springer.

Jackson, Brad & Ken Parry (2008). *A Very Short, Fairly Interesting and Reasonably Cheap Book about Studying Leadership.* London: SAGE.

Kotter, John (2001). What leaders really do. *Harvard Business Review. Special Issue on Leadership* 79.11: 85–96.

Ladegaard, Hans (2012). Rudeness as a discursive strategy in leadership discourse: Culture, power and gender in a Hong Kong workplace. *Journal of Pragmatics* 44: 1661–79.

Lowe, Sid (1998). Culture and network institutions in Hong Kong: A hierarchy of perspectives. A response to Wilkinson: 'Culture institutions and business in East Asia'. *Organization Studies* 19.2: 321–43.

Marra, Meredith, Stephanie Schnurr & Janet Holmes (2006). Effective leadership in New Zealand workplaces: Balancing gender and role. In J. Baxter (ed.), *Speaking Out: The Female Voice in Public Contexts*. Basingstoke: Palgrave Macmillan. 240–60.

Northouse, Peter (1997). *Leadership. Theory and Practice*. London: SAGE.

Redding, S. Gordon (1990). *The Spirit of Chinese Capitalism*. Berlin/New York: Walter de Gruyter.

Rost, Joseph (1998). Leadership and management. In Gill Robinson Hickman (ed.), *Leading Organizations. Perspectives for a New Era*. London: SAGE. 97–114.

Schnurr, Stephanie (fc). Leadership. To appear in Bernadette Vine (ed.), *Handbook of Language in the Workplace*. Abingdon: Routledge.

Schnurr, Stephanie & Angela Chan (2011). When laughter is not enough. Responding to teasing and self-denigrating humour at work. *Journal of Pragmatics* 43: 20–35.

Schnurr, Stephanie & Angela Chan (2009). Leadership discourse and politeness at work. A cross cultural case study of New Zealand and Hong Kong. *Journal of Politeness Research* 5.2: 131–57.

Schnurr, Stephanie, Angela Chan, Joelle Loew & Olga Zayts (fc). Leadership and culture: When stereotypes meet actual workplace practice. To appear in Cornelia Ilie & Stephanie Schnurr (eds), *Challenging Leadership Stereotypes through Discourse: Power, Management and Gender*. Delhi: Springer.

Schnurr, Stephanie & Bernie Mak (2011). Leadership and workplace realities in Hong Kong. Is gender really *not* an issue? *Gender and Language. Special Issue on Gender and Language in the Workplace* 5.2: 337–64.

Schnurr, Stephanie & Olga Zayts (2013). 'I can't remember them ever not doing what I tell them!' Negotiating face and power relations in 'upwards' refusals in multicultural workplaces in Hong Kong. *Intercultural Pragmatics* 10.4: 593–616.

Schnurr, Stephanie & Olga Zayts (2012). 'You have to be adaptable, obviously.' Constructing cultural identities in multicultural workplaces in Hong Kong. *Pragmatics* 22.2: 279–99.

Schnurr, Stephanie & Olga Zayts (2011). Constructing and contesting leaders. An analysis of identity construction at work. In Jo Angouri & Meredith Marra (eds), *Constructing Identities at Work*. Houndmills: Palgrave. 40–60.

Selmer, Jan & Corinna de Leon (2003). Culture and management in Hong Kong SAR. In Malcolm Warner (ed.), *Culture and Management in Asia*. London: Routledge Curzon. 48–65.

Wenger Etienne (1998) *Communities of Practice. Learning, Meaning, and Identity*. Cambridge, UK: Cambridge University Press.

Westwood, Robert I. (1992). Culture, cultural differences, and organisational behaviour. In Robert I. Westwood (ed.), *Organisational Behaviour: Southeast Asian Perspectives*. Hong Kong: Longman. 27–62.

Wodak Ruth, Winston Kwon & Ian Clarke (2011). Getting people on board. Discursive leadership for consensus building in team meetings. *Discourse & Society* 22.5: 592–644.

Wong, Jonny, Philco Wong & Li Heng (2007). An investigation of leadership styles and relationship cultures of Chinese and expatriate managers in multinational companies in Hong Kong. *Construction Management and Economics* 25: 95–106.

Yukl Gary (2002). *Leadership in Organizations* (5th edn). Upper Saddle River, NJ: Prentice Hall.

Zayts, Olga, Stephanie Schnurr & Srikant Sarangi (fc). Shared expertise in negotiating future actions in the genetics case conferences. To appear in Srikant Sarangi & Per Linell (eds), *Team Talk: Decision Making across Boundaries in Health and Social Care Professions*. London: Equinox.

5 Moving beyond stereotypes. Constructing and negotiating identities at work

I'm not here forever so it's much better to sacrifice the gweilo.[1]
(Susan, expatriate from the UK and Head of Department at
a large international financial corporation in Hong Kong)

Introduction

Following on from the previous chapter where we have analysed and discussed some of the ways in which people claim and negotiate leadership roles and identities, in this chapter we further explore the topic of identity construction. The central role of identity in workplace interactions has long been established. It has been argued that the ways in which people perceive themselves and those they work with are important aspects of workplace interactions (e.g. Van de Mieroop & Clifton 2012; Angouri & Marra 2011; Schnurr 2013; Van de Mieroop & Schnurr fc). This is also the case for the participants in our corpus, who constantly construct and negotiate their own and each other's identities as they – more or less actively and sometimes strategically – position themselves in relation to others.

As we have seen throughout the previous chapters, in the interviews participants readily and frequently mobilise relatively static cultural[1] categories, such as '*Hong Kong people*', '*Chinese people*' and '*Westerner*' to which they orient when constructing their own identity and that of the people they work and interact with. Susan's quote at the beginning of this chapter is a particularly interesting example of this. During the interview that we did with her after data collection, she describes herself as a '*gweilo*' in her company who can easily be replaced. She thereby makes visible her outsider status as an expatriate (originally being from the UK and having moved to Hong Kong for a temporary work assignment almost three years ago). She also acknowledges the fact that, for her, Hong Kong is merely one stop on her career path. However, her use of the term '*gweilo*' to refer to herself is rather ambiguous in this context and performs various functions in terms of identity construction. On the one hand, it enables her to emphasise her outsider status as a '*Westerner*' and a '*foreigner*' (which are other identity categories that she frequently mentions throughout her interview), while on the other hand, by using the specific locally coined term '*gweilo*' she simultaneously signals her knowledge of Hong Kong local practices (namely to refer to Westerners as '*gweilos*'). This connotation and function of the term '*gweilo*' in particular could be interpreted as an attempt to claim belonging to the local culture. Susan thus positions herself somewhere in between the expatriate Western community and the Hong Kong local community.

This chapter closely examines some of the discursive processes through which Susan and others enact and negotiate their various professional and social identities in their workplace interactions. We will link these observations to notions of first- and second-order culture. First, we briefly explain the concept of identity, then analyse and discuss some examples of identity construction.

Constructing and negotiating identities

Our understanding of identity is firmly based on recent constructivist conceptualisations which view identity construction as a dynamic and inherently collaborative process that is enacted throughout an interaction as interlocutors orient to each other and negotiate their expectations, roles and responsibilities (e.g. Bucholtz & Hall 2005). Just like 'culture', we understand identity as 'something that people *do* which is embedded in some other social activity, and not something they "*are*"' (Widdicombe 1998: 191; our emphasis). According to this view, then, identities are not assigned a priori (e.g. based on someone's job title), but are the product of ongoing negotiations among interlocutors.

Moreover, the various identities that interlocutors construct and literally talk into being are always, to some extent, inter-subjectively created and enacted by drawing on and trying to reconcile different and often contradictory aspects. Identities are 'never unified and [. . . are] increasingly fragmented and fractured; never singular but multiply constructed across different, often intersecting and antagonistic, discourses, practices, and positions' (Hall 2000: 7). As a consequence, we need 'to speak of identities in the plural, considering that every social agent – whether individual or collective – can actualize, mobilize, or produce identities according to the context' (Deschamps & Devos 1998: 3). Interlocutors may draw on and construct different, sometimes opposing identities simultaneously and, as we have seen in Susan's quote at the beginning of the chapter, they often do this by positioning themselves in relation to others. This view of identity as dynamic and emergent is also reflected in Bucholtz and Hall's (2005) framework, which proposes five principles of identity construction. The two principles that are most relevant to our interest here are the indexicality principle and the relationality principle.

The indexicality principle captures some of the processes and mechanisms through which identities are constructed and claimed throughout an interaction. It emphasises the ongoing identity work that interlocutors undertake during an interaction. They do this not only by explicitly setting up identity categories, such as Susan's use of the term '*gweilo*', but also by implicitly positioning themselves and others, for example by taking a particular stance or by using linguistic structures that are associated with a particular identity, as we illustrate in the examples below. In this way, specific linguistic forms, such as the frequent use of interruptions or hesitation markers, are implicitly associated with certain identities via the interactional stances that they evoke (Ochs 1993).

The relationality principle emerges around the idea that identities are not constructed in isolation, but are intersubjective achievements. According to Bucholtz and Hall (2005), this principle lies at the heart of their framework. It states that identities 'are never autonomous or independent, but always acquire social meaning in relation to other available identity positions and other social actors' (Bucholtz & Hall 2005: 598). That is, while setting up one kind of identity, interlocutors at the same time create other identities. As the examples discussed in the previous chapters have shown, this may be the case, for instance, where expatriates more or less explicitly position themselves in opposition to '*the locals*' they work with (see also Example 5.1).

We have chosen six examples here to capture the complexities involved in these processes of identity construction and negotiation, and to discuss some of the ways in which the notions of first- and second-order culture may be relevant. We first describe how interlocutors may construct their identities by mobilising cultural$_1$ categories, and how they sometimes explicitly position themselves as a member of their particular company. We then illustrate how the processes of identity construction are embedded in interlocutors' orientation to the interactional context.

Mobilising cultural$_1$ categories when constructing identities

There are at least two different ways in our data in which interlocutors more or less explicitly mobilise and orient to cultural$_1$ categories when constructing their identities. First, there is an abundance of examples where participants mention membership in specific cultural$_1$ categories in the interviews and use this as explanation for perceived differences between themselves and others. Second, there is – albeit very limited – evidence in our corpus of authentic workplace interactions of instances where interlocutors make their culture$_1$ perceptions explicit and relevant in the ongoing interaction – for example by explicitly referring and orienting to the socio-cultural background of interlocutors. We provide one example to illustrate each below.

In most of the interviews that we conducted with expatriates, we did not specifically ask them about identity, and yet, throughout their accounts of what it is like to work and live in Hong Kong, most of them engaged in identity work. For example, when describing their (professional) roles, they at the same time mobilised specific identity categories that are closely linked to their professional title or institutional role – such as '*Head of Department*', '*owner of a language teaching company*', '*junior partner*', '*nurse*', etc. Moreover, and perhaps more interesting for our focus on language and 'culture' at work, many of our expatriate interviewees commented on their 'special' or outsider status in their workplace – just like Susan calling herself a '*gweilo*'. They frequently referred to themselves as '*foreigner*' and '*expatriate*', thereby actively positioning themselves in opposition to the people they work with, i.e. '*the locals*'. This creation of an 'us' versus 'them' dichotomy was further supported by the frequent mentioning of cultural₁ categories – such as '*the Australians*' and '*people in the Netherlands*' – which were often used to set themselves in opposition to their local colleagues and clients. Example 5.1 is a good illustration of this.

Example 5.1

Context: Interview with Tobias, a managing director of a large telecommunications company, who has been living in different parts of Asia for over 17 years. He is originally from the UK and at the time of data collection, he managed more than 1,000 employees, most of whom were local Hong Kong Chinese. Prior to this excerpt Tobias has admitted that although he has lived in Hong Kong for almost two decades he does not speak any Cantonese. IR – interviewer.

1	Tobias:	I found that very, um (.) the locals didn't like me learning Cantonese.
2	IR:	Why?
3	Tobias:	I -(.) Why do they feel like that? I-I don't know. I guess they'd like
4		to have their secrets,=
5	IR:	Mm.
6	Tobias:	=and feel separate. Um, the way they would show it would be,
7		even if you practice a simple phrase, um, very condescending
8		attitude, like, wow, you can say good morning in Cantonese, fantastic.
9		And that sort of attitude always put me off. If it's that hard to
10		just get a very simple conversation going without commenting on
11		that you were having a conversation,=
12	IR:	Mm.
13	Tobias:	=Um, it (.) I-I'm...maybe, for five minutes a year, I think, Gosh, I
14		wish I could understand what they were saying, but that's not
15		enough to get me to go and learn Cantonese and, uh, um,
16		as I was saying earlier, I actually enjoy not speaking Cantonese
17		and listening to-so that I can't understand what's going on,
18		on the street, or other people can't connect with me.
19		You don't hear the jabbering that other people are doing and
20		understand what rubbish they're talking about.

In the beginning Tobias explicitly mentions the identity category of '*the locals*' (line 1) to refer to his Hong Kong Chinese employees, and positions himself in opposition to '*them*'. This oppositional stance is reflected in his use of pronouns throughout, whereby he creates a 'them' versus 'me' dichotomy. Like Susan in the quote at the beginning of the chapter, he portrays himself as an outsider who is not part of the 'local' in-group ('*I guess they'd like to have their secrets [. . .] and feel separate*' (lines 3, 4 and 6)). He seems to feel deliberately excluded by '*them*' due to his lack of Cantonese, which is described here as the key to achieving in-group membership. Interestingly, however, as becomes clear towards the end of this excerpt, Tobias does not seem to mind being excluded from this particular in-group, and he emphasises that he actually '*enjoy[s]*' it (lines 15 and 16). He supports his claims by negatively describing these '*other people*' (e.g. by implying that he actually does not want them to '*connect with me*' (line 17), and by referring to their '*jabbering*' (line 18) and the '*rubbish they're talking about*' (line 19)). Through his choice of pronoun he also reveals a rather negative and condescending attitude towards these others, which further adds to the distance he creates between himself and them.

The next example is one of the rare instances in our corpus where interlocutors explicitly orient to culture$_1$ in their workplace interactions – in this case by enquiring about nationality. This excerpt occurred during a telephone counselling consultation between a nurse and a new mother, whose newborn has been diagnosed with G6PD deficiency. G6PD deficiency is a mild genetic condition related to an enzyme deficiency. In the worst-case scenario the condition can lead to a haemolytic reaction and even fatality, but it can be very well managed by avoiding certain substances (e.g. certain foods, such as fava beans, or some Chinese medications). The call takes place shortly after the mother has delivered the baby, while she is still on the maternity ward.

Example 5.2[2]

Context: Prior to the phone call the mother, who had not heard about G6PD deficiency before, has received an information leaflet containing important information about the condition, including some pictures of the substances that the baby (or herself while breastfeeding) must not consume or get exposed to. The nurse is Hong Kong Chinese and the mother is Filipino.

1	Nurse:	Okay? So, firstly, you don't give any medicine to your baby by
2		your own.
3	Mother:	Okay.
4	Nurse:	.h Actually, are you Indian or Pakistani?
5	Mother:	No, eh is eh Filipino.
6	Nurse:	Oh! Filipino. So do you have any (.) I mean traditional herb, (.) or
7		medicine in Philippine for the baby?
8	Mother:	No.
9	Nurse:	No, so that's fine. So you just .h ah stick to the rules, okay? No
10		matter it is your family ah traditional medicine or whatever.
11		Just don't give the baby
12		any kind of medicine or drug without seeing doctor.

((10 lines omitted))

| 13 | Nurse: | Don't feed your baby with the broad bean, (.) or the fava bean. |

| 14 | | Do you see the number three? ((refers to a patient |
| 15 | | information leaflet)) |

((7 turns omitted in which the nurse continues with her explanations))

16	Mother:	What does it mean of broad bean?
17	Nurse:	Broad bean, it is a kind of bean.
18	Mother:	Bean?
19	Nurse:	Yeah, look like the kidney shape. And it is quite big. .h And some
20		people use it as a snack. .h So if you go to those shops selling
21		the snack, you ask them for the broad bean, they would show you.
22		Usually they are very (.) quite big,
23		I mean compare with other kind of bean. Okay?
24	Mother:	Okay.
25	Nurse:	They are quite big and slightly brownish color.
26	Mother:	Okay.
27	Nurse:	And some are (.) have the brown hard coat, okay? And look like
		a kidney.

((6 lines omitted))

28	Nurse:	Okay. So if- if you are not sure how it look like, you can (.) go
29		to those shop selling the snack and then ask them for broad bean.
30		Then they will show you.
31		Okay.
32		Okay? Just don't feed your baby with the broad bean,
33		then will be okay

((. . .))

What is particularly interesting about this example is how culture$_1$ is made relevant here when the nurse asks the mother about her socio-cultural background: '*actually are you Indian or Pakistani?*' (line 4). This explicit orientation to culture$_1$ is particularly relevant in the context of this consultation, as it is used by the nurse as an entry into checking whether the mother (who is here being assigned an identity based on her membership in a particular national group) would routinely give any '*traditional herb, (.) or medicine*' (lines 6 and 7) to the baby – which, as the nurse repeatedly stresses throughout, needs to be avoided at all costs. By explicitly describing the mother as '*Indian or Pakistani*', the nurse also makes relevant the socio-cultural context in which this interaction takes place: it is the specific context of genetic counselling in Hong Kong that gives meaning to her questions and information regarding certain Chinese medicinal products which individuals with the condition should not consume or be exposed to.

Based on the mother's response in which she categorises herself as '*Filipino*' (line 5), the nurse proceeds with the information delivery – but in ways that go beyond the traditional role of nurses as information providers. Due to the mother's self-categorisation as belonging to the particular cultural$_1$ group of '*Filipino*', then, the nurse (rightly) assumes that the mother is not familiar with a particular type of bean that can cause harm to the baby, namely the so-called broad bean (line 13). In what follows, the nurse takes on the role of a cultural broker or mediator (Zayts & Schnurr 2014), in which she spells out particular practices that she associates with different cultures$_1$. She thereby mediates or translates knowledge that she ascribes to the local Hong Kong culture$_1$ in various ways to ensure that the mother has sufficient information about that bean (line 13 onwards).

After some initial misunderstanding, which seems to be – at least partly – due to the mother's non-native English proficiency, the nurse addresses the mother's uncertainty about what a broad bean is by providing further explanations. For example, she describes its shape ('*kidney shape. And it is quite big*' (line 19)) and colour ('*slightly brownish*' (line 25)), and she also explains what people in Hong Kong typically use it for ('*as a snack*' (line 20)). Since these explanation attempts seem to have little effect, the nurse eventually informs the mother where she can find broad beans ('*those shop selling the snack*' (line 30)) and suggests that she ask '*them*' (presumably the people selling the beans) to show these particular beans to her (lines 30 and 31). She thereby moves beyond a description of the bean's appearance and sets up two different, and in this case opposing, subject positions for the mother ('*you*') on the one hand, and local Hong Kong people who eat and sell the bean ('*they*') on the other hand. Interestingly, in this 'you' versus 'them' dichotomy she places herself between the mother ('*you*') and the Hong Kong locals ('*they*'). Thus, in contrast to the mother, in this exchange the nurse refuses to explicitly categorise herself as a member of either group. By positioning herself in between these two groups of people, the nurse is not claiming an in-group status with either the mother or the Hong Kong locals. In other words, although the mother is constructed as a foreigner who lacks certain cultural$_1$ knowledge, the nurse is at the same time portrayed as a mediator and a facilitator between the (foreign) client and the locals. This professional identity of the nurse, which draws heavily on the non-traditional nursing role of cultural broker and mediator, arises out of the need to adhere to a clinical agenda while at the same time responding to the specific demands nurses in Hong Kong regularly face (see also Zayts & Schnurr 2014).

In this example, participants make their culture$_1$ beliefs explicit and orient themselves to these first-order notions of culture as they construct their own and each other's identities – in close relationship to (perceived or assumed, as well as sometimes actual) membership in different groups. As this excerpt has shown, these identities are often closely intertwined with each other, and are, in fact, constructed in relation to each other: by constructing the mother's identity as '*Filipino*' and non-local, the nurse at the same time positions herself as a mediator who has the local knowledge that the mother lacks.

However, examples like these, where interlocutors explicitly mention and draw on often relatively rigid identity categories that establish a link between membership in a certain culture$_1$ group and specific behaviours and knowledge, are the exception in our corpus. In fact, in most of the interactions we recorded, participants do not make any references to culture$_1$. Thus, while in the interviews they regularly mobilise and reproduce first-order notions of culture, it almost seems like there is no interactional space for such often-stereotyping claims in their actual workplace encounters. Rather, in most workplace interactions, interlocutors draw on a wide range of discursive strategies in order to construct and negotiate their own and each other's identities. As we discuss in more detail in the next sections, they thereby orient to and negotiate the norms and practices associated with the interactional context in which they interact (as reflected in the notion of culture$_2$), while at the same time often challenging culture$_1$ stereotypes. But before discussing this in more detail, we first illustrate how in the interviews, participants sometimes used other collectives, such as their company, as a reference point to which they positioned themselves in relation when constructing their professional identities.

Mobilising company membership as an important aspect of professional identity

In this section we focus on Martin, an expatriate from the Netherlands, who at the time of recording had been working and living in Hong Kong for over six years. We explore how he constructs and negotiates with the interviewers his professional identities by positioning himself in relation to the company he works for. Martin is one of the partners of Company K, a large financial corporation with branches in over 150 countries across the world.

Martin is an excellent case to illustrate how interlocutors not only orient to culture$_1$ when constructing their professional identities in the interviews, but may, in fact, draw on other aspects that they consider to be particularly relevant for an understanding of who they are and how they want to portray themselves in front of the (expatriate) interviewers. As becomes clear throughout the interview, for Martin, being a member of the specific organisation he works for is an important part of his professional identity. This is reflected, for example, in the observation that he repeatedly draws on organisational jargon, thereby not only constructing his professional identity, but also highlighting the fact that his views are very much in line with the aims and objectives of the company he works for. For example, he frequently uses the inclusive first-person plural pronoun '*we*' when talking about Company K, as in '*we, over the last five years, have really tried as a firm to become globally uniform*'. With comments like this, he not only reiterates and, thus, reinforces organisational discourses (here of becoming '*globally uniform*'), but also explicitly aligns with the company's views and goals. In fact, at several points during the interview it becomes clear that he has internalised (and is proud of) the company's aims and objectives – for example, when he spontaneously recites the (rather lengthy) list of company values. Clearly, for Martin, being a member of Company K (rather than of a different company) is an important aspect of his professional identity and affects the ways in which he portrays himself during the interview. Examples 5.3 and 5.4 illustrate this and show how Martin constructs his professional identity by emphasising the similarities and shared ground between himself and the company.

Example 5.3

1	Martin:	This part, this part of the world, uh, in particular at this time, I don't
2		think there's anything comparable to it in terms of its
3		China being the, you know, a stone throw away.
4		Uh, there's never ever, I think, gonna be such growth
5		as we're currently experiencing
6		Company K-wise but also economy-wise. Um, the region itself, as I
7		said, we have a number of smaller Company K practices where, in my
8		particular case I do quite a bit of work, that doesn't apply to 99
9		percent, I would say most of me eighteen thousand colleagues.
10		But, for me, that's an interesting experience as working in places
11		like Vietnam, Taiwan, Thailand, Indonesia, Malaysia, uh,
12		Philippines. Um, and then
13		living in this part of the world I think is, is not bad either. You know, in
14		two hours you're on a nice beach resort.

In this extract Martin portrays himself as embracing the globalisation and cultural diversity that Company K propagates (e.g. '*working in places like Vietnam, Taiwan, Thailand, Indonesia, Malaysia, uh, Philippines*' (lines 10–11)). He adapts the company's perspective of viewing these trends as a highly valued experience (e.g. '*that's an interesting experience*' (line 9)) rather than as a challenge. His frequent use of the first-person inclusive pronoun '*we*' further emphasises this alignment and identification with Company K. However, at the same time Martin also to some extent distances himself from his '*eighteen thousand colleagues*' (line 8) and sets himself apart by highlighting his uniqueness (e.g. '*that doesn't apply to 99 percent*' (line 9)). He thereby manages to carve out a space in which he positions himself within the company's dominant discourses of growth and development (e.g. lines 4–5), as well as of globalisation and cultural diversity. Example 5.4 illustrates this further.

Example 5.4

Context: When asked to describe the ideal Company K employee, Martin produces the following narrative.

1	Martin:	So, yeah, you <u>do</u> look for somebody who's open and er: outgoing
2		and willing to communicate- communicate in England (.), in English.

3   Um, I remember years ago in Holland, (.) and perhaps it's not so much
4   the case here yet because it's just a different culture but (.) Company K
5   put an ad on the television or newspapers, I can't remember which
6   said If you finished your university degree in three years, which
7   typically you would do <u>four</u> in Holland, if you finished it in three,
8   or maybe it said even four, er,
9   please make, please make a trip around the world and then
10   come and speak to us. In other words, (.) we would <u>like</u> you to have
11   a little bit more than just your university focus on hopes and studies
12   and, uh, stuff like that. Um, so, yeah, it's (.) somebody who is a
13   bit <u>more rounded</u> than just, than just somebody who's
14   focused on the university.

In between this enumeration of fairly abstract talents (e.g. openness, being outgoing and communicative (lines 1–2), and '*a bit more rounded*' (lines 11–12)), Martin inserts a relatively short story (lines 3–9) that serves as a clarification. In this brief narrative, Company K acts as the protagonist, inciting potential recruits to '*make a trip around the world*' (line 9) to gain some intercultural experience, and to develop competence in interacting with different 'cultures'. This story is in line with the company's official discourse of global uniformity, which, as Martin repeatedly mentions throughout the interview, embraces cultural diversity and is a crucial aspect of the company's vision, to which he claims to strongly adhere. By telling this little anecdote he at the same time portrays himself as a representative of Company K, a 'global citizen' who values this experience that can be gained by making a '*trip around the world*' (line 9). He thereby aligns with the master narrative of embracing 'cultural diversity' as propagated by his company.

Moreover, by recounting the practices of Company K in the Netherlands (line 3), where this multinational company has its headquarters, Martin explicitly makes culture$_1$ relevant as a discerning feature and an essential explanatory factor (line 4). He thus frames his story as being related to what he perceives to be a difference between the Netherlands and Hong Kong. Though his statement is hedged ('*perhaps*' (line 3)), it nevertheless reflects his hierarchical view in which the practices displayed by the Dutch branch of the company are set up as goals which the Hong Kong branch has not '*yet*' reached (line 4). Through this process of reducing the differences between Company K's offices in Hong Kong and the Netherlands to culture$_1$ as an explanatory factor ('*just a different culture*' (line 4)) and by constructing the former as immature, Martin simultaneously constructs and makes relevant his own identity of being Dutch. It is, of course, quite ironic that this reductionist view of cultural$_1$ differences and the subsequent hierarchical construction of Hong Kong versus the Netherlands is actually established by means of a story about Company K's (and by implication, Martin's) awareness and appreciation of the importance of intercultural competence and openness to other cultures$_1$.

These short fragments show how Martin's professional identity is closely intertwined with his membership in Company K. This is reflected, for example, in the ways in which he relates to and draws on company discourses of openness and appreciation of cultural diversity. He constructs his individual professional identity as being strongly influenced by his membership in this specific company. By drawing on institutionalised discourses and adapting and reproducing the company's perspective throughout the interview, Martin also uses institutionalised forms of power and ideology to confirm and support his identity claims as a member of Company K. What is particularly interesting about these examples, then, is not only the fact that Martin celebrates his expatriate status and the cultural$_1$ experience that comes with it, thereby making first-order notions of culture relevant, but that he constructs his professional identity as closely related to the company that he works for.

In contrast to Examples 5.1–5.4, in which interlocutors set up specific subject positions for themselves and others in more or less explicit ways (e.g. by refer-ring to '*the locals*', '*Indian or Pakistani*' and '*Company K*'), in the next section we explore some of the discursive, and less explicit, processes through which participants construct and negotiate their own and each other's identities throughout an interaction. Although they draw on the same processes – such as indexicality and relationality – rather than making first-order notions of culture explicit, interlocutors primarily orient to the immediate context in which an interaction takes place.

Orienting to the interactional context

We have chosen two examples here to illustrate how interlocutors construct and negotiate their own and each other's identities by drawing on a wide range of discursive strategies which index specific roles and identities that are available to them within the constraints of the interactional context in which they operate. In line with the indexicality and relationality principles, participants not only portray themselves as a particular professional, expert, client, mother, etc., but also position themselves in relation to others. This may be harmonious (as in Example 5.5) or it may involve interactional struggles (as in Example 5.6).

Example 5.5 occurred during a prenatal screening consultation for Down's syndrome in a public hospital in Hong Kong. The interaction takes place between an expectant first-time mother who is 37 years old and from the Philippines, and a nurse who is Hong Kong Chinese. The mother does not have any prior experience or knowledge of Down's syndrome and attends the consultation on her own.

Example 5.5

Context: This extract occurs after the nurse has outlined various testing options to determine the mother's risk of having a child with Down's syndrome, and now asks the client to make a decision whether she would like to pursue any of these options. The nurse is Hong Kong local and the client from the Philippines. The interaction was conducted in English.

```
 1  Nurse:   Huh huh. so um: what do you prefer?
 2  Mother:  Uh uh as a nurse, [huh huh]=
 3  Nurse:   [°um°, yes] ((smiles and nods))
 4  Mother:  =because of course you may know better than I do when it comes to
 5           medical thing. So what do you suggest? Whether I have a blood
 6           test or the- do I have the: amni:=
 7  Nurse:   = an invasive [test].
 8  Mother:  [.h In]vasive test?
 9  Nurse:   °Um:° .h Yeh. Where's your husband?
10  Mother:  My husband is in Phi[lippines].
11  Nurse:   [in Phi]lippines. Um huh. .h nah depends on
12           your- on your preference. .h um each test has its um advantage and
13           disadvantage.
14  Mother:  Yeh.
15  Nurse:   For the screening test, it is safe.
16  Mother:  Ok.
17  Nurse:   But less accurate. Eighty percent accurate. With the invasive test,
18           it is accurate. But with the- the little bit risk of miscarriage
19           one in two hundred. .h so .h em: whether you want to have an
20           accurate test, or you want to have a safe test. If you want to have
21           an accurate test, then you go for amniocentesis.
22           .h but if you think that oh (..) I want to have a safe test,
23           then screening test is the choice.
24           I think it's better to discuss with your husband first.
25  Mother:  Ok. ((smiles)) huh huh h that's right. h
26  ((Nurse smiles))
27  Nurse:   You can check it up. .h I can make you a copy and then you discuss
28           with him first. Because today you are seventeen weeks.
29  Mother:  Yes.
30  Nurse:   Um: there's still time for considering the test.
31  Mother:  Yeah. Yeah. °ok.°
```

Throughout this exchange interlocutors construct their own and each other's identities by orienting to the specific interactional context in which this interaction takes place. They portray themselves as '*nurse*' (i.e. as someone who has more expert knowledge) and as client (i.e. as someone who has less expert knowledge) and they largely uphold the interactional rights and responsibilities associated with these roles. For example, in the beginning the client explicitly mentions the professional identity category of '*nurse*', thereby assigning the medical provider membership in that category. This move is also used by the client to explain why she is asking for advice: '*you may know better when it comes to medical thing*' (lines 4 and 5). She thereby constructs the nurse as the more knowledgeable party and at the same time sets up specific expectations and obligations that are associated with this profession. These expectations may of course differ among interlocutors, and indeed, in these consultations there is often a huge discrepancy between the mothers' expectations (namely to receive advice from the nurses) and the nurses' behaviour (namely to adhere to the ethos of non-directiveness (as elaborated in Chapter 3) and to ensure the patient reaches her decision autonomously).

However, as we can see from the nurse's responses to the patient's request for advice, rather than collaborating with the mother's attempt to construct her as a more knowledgeable advice giver, the nurse adheres to the institutionally prescribed role of nurse as information provider. She thus explicitly states that the decision lies with the mother (lines 11 and 12), which is followed by further information delivery outlining the available choices (lines 15–23). Interestingly, the nurse mobilises the identity of 'wife', which she implicitly assigns to her client when enquiring about her '*husband*' (line 9). This marital identity also becomes relevant again later when the nurse rejects the client's request for advice by suggesting she should discuss the various options with her husband instead (lines 22 and 23, 26 and 27), to which the expectant mother seems to agree (lines 24 and 28). All these behaviours by the nurse can be interpreted as indexing a knowledgeable and relatively powerful stance which, in turn, contributes to constructing the nurse's professional identity – in close relation to the woman's identity as a less knowledgeable, uncertain wife and soon to be mother.

As we argued in Chapter 3, many of the behaviours displayed by interlocutors in this example seem to be aligned with previous research on counselling discourse in Asia, which has noted that patients of Asian background tend to expect a more directive treatment and to be told what to do (Johnson & Nadirshaw 2002; Zayts et al. 2012). This impression is further reflected in a comment from one of the patients in our dataset, who in the interview after the consultation told us that '*she [i.e. the nurse] said 'take the test' and I took the test*'. In these instances, it seems that the behaviours displayed by interlocutors during their actual workplace interaction reflect and reinforce claims about first-order notions of culture (cf. the request for advice by the client in Example 5.5). As we have emphasised in previous chapters, however, it is crucial to take a more critical stance towards such often-stereotyping generalisations. In fact, interlocutors' behaviour in this extract could also be accounted for by alternative explanations, such as by making reference to the 'activity type' of genetic counselling.

The notion of activity type was introduced by Levinson (1979) to refer to relatively conventionalised communicative practices that take place in a particular context. Activity types are characterised by specific constraints about what is said and done in a particular encounter, and how these contributions are interpreted by participants. It is thus closely related to our notion of culture$_2$ as locally developed and negotiated practices and behaviours that are considered by interlocutors as appropriate and politic (as discussed in more detail in Chapter 2). According to this line of thinking, then, if we acknowledge that participants may have different expectations about what is going to happen during a specific activity and also about 'what will count as allowable contribution' (Levinson 1992: 73), then we can make sense of the behaviour displayed by the nurse and the expectant mother in Example 5.5 without necessarily having to draw on first-order claims about 'culture' in Chinese institutional contexts.

More specifically, rather than ascribing the client's behaviour to culture$_1$ norms (e.g. the client's attempts to transfer her decision making responsibilities to someone in a more powerful position), it could also be explained in terms of interlocutors' awareness (or lack) of the norms that characterise the specific activity type of genetic counselling, as captured in culture$_2$ (cf. Zayts & Pilnick 2014). In other words, the mother's behaviour could be understood as an expression of her expectation that she will receive advice during this genetic counselling session from the nurse about further procedures, and also of her lack of awareness of the nurse's commitment (which is tied to her professional role) to not giving direct advice and to ensuring that her clients reach their decisions regarding testing options autonomously (for a similar line of argument see also Campbell & Roberts 2007; Sarangi 1994). Thus, rather than basing an interpretation of interlocutors' behaviours on assumptions about culture$_1$-specific behaviours, it is more productive to understand them in the specific context in which they occur, where practices are closely related to specific activity types, which, in turn, form integral parts of culture$_2$.

However, as the next example illustrates, there is clearly some variation in the ways in which interlocutors orient to the specific roles that are associated with an activity type. It is important to bear in mind that roles and identities are continuously actively negotiated throughout an interaction, and that interlocutors also sometimes challenge and resist each other's identity claims. The next example illustrates this. Like Example 5.2, it is taken from a telephone consultation between a mother of a newborn baby who has been diagnosed with G6PD deficiency and a nurse.

Example 5.6

Context: While the mother is still on the maternity ward, the nurse talks to her on the telephone about her child's diagnosis. The nurse is Hong Kong local and

the mother from Mainland China. The consultation is conducted in Cantonese,
the mother's second language.

1	Nurse:	所以, 要預防嘅話, 嗽呀:, (.) 媽咪, 頭先你講過喇有
		So, for prevention, so:, (.) Mommy, you have just said
2		大部份嘅中藥係唔可以食.
		he can't take most of the Chinese medicines.
3		嗽呀, (.) 其實呢主要就係五種.
		So, (.) actually there are five main types.
4	Mother:	係.
		Yes.
5	Nurse:	係啦. 嗽呀, 你記唔記得係邊五種呀?
		Yes. So, do you remember which five?
6	Mother:	唔記得.
		I don't remember.
7	Nurse:	唔記得? 嗥, 嗽, 我, (.)
		You don't? Well, so, I, (.)
8	Mother:	單張嗰到有冇㗎?
		Does the leaflet have the information?
9	Nurse:	單張呢有嘅, 不過, 不過如果問媽咪, 你, 你自己點樣做呀?
		The leaflet does have it, but, but if I ask Mommy, you, what will you do?
10	Mother:	uh:
11	Nurse:	即係你, 自己本人啊, 因為你知你有呢個病㗎嘛?
		I mean you, yourself, because you know you have this deficiency, right?
12	Mother:	我, 我, 我知道邊啲唔食得或者唔好接觸. (.)
		I, I, I know what I can't eat or touch. (.)
13	Nurse:	嗽呀, eh: 譬如, 嗥, 因為你頭先話你又唔記得咗
		So, uh: like, ok, since you just said you don't remember
14		邊啲中藥唔食得喇, 嗽樣如果你=
		what kinds of Chinese medicines you can't take, then if you=
15	Mother:	=所以我咩中藥都唔食囉.
		=So I don't take any Chinese medicines.

This is a particularly interesting example from the angle of identity construction, as it illustrates the identity struggles (cf. Van de Mieroop & Schnurr fc) of the nurse and the mother over expert knowledge. More specifically, the mother, through her challenging behaviour, considerably undermines the nurse's attempts to construct herself as a more knowledgeable expert whose role it is to provide information about the baby's condition to the mother. For example, the nurse's initial question to the mother about which specific ingredients the baby needs to avoid (line 5) seems relatively directive and almost condescending considering that the mother has informed the nurse in the previous part of the consultation (not included in the extract) that she knows about the Chinese medicine as she has the condition herself. In responding, the mother delegitimises (to use Bucholtz & Hall's (2005) term) the nurse's role as information provider by undermining her attempt to repeat this information and to portray herself as an expert or information provider (i.e. as someone who knows better and whose responsibility it is to ensure that the mother has sufficient knowledge about the condition and can manage her child after hospital release).

This challenge becomes even more explicit in line 12 when the mother continues to refuse to cooperate with the nurse by categorically stating '*I, I, I know what I can't eat or use*' rather than demonstrating her knowledge of the Chinese medicinal products that she (and, more importantly, her newborn baby) should avoid. This rather harsh reaction of the mother may at least partly be a response to the nurse's diminutive reference '*Mommy*' (lines 1 and 9) and her way of talking, which may be perceived as patronising and as resembling class-room interaction rather than genetic counselling. By refusing to cooperate with the nurse's attempts to construct her own and the mother's positions in this interaction, the mother at the same time prevents the nurse from enacting those activities which are traditionally assigned to the nurse role and which index that particular professional identity.

Interestingly though, in spite of the mother's repeated challenges, the nurse continues with her attempts to act out her institutionally prescribed role of information provider (e.g. her justification of another attempt at information delivery in lines 13–14). But before she gets the opportunity to start providing the information, the mother interrupts her with another categorical statement ('*So I don't take any Chinese medicine*' (line 15)). The mother thereby, again, dele-gitimises the nurse's attempt to maintain the institutionally assigned role as an information provider, and also challenges the nurse's attempts to construct her professional identity in line with these institutional and job-specific demands.

The mother's challenges of the nurse's attempts to construct her professional identity in Example 5.6 are clearly in stark contrast to the behaviour of the expectant mother in Example 5.2. Rather than harmoniously co-constructing the nurse as an expert and information provider in line with the institutional guide-lines for the profession of a nurse, the mother in Example 5.6 repeatedly resists and challenges the nurse's attempts to construct an institutionally sanctioned hierarchy between herself and the mother. The mother ultimately portrays herself as a knowledgeable expert: '*I know what I can't eat or touch*' (line 12). She thereby at the same time also challenges those culture$_1$ claims which portray 'the Chinese' as respecting and upholding asymmetrical power relations as claimed in some earlier literature (e.g. Chee & West 2004; Selmer & de Leon 2003) and as discussed in previous chapters.

Discussion

This chapter has explored some of the processes through which questions of identity are linked to first- and second-order notions of culture – both in partici-pants' interviews and in their actual workplace interactions. We have identified and described three aspects of identity construction that emerged in our data. The first aspect referred to how interlocutors mobilise and orient to culture$_1$ categories – both in the interviews when positioning themselves in relation (and often in opposition) to others, as well as (albeit relatively rarely) in their actual workplace interactions, where they sometimes made explicit reference to interlocutors' nationalities. The second aspect of identity construction referred to those instances where participants mentioned membership in a particular company (rather than a profession or culture$_1$) as a relevant aspect of their professional identity. And the third aspect referred to the ways in which interlocutors constantly orient to the interactional context in which an encounter takes place.

As we have shown in our analyses and discussions, in these processes of identity construction, questions of who people are and how they perceive themselves in relation to others are closely related to first- and second-orders of culture. First-order culture was particularly relevant in those instances where interlocutors explicitly mentioned identity categories that suggest a direct link to culture$_1$, such as Susan's use of the local term '*gweilo*' in the quote at the beginning of the chapter, and the overt mentioning of cultural$_1$ categories in Examples 5.1 and 5.2. However, such instances are relatively rare in our corpus, and in contrast to the interviews, there are very few among the naturally occurring workplace interactions that we recorded. Rather than making explicit reference to culture$_1$ when constructing and negotiating identities in their workplace interactions, participants mainly oriented to the specific context in which an encounter took place and mobilised various professional (and lay) identities associated with it (cf. Examples 5.5 and 5.6). As we have illustrated, throughout their workplace interactions interlocutors draw on a wide range of discursive strategies to construct and negotiate their own and each other's identities in ways that reflect, reinforce and contribute to constructing culture$_2$ and the locally developed and negotiated practices that are considered to be appropriate and politic behaviours in the specific context in which their interaction takes place.

Thus, although it has been argued by previous research that people's identities are located in the wider socio-cultural context in which an interaction takes place (e.g. Kidd & Teagle 2002), our analyses have demonstrated the crucial importance of considering locally developed practices and understanding identity construction processes in the context of the specific activity type at play. The notion of activity type enables us to acknowledge that interlocutors orient to and negotiate their expectations of what is going to happen during a particular encounter, which also affects the identity claims they make for themselves and others, as well as the ways in which they either acknowledge and reinforce or challenge and reject each other's attempts to construct specific identities. These processes of identity construction and negotiation take place in the context of culture$_2$. In other words, they are closely linked to the localised norms and practices that characterise a particular profession, a specific professional context or a particular activity type. They are, therefore, not primarily a reflection of first-order culture.

In the next chapter we continue our discussion of the topic of identity construction and 'culture' (in both first- and second-order meanings), and focus on an aspect of identity that is particularly relevant in a workplace context: gender.

Notes

1 *Gweilo* is a Chinese term which literally means '*ghost*'. It is frequently used by Hong Kong locals to refer to Western (i.e. stereotypically Caucasian or 'White') expatriates.
2 Example 5.2 and 5.6 are also discussed in Zayts & Schnurr (2014), and the analysis in this chapter draws on this previous work; and Example 5.5 appears in Zayts & Schnurr (2012).

References

Angouri, Jo & Meredith Marra (2011). *Constructing Identities at Work.* Basingstoke: Palgrave Macmillan.

Bucholtz, Mary & Kira Hall (2005). Identity and interaction: A sociocultural linguistic approach. *Discourse Studies* 7.4–5: 585–614.

Campbell, Sarah & Celia Roberts (2007). Migration, ethnicity and competing discourse in the job interview: Synthesizing the institutional and personal. *Discourse & Society* 18: 243–71.

Chee, Harold & Chris West (2004). *Myths about Doing Business in China.* Basingstoke/ New York: Palgrave Macmillan.

Deschamps, Jean-Claude & Thierry Devos (1998). Regarding the relationship between social identity and personal identity. In Stephen Worchel, Francisco Morales, Dario Paez & Jean-Claude Deschamps (eds), *Social Identity.* London: SAGE. 1–12.

Hall, Stuart (2000). Who needs identity? In Paul Du Gay, Jessica Evans & Peter Redman,(eds), *Identity: A Reader.* London, SAGE. 15–30.

Johnson, Amanda Webb & Zenobia Nadirshaw (2002). Good practice in transcultural counseling: An Asian perspective. In Stephen Palmer (ed.), *Multicultural Counselling: A Reader.* London: SAGE. 119–28.

Kidd, Warren & Alison Teagle (2002). *Culture and Identity.* Houndmills: Palgrave.

Levinson, Stephen C. (1992). Activity types and language. In Paul Drew & John Heritage (eds), *Talk at Work: Interaction in Institutional Settings.* Cambridge, UK: Cambridge University Press. 66–100.

Levinson, Stephen C. (1979). Activity types and language. *Linguistics* 17: 365–99.

Ochs, Elinor (1993). Constructing social identity: A language and socialization perspective. *Research on Language and Social Interaction* 26.3: 287–306.

Sarangi, Srikant (1994). Accounting for mismatches in intercultural selection interviews. *Multilingua* 13.1/2: 163–94.

Schnurr, Stephanie (2013). *Exploring Professional Communication. Language in Action.* Abingdon: Routledge.

Selmer, Jan & Corinna de Leon (2003). Culture and management in Hong Kong SAR. In Malcolm Warner (ed.), *Culture and Management in Asia.* London: Routledge Curzon. 48–65.

Van de Mieroop, Dorien & Jonathan Clifton (eds) (2012). *Pragmatics. Special Issue on Institutional Identities* 22.2.

Van de Mieroop, Dorien & Stephanie Schnurr (eds) (fc). *Identity Struggles. Evidence from Workplaces around the World.* Amsterdam: Benjamins.

Widdicombe, Sue (1998). Identity as an analysts' and a participants' resource. In Charles Antaki & Sue Widdicombe (eds), *Identities in Talk*. London: SAGE. 191–206.

Zayts, Olga & Alison Pilnick (2014) Genetic counseling in multilingual and multicultural contexts. In Heidi Hamilton & W.-Y. Chou (eds), *Handbook on Language and Health Communication*. London and New York: Routledge. 557–72.

Zayts, Olga & Stephanie Schnurr (2014). More than 'information provider' and 'counselor'. Constructing and negotiating roles and identities of nurses in genetic counseling sessions. *Journal of Sociolinguistics* 18.3: 345–69.

Zayts, Olga & Stephanie Schnurr (2012). 'You may know better than I do': Negotiating advice-giving in Down's Syndrome screening in a Hong Kong prenatal hospital. In Holger Limberg & Miriam Locher (eds), *Advice in Discourse*. Amsterdam: John Benjamins. 195–212.

Zayts, Olga, V. Yelei Wake & Stephanie Schnurr (2012). Chinese prenatal genetic counseling discourse in Hong Kong: Health care providers' (non)directive stance, or who is making the decision? In Yulin Pan & Daniel Kádár (eds), *Chinese Discourse and Interaction: Theory and Practice*. London: Equinox. 228–47.

6 Gender. The interplay between the 'local' and the 'global'

There's a gender implication for everything you do.
(Gillian, member in one of the District Councils in Hong Kong)

Introduction

In this chapter we continue the discussion in the previous chapters about the role of culture$_1$ and culture$_2$ in the workplace context, and explore some of the ways in which this analytical distinction can be applied to an analysis of gender, and, more specifically, how it may enable us to better understand the interplay between local practices and global issues.

Hong Kong provides an interesting site for investigating gender and culture in both its first- and second-order meanings. Although Hong Kong is a city where Eastern and Western traditions blend in complex ways (Chan 2005; Cheng 2003), it has been claimed that traditional Chinese values and practices remain strong in many aspects of society, including many workplaces – such as the belief that women's place is typically viewed as the home (De Leon & Ho 1994) and the existence of hierarchical and often patriarchal family structures which are also enacted in many workplaces where fathers and (typically male) leaders are seen as absolute authority figures (see also Chapter 5 and e.g. Chee & West 2004; Cullen 1999; Lee 2004; Schnurr 2010; Ladegaard 2012). These gendered structures are often viewed as a reflection of culture$_1$, as Selmer and De Leon (2003: 55) maintain: '[l]egitimized by traditional cultural values still prevalent in modern Hong Kong, the hierarchical and patriarchal relationships of the family are replicated in the organizational structures' (see also Hong Kong Council of Social Service 2012).

However, in spite of these links of first-order notions of culture with gender, there is an ongoing debate both in the media[1] and among academics as to whether gender is indeed an issue in Hong Kong. The contradiction between the claim that 'sexual inequalities no longer exist in Hong Kong' (Women and Media Concern Group, AAF 1992: 183) and prevailing evidence of 'unequal employment and promotion opportunities, lesser pay and fewer leadership positions' for women (The Women's Foundation 2006: 19) makes an investigation of gender and 'culture' in Hong Kong an important and rewarding undertaking.

Drawing on a combination of culture$_1$ and culture$_2$ examples, this chapter challenges some of the prevailing assumptions about the role of gender in Hong Kong workplaces. It identifies and critically discusses some of the gendered assumptions and practices that characterise many workplaces in Hong Kong – many of which are typically associated and explained with reference to culture$_1$. These 'global' assumptions about the gender order and the roles of men and women – which are often closely reflected in participants' first-order notions of culture – are then contrasted with a fine-grained analysis of the local practices that interlocutors draw on in their workplace interactions while at the same time orienting to, enacting and actively constructing second-order notions of culture.

Background: Gender in Hong Kong workplaces

In our previous research on gender in Hong Kong workplaces, we have found that the various advancements for women reported in the media have primarily taken place on the surface, and that gender discrimination is still an important issue in Hong Kong. We have argued that while on the surface, 'Hong Kong appears to be a very modern and progressive society where women enjoy more privileges than in many other Asian countries, our critical analysis of discourses in two important public contexts [workplaces and advertisements] seems to indicate relatively little progress in terms of symbolic capital wielded by women in the society (Bourdieu 1991; Cameron 2006)' (Kang & Schnurr 2010: 185). These findings are also supported by other studies which observed that strong gender norms and traditional role differentiations, which often discriminate against women in various contexts, prevail in Hong Kong (e.g. Ebrahimi 1999; Lee 2003; De Leon & Ho 1994; Ngo 2001; Lee & Fung 2006; Hong Kong Council of Social Service 2012; Saidi 2015).

This discrimination is reflected in the workplace context where women are often disadvantaged in terms of salary and promotion opportunities (Hong Kong Council of Social Service 2012; The Women's Foundation 2006; see also Chow 1995; Lee 2003; Pearson & Leung 1995; Ebrahimi 1999). According to key statistics, in 2009 women's monthly income was 70 per cent less than that of men (Hong Kong Council of Social Service 2012: 14). Moreover, in 2009, on average only 7.6 per cent of board members in Hong Kong were women[2]; and in a recent report published in 2015, it is stated that there is currently only one female Chairperson of the Boards for Hong Kong's leading companies (Community Business 2015).

One of the reasons for the endurance of this glass ceiling seems to be related to upholding traditional role differentiations along gender lines, as reported in previous studies. For example, Yeung et al. (2004: 509) observed that of the almost 200 female managers they interviewed in China and Hong Kong, over 90 per cent 'agreed or very much agreed with the statement that "career women should not expect to shirk their household responsibilities"'. Similarly, a study by Pearson and Leung (1995: 8) found that 'the family is accepting of a wife and mother working as long as she continues to maintain her domestic responsibilities' (see also Lee 2003, 2004; Hong Kong Council of Social Service 2012).

It seems that this 'attitude of cosy complacency' (Pearson & Leung 1995: 18), stemming from claims that gender is not an issue (any more) in Hong Kong and thereby ignoring gender issues, does not adequately reflect the workplace realities of many women. The following quotes, which are taken from Mahtani (2006) who conducted interviews with 22 women leaders from different sectors and industries in Hong Kong, illustrate the relevance of gender issues in the landscape of today's Hong Kong further.

Example 6.1

Female leader 1:   *Traditionally women are supposed to belong more to the home, to play a major role in the family. Modern women also go out [to work], contributing to society, to become leaders. They have to take up more roles. Women have to work extra hard, to be more efficient with their time usage.* (Mahtani 2006: 27)

Example 6.2

Female leader 2:   *People would be very critical if [they] had to promote a female instead of a man because people still continue to believe men are more capable than females, that men can devote more in terms of time, devotion, and energy.* (Mahtani 2006: 28)

Example 6.3

Female leader 3:   *At all times, I have to prove that I am no worse, but even better than a male colleague . . . in terms of commitment and results. If women want to achieve the same position as a man, women have to work harder.* (Mahtani 2006: 28)

While we do not want to claim that this sample is representative of the experience of women in leadership positions in Hong Kong, these quotes by different female leaders are nevertheless a strong indication that gender is still very much an issue – especially for women at the top. Among the issues mentioned by the women interviewed by Mahtani were their struggles with balancing the often competing demands of traditional role expectations – especially regarding fulfilling familial duties and pursuing a professional career (see also Chapter 7) – and the feeling of being disadvantaged in terms of promotion opportunities and career development and progression. These aspects were also brought up in an interview that we conducted with Sabitha, a very successful (and highly acclaimed) leader in her field (see also Chapter 4). Asked about her experiences as a female leader in Hong Kong, she expressed her belief that in Hong Kong '*leadership and corporate life have been described in a certain way and mostly by men*' so that certain discourses – such as the discourse of work–life balance (see also Chapter 7) and discourses of motherhood and femininity – are often ignored and are simply not part of the hegemonic, mainstream leadership discourse. The comments of the women leaders in Examples 6.1–6.3 and evidence from recent research (e.g. Schnurr & Mak 2011; Ladegaard 2012) certainly reinforce this impression.

Further evidence of gender discrimination in Hong Kong workplaces is provided by Lee et al. (2008 as referred to in Ladegaard 2012), who found that the vast majority of their (male and female) respondents claimed that they would prefer to work for a male leader, while only 27 per cent said they preferred a female leader. These preferences were often explained by reference to gender stereotypes of what informants considered to be typical characteristics of male and female leaders. Not surprisingly perhaps, given the evidence reported above, 63 per cent of the stereotypes mentioned for male leaders were positive (such as being 'efficient' and 'easy-going') while a staggering 60 per cent of the stereotypes produced for female leaders were negative (e.g. being 'emotional' and 'obsessed with details').

In addition to the overwhelming evidence already provided by previous research, we also found evidence in our corpus of other instances where gender comes to the fore, such as participants' stereotypical comments about men and women, as in Example 6.4 (see also Schnurr (2013) for the discussion of further examples).

Example 6.4[3]

Context: During one of the regular meetings of one of Hong Kong's District Councils. Participants are discussing how to make the Council's various activities and plans more appealing to women. Bob, one of the members of the Council who is Hong Kong Chinese, explains what he perceives to be the 'needs' of women and men.

1 Bob: Then I think what kinds of needs these are? (.) when it comes to the
2   male, it is very simple, we like playing soccer we like watching
3   soccer matches, we like wrestling. Females watch Ladies' New Looks'
4   and something like Afternoon Tea

In his comment about the '*needs*' (line 1) of men and women, Bob heavily draws on and at the same time reinforces stereotypical views of men and women. By describing men as being mainly interested in '*playing soccer*', '*watching soccer matches*' and '*wrestling*' (lines 2 and 3), he portrays them as focusing on sports and physical activities, while women, on the other hand, are portrayed as being more passive, namely as watching TV programmes about fashion ('*Ladies' New*

Looks') and household-related topics (*'Afternoon Tea'*) (line 4). By describing men and women as being interested in and doing essentially different things, he at the same time actively creates a gender dichotomy. With his short comment, then, Bob not only evokes and draws on some of the stereotypical roles that have traditionally been assigned to men and women, but he also reproduces them to some extent and brings them into the context of his workplace. Although it becomes clear later in the interaction that Bob is aware of the fact that he was stereotyping, this discourse of gender differences is nevertheless derogatory and discriminates against women, who are portrayed in line with traditional and rather restricted models of role differentiation.

The existence of gendered discourses underlying and informing comments expressed in Examples 6.1–6.4 is often explained by reference to culture₁ perceptions, which describe Hong Kong as a relatively masculine society with largely patriarchal relations, as explained in Chapter 4 (e.g. Hofstede 1980; De Leon & Ho 1994; Ngo 2001; Lee 2003; Schnurr & Mak 2011). However, these claims about gender and Hong Kong largely draw on first-order notions of culture and make generalisations on a relatively abstract level while ignoring more locally negotiated practices (as captured in second-order notions of culture). We address this issue in later sections of the chapter, where we explore some of the ways in which gender is enacted on the local level. But first, we will briefly describe what gender is and why it is relevant in a workplace context.

What is gender and why is it relevant at work?

Following recent research, we understand gender as a performance, as something that people *do*, rather than as an attribute (based on biological features) that people possess (e.g. Butler 1990; West & Zimmerman 1987). This definition is very much in line with our dynamic understanding of culture (in its first- and second-order meanings) as a dynamic process or performance, as outlined in Chapter 1. Gender, like 'culture', is thus best researched 'in action', i.e. by exploring some of the ways in which people *do* it. A good illustration of this is Gillian's quote at the very beginning of the chapter, where she makes explicit reference to gender, or Examples 6.1 to 6.4 where participants draw on specific gendered discourses that position men and women in certain ways, thereby reinforcing traditional (often stereotypical and discriminatory) role expectations of women and men. In all these instances, gender is explicitly made relevant through interlocutors' comments and is thereby brought to the fore. Another, albeit often less explicit, way in which gender may be enacted in a workplace context is by drawing on elements of so-called gendered speech styles. Table 6.1 summarises what Holmes (2000) and others describe as feminine and mascu-line speech styles.

Although the notion of gendered speech styles has to be treated with caution (e.g. Cappella 2015), they are nevertheless generally considered as a good starting point to understand how certain behaviours are gendered (i.e. associated with

Table 6.1 Widely cited features of feminine and masculine interactional styles (based on Holmes 2000)

Elements of a feminine interactional style	Elements of a masculine interactional style
Facilitative	Competitive
Supportive feedback	Aggressive interruptions
Conciliatory	Confrontational
Indirect	Direct
Collaborative	Autonomous
Minor contribution (in public)	Dominates (public) talking time
Person-/process-oriented	Task-/outcome-oriented
Affectively oriented	Referentially oriented

the ways in which men or women are stereotypically assumed to be talking). There is ample evidence, however, that actual workplace practices are much more complex and that both men and women regularly (and sometimes strategically) draw on and combine elements of both styles (e.g. Holmes 2006; Schnurr & Mak 2011; Mullany 2007).

By using elements of these speech styles, people at work not only construct their gender identities but also at the same time create their professional identities (as discussed in more detail in the previous chapter). More specifically, as Cameron and Kulick (2003: 58) maintain, 'the same way of speaking signifies both a professional identity and a gendered identity, and in practice these are difficult to separate: the two meanings coexist, and both of them are always potentially relevant' (see also Holmes & Schnurr 2005).

One problem that is closely related to this distinction between feminine and masculine speech styles, and the stereotypical assumptions underlying it, is often referred to as the double-bind. The double-bind describes the situation where women at work find themselves caught between the competing expectations of behaving (and talking) in ways that are stereotypically associated with femininity (e.g. by drawing on elements of feminine speech styles) and displaying behaviour that is considered professional and appropriate for their institutional role. This dilemma is particularly acute for women in leadership positions who often struggle with being perceived negatively (e.g. too aggressive and too masculine) when drawing on elements of masculine speech styles, while being judged as too feminine and unprofessional when using elements of feminine speech styles (e.g. Mullany & Litosseliti 2006; Pauwels 2000; Brewis 2001; Peck 2000). Although these perceptions seem to be changing (e.g. Fletcher 2004), elements of feminine speech styles, such as being supportive, collaborative and facilitative, tend to be evaluated more positively when displayed by men (e.g. Sinclair 1998).

While it would go beyond the scope of this chapter to discuss all of the gender issues that prevail in workplaces in Hong Kong in great detail, our aim here is to illustrate some of the ways in which gendered (and often stereotypical and discriminatory) discourses extant in many of these workplaces are often explained via first-order notions of culture, while specific interactional behaviours (such as displaying elements of gendered speech styles) are closely linked to second-order notions of culture. Thus, in order to better understand the role of gender in Hong Kong workplaces, both first- and second-order notions of culture are useful concepts, because they provide frequently mentioned 'global' explanations for the gender order and gendered role expectations, as well as insights into actual (gendered and gendering) practices at the 'local' level in specific workplaces (see also Litosseliti 2006; Sunderland 2004). We further discuss this last point in the next section as we examine some of the ways in which interlocutors *do* gender in their everyday workplace interactions.

Local practices

In this section we look at several examples from two different workplaces in Hong Kong to explore the role of the local context and locally negotiated practices through which gender is enacted on the micro-level of an interaction (captured in our notion of culture$_2$). We take as a starting point a question raised in an article by Ladegaard (2012) which explicitly establishes a link between culture$_1$ and issues of gender. Based on his analysis of two female leaders in a small factory outlet in Hong Kong, Ladegaard (2012: 1675) speculates that 'normatively masculine and feminine management styles may be culture specific, in terms of perception as well as actual behaviour'. Guided by his observations and those made in some of our own earlier work (e.g. Schnurr 2010), which show women leaders in Hong Kong displaying relatively direct and sometimes aggressive behaviours, Ladegaard poses the question as to whether 'normatively masculine and feminine management styles are culture specific', and whether 'female leaders in Chinese contexts are allowed, or maybe even expected, to behave more aggressively' (Ladegaard 2012: 1674). Although we do not have the space to answer these questions exhaustively, in what follows we provide case studies of two female leaders in Hong Kong who display different behaviours, thereby questioning such generalising assumptions about potential, explicit links between first-order notions of culture, gender and normative or preferred leadership styles and behavioural patterns.

Both of the women in our case studies are very successful in their careers, and have founded popular language learning centres. They are thus good examples of the increasingly growing numbers of female entrepreneurs in the Hong Kong workforce (e.g. The Women's Foundation 2006). We have chosen seven examples here to illustrate some of the diverse ways in which these two women do gender by drawing on and skilfully combining elements of masculine and feminine speech styles when achieving their workplace objectives.

Case study 1: Janet

Our first case study focuses on Janet, who is the owner of the language learning centre Lingsoft Inc. At the time of data collection she has been living in Hong Kong for almost 30 years. When she moved to Asia (from the UK) she first worked as an English language teacher for the British Council before founding her own company. Janet's company currently employs 15 Hong Kong locals.

In line with the observations made by the previous literature, in the interactions that we recorded at Lingsoft Inc. Janet often displays elements of a masculine speech style – especially when getting things done and assigning tasks that have a strict deadline, as in Examples 6.5–6.7. There is also, however, ample evidence in the data of collaborative and consultative behaviour which is often associated with a feminine style (e.g. Marra et al. 2006), as evidenced in the team's decision-making practices (cf. Example 6.8).

Example 6.5

Context: During a regular team meeting at Lingsoft Inc. The meeting is chaired by Janet. Katja, Tanya and Clarisse, three of the employees, are discussing who is going to sign off an information leaflet which needs to be sent off to the customers soon.

1	Katja:	You wanna sign that? You need to sign that, right?
2	Janet:	Yeah, I was in a meeting, so I can't write it. But I'll go through
3		the (pictures), around, and it's ok.
4	Katja:	Ok (.) in your case.
5	Janet:	You do it. No no no, not till next week. I need it today. This
6		should go out with speed. That should go out within 24 hours
7		at the meeting. So that has to be printed out.
8	Tanya:	(Name) letter and the price for that.
9	Clarisse:	Yes.
10	Tanya:	Ok, thank you.

At the beginning of the extract Katja reminds Janet to sign off the brochure (line 1), but since Janet did not attend the meeting where this was discussed, she rejects this request and instead offers to look at the pictures and make sure they are okay (lines 2–3). Rather than doing the task herself, she then assigns it to Katja in a very direct, explicit and unmitigated way – '*you do it*' (line 5) – which is followed up by several equally direct and potentially face-threatening instructions: e.g. '*I need it today*' (line 5). Especially the repeated use of the negation marker '*no*' (line 5) and the repeated and precise indication of time ('*within 24 hours*' (line 6)) make these instructions seem rather challenging and perhaps even confrontational. Moreover, Janet's exclusive focus on task-/outcome-oriented aspects (as reflected, for example, in the absence of any mitigation strategies) and her autonomous way of giving these instructions are indexing a masculine speech style.

In addition to those instances where Janet tells her subordinates explicitly what they need to do, she also often assigns tasks and makes sure her team members know what they are expected to do by drawing on the more implicit, and more face-saving, strategy of asking questions. Examples 6.6 and 6.7 are also taken from team meetings at Lingsoft Inc.

Example 6.6

1 Janet: So they- can you speak to them about (xxx)?
2 Clarisse: Yes.
3 Janet: Okay.

Example 6.7

1 Janet: Okay. Um, once we've moved onto another, another issue, can you go
2   and just check that for me?
3 Clarisse: Yeah.

Like in Example 6.5, in Examples 6.6 and 6.7 Janet is clearly the one in charge, and again, her interactional behaviour incorporates several elements of a masculine style, such as being direct (e.g. the choice of '*can*' rather than '*could*'), short and to the point with hardly any affective orientation (e.g. the absence of '*please*' or '*thank you*'). However, since these are clearly relatively small and routine tasks that need to be done, this direct interactional style and the absence of more affectively oriented strategies are perhaps not surprising (e.g. Holmes & Stubbe 2003).

Through her behaviour in Examples 6.5–6.7 Janet portrays herself as an autonomous and perhaps sometimes autocratic leader who is clearly in charge. These identities are largely evoked through her frequent use of elements of a masculine speech style, as well as the stances of authority, power and decisiveness that they evoke (see also Chapter 5). These observations thus provide further support for the findings of earlier research (e.g. Ladegaard 2012; Schnurr 2010) and could be understood as being in line with culture[1] perceptions according to which women leaders in Hong Kong are being allowed or even expected to display behaviours typically associated with masculine speech styles.

However, looking at some of the decision making episodes of Janet and her team (see also Chapter 3), a rather different and more nuanced picture emerges which shows Janet often taking a back-seat and letting her team members actively contribute to the discussion, as in Example 6.8.

Example 6.8

Context: Low attendance rate among students is one of the difficulties Lingsoft Inc. faces each year, and so team members are discussing how to prevent this from happening, and how to make sure students continue attending their classes during the summer. Valerie and Ivan are two other employees at the language learning centre.

1	Janet:	[.h So], I think just during the summer can we just say the parents
2		got you know (xxx) summer. Um, Mrs. Fenner will, assess the child during
3		her, during the class. So we'll give her free, free class
4		and Mrs. Fenner will do the assessment during the class.
5	Katja:	[Mm.]
6	Valerie:	Also free of charge for the-, for the-=
7	Katja:	Assessment.
8	Valerie:	=for the first class.
9	Janet:	And then I will do it as an assessment, Vicky, to save time (xx)
10		got here really quickly.
11	Ivan:	Okay.
12	Valerie:	That's good, that's better. If not we can't, encourage- encourage
13		them to come here I just pay three hundred ninety eight.
14		[((laughs))]
15	Ivan:	[((laughs))] Mm-hmm, okay. U:m, okay. I do that, mm-hmm.
16	Janet:	Okay.

Although Janet is clearly involved in this decision making episode (as is reflected in the fact that she is the only one to make substantial suggestions (lines 1–4, 9–10), and also the one who has the last word (line 16)), the decision making is a team effort in which the various members participate. This collaborative way of coming to a decision here is set up by Janet in line 3 when she uses the inclusive first-person plural pronoun '*we*' to signal conjoint ownership of the issue. This is picked up by various team members who conjointly and collaboratively work towards finding a solution. Particularly noteworthy here are the ways in which team members contribute to and complete each other's sentences (lines 6–9), their frequent expressions of agreement and positive responses (lines 6–8), their use of humour and joint laughter involving several team members (lines 14–15) and Ivan's offer to take on some of the tasks that are involved. Thus, although Janet plays an active role in this decision making episode and is the one to ratify it at the end (line 16), her overall speech style displayed in this example is very different compared to Examples 6.5–6.7. In this excerpt she employs several strategies associated with a feminine speech style, such as facilitative formulations and taking a collaborative approach (e.g. by allowing participants to contribute).

Throughout the various meetings that we have recorded at Lingsoft Inc., we observed Janet displaying a wide range of different behaviours – sometimes being more direct and task-oriented (which is typically achieved by drawing on elements of a masculine speech style), while at other times being more facilitative and encouraging collaboration (by drawing on elements associated with a feminine speech style). Clearly, the interactional behaviour displayed by Janet – even within a single meeting – is very complex and she skilfully draws on and combines elements of both masculine and feminine speech styles. These observations support our earlier research on another female leader in Hong Kong, Sabitha (see Chapter 4), where we also identified differing interactional behaviours in different contexts, such as regular staff meetings, one-to-one interactions with colleagues and weekly emails (Schnurr & Mak 2011). In the meeting and emails, Sabitha, like Janet, used many of the elements ascribed to a masculine speech style and indexed masculine ways of behaving, such as being competitive, confrontational, direct, autonomous and task-oriented. A very different picture emerged, however, in her one-to-one interactions with her colleagues, where she put much more emphasis on relational aspects, involving people and making sure they were happy to do the work that was assigned to them.

These observations of very different and, one could even argue, contrasting behaviours displayed by the leader within their organisation clearly demonstrate that there is no single way of doing leadership and of behaving in a workplace context (see also Chapter 4). On the contrary, Sabitha, Janet and our other participants regularly and skilfully draw on and combine different elements of masculine and feminine speech styles to suit their purposes and to achieve their transactional and relational workplace goals.

So, while we found evidence in the data of behaviours that seems to reinforce claims about gender and first-order notions of culture, we also found ample evidence of behaviours that contradict these expectations. As we have argued in the previous chapters, Janet's interactional behaviour, and the ways in which she gets things done and makes decisions with her team, cannot adequately be explained by sole reference to first-order notions of culture but need to be understood in the local context of her workplace and the specific practices that are considered normative among members (as in second-order notions of culture). We now look at one more case study, before discussing in more detail the crucial role of culture$_2$ in this context and how a combination of analysing first- and second-order culture may provide a useful framework for understanding gender at work.

Case study 2: Lily

Our second case study focuses on Lily, the co-founder and co-owner of another language learning centre, Sandcastle, in Hong Kong. Like Janet, Lily grew up and was educated in the UK. At the time of data collection she had been living in Hong Kong for two years. Her husband is Hong Kong Chinese, and they have moved to Hong Kong permanently. What is particularly noteworthy about Sandcastle is its very supportive and collaborative atmosphere – this '*aura in the centre of happiness and friendliness and warmth*', as members have described it. In the interviews, staff members have explicitly commented on the respectful ways in which they deal with each other at all times. The managers, Lily and

Jenny, emphasised that they treat their staff as their '*friends*' and '*actually care*' about their well-being and want them '*to be happy at work*'. Thus, unlike Lingsoft Inc., a lot of emphasis is put on relational or affective aspects, which is also reflected in members' interactional behaviours, as Example 6.9 demonstrates.

Example 6.9

Context: During one of their regular team meetings, staff members discuss Chloe's idea to incorporate information about new activities and courses offered by Sandcastle on the company's website. Chloe is the company's receptionist.

1	Chloe:	That's really good to have a link showing all the new stuff on the
2		website. And I was wondering if we could send, just because I was
3		going to send an email to a couple of parents, ((a student's name))'s
4		mom and ((a student's name))'s mom. They want to do extra stuff.
5		And I have an idea that we could do it to all the parents in our
6		database. Send an email that they can click through automatically to
7		the links.
8	Jenny:	Oh, brilliant.
9	Chloe:	How's that?
10	Lily:	But then there's gonna be in the newsletter now.
11	Chloe:	Oh, yes. Then it's doubling up.
12	Lily:	Maybe- maybe better just to do the newsletter.
13	Chloe:	Okay.
14	Lily:	'Cause the parents don't like it by emails.
15	Chloe:	Sure.
16	Lily:	It was a good idea, though.
17	Chloe:	°It's fine.°

Although there is a lot to say about this example, we focus here on the ways in which Lily reacts to Chloe's suggestion. Rather than declining Chloe's suggestion right away, Lily expresses her concern about potential overlaps with the information included in the newsletter and parents' potentially negative reactions (lines 10 and 14). She thereby implicitly articulates her disagreement and expresses her opinion in a very mitigated and face-saving way. Chloe seems to understand the message and to share these concerns, as her agreeing minimal responses indicate (lines 13, 15, 17). What is particularly interesting about this example is Lily's encouraging comment towards the end, '*It was a good idea, though*' (line 16), with which she brings the discussion to an end while at the same time acknowledging Chloe's efforts and expressing her appreciation. She thereby enhances Chloe's face, which further mitigates the potential face-threat of the rejection of her suggestion. Through these behaviours, Lily manages to keep her subordinate motivated and feeling appreciated in spite of her rejection. As Chloe's final reply indicates, this is achieved successfully here.

This example is thus an excellent illustration of the supportive and collegial atmosphere that characterises Sandcastle – one aspect of which is members' interactional behaviours. When criticising her subordinate and ultimately rejecting her suggestion, Lily draws on several elements of a feminine style: her contributions are indirect, conciliatory and affectively oriented. This kind of behaviour is thus in sharp contrast to the behaviour displayed by Janet in Examples 6.5–6.8, and it also challenges some of the claims made in earlier research about the relatively masculine behaviour of women leaders in Hong Kong as an alleged reflection of culture$_1$. The next example illustrates this further by showing that members of this team often volunteer, rather than being explicitly assigned to do a particular task.

Example 6.10

Context: During the same meeting. Participants are organising an upcoming event at the beginning of the academic year.

```
 1 Lily:    ((clicking her fingers)) Do you want me to do the introduction?
 2          (.)
 3 Jenny:   hhh coming up end of September, yeh?
 4 Lily:    Yeah.
 5 (.) ((noise of children playing outside the meeting room))
 6 Jenny:   I- I do a little write up on the parents' evening, and then just again ah
 7          (xxx) a little bit more.
 8 Lily:    Okay. (.) I'll do the welcome. And I'll try to find something funny also.
 9          Something light hearted.
10          (.)
11 Jenny:   °Yeh.°
12 Chloe:   And what would you like me to do?
13 Jenny:   What'd you like to do? What do you think would be nice to have in a
14          newsletter?
15 Lily:    Did you do (xxx)?
16 Chloe:   No.
17 Jenny:   May be, ah you can do (xxx)? Maybe huge word introducing-
18          introducing a new staff, °yeah°.
19 Chloe:   Okay. Would it be (xxx), °do you think?°
20 Lily:    Do you want to try a- a different introduction, so Sandcastle, so from
21          our viewpoint, saying, you know, at Sandcastle (.) we've got three
22          new teachers?
23 Chloe:   Sure. And then it's kinda (xxx). (.) Sure.
```

While it could perhaps be expected that Lily, one of the co-owners, takes on part of the responsibility of organising the upcoming event by volunteering to do the introduction (line 1), Chloe's question '*And what would you like me to do?*' (line 12) seems more noteworthy. In fact, there is ample evidence in the data from this workplace of team members asking what they can do to help, and sometimes offering to take on specific tasks. Jenny's behaviour of asking her subordinates what they would like to do (line 13) and then making a suggestion (lines 13–14, 17–18) – rather than explicitly assigning them tasks – is in line with the practices that characterise the collaborative and supportive atmosphere of Sandcastle. Interestingly, Lily's suggestions are formulated relatively tentatively (with a lot of mitigation strategies) and leave room for Chloe to decline. In a sense, these suggestions almost seem like options rather than directives. After Chloe has agreed to take on a particular task (line 19), Lily provides some further, more concrete suggestions (lines 20–22) in the form of an interrogative ('*Do you want to try*') rather than a declarative and chooses the lexical item '*try*' rather than '*do*' – which again, leaves room for Chloe to decline or make an alternative suggestion.

This example thus nicely shows that members of this team, including Lily, regularly draw on elements of a feminine speech style. Moreover, Lily's supportive and collaborative behaviour reflects, reinforces and actively contributes to constructing the normativity of such behaviours in this particular workplace. However, even in this supportive and collaborative workplace environment, we find instances of concise, direct ways of uttering directives – reminiscent of elements of masculine speech styles – as the next example shows.

Example 6.11

Context: During the same meeting. Participants are discussing the possibility of one of their students doing a trial class and what dates might be best for this.

1 Lily: °So what about the trial this week? Can you explain?°
2 Penny: Ok. °Emmm there's a lot.°
3 Lily: Just the highlighted ones.
4 Jenny: [Yeh.]
5 Penny: [Ok.] Ah, a lot. Ah, <u>Mon</u>day, two o' clock past. Actually,
6   all is half past.
7   ((checking the schedule))

In contrast to the other examples from Lily's team at Sandcastle discussed above, this one is markedly different in that it shows Lily being direct and almost demanding. Her request for further information and explanations from Penny is uttered by two consecutive questions, whereby the latter repeats the former in that it is more explicitly asking for the same thing, namely some explanations (line 1). The direct style in which these questions are articulated (without any mitigation strategies) is responded to by Penny with hesitation markers and an evasive attempt at an answer ('*Ok. Emmm there's a lot.*' (line 2)). Only after Lily provides some further clarification (line 3), albeit again with only very little facework ('*just*'), does Penny seem to understand ('*OK. ah*') and she provides some further information as requested (lines 5–6).

We have included this example here to show that even in relatively supportive work environments where members' interactional behaviours are characterised by high levels of collaboration and a regular usage of elements associated with a feminine speech style, we do find some variation, and at times members also draw on elements ascribed to a masculine speech style, such as directness and confrontation. As we have argued in some of the previous chapters, there is clearly more than one way of talking and behaving in any workplace, and members do indeed display different behaviours – some of which may be associated with feminine and others with masculine speech styles.

Discussion

Drawing on a combination of culture$_1$ and culture$_2$ examples, this chapter has challenged some of the prevailing assumptions about the role of gender in Hong Kong workplaces. We have started by identifying and critically discussing some of the gendered assumptions and practices that characterise many workplaces in Hong Kong, which are often associated with first-order notions of culture, such as patriarchal and relatively hierarchical structures. As our analyses of two case studies of successful women professionals have shown, however, these 'global', first-order culture assumptions about the gender order and the roles of men and women cannot adequately explain the complex and diverse picture of how actual people *do* gender in their everyday workplace interactions. Rather, as we have argued in this and the previous chapters, these ways of behaving and doing gender are closely intertwined with the local practices that interlocutors construct and constantly shape, reinforce and sometimes challenge as they orient to, enact and construct second-order cultures.

Gender at work is an important topic and one which comes in different forms and disguises. In addition to the rare moments where participants explicitly comment on gender issues, thereby bringing gender to the fore, as discussed in the first part of this chapter, a variety of more implicit, subtle ways exist in which gender is made relevant in participants' everyday workplace experiences. One way in which gender is regularly, perhaps daily, enacted and (re-) constructed by interlocutors is via elements of speech styles typically associated with masculinity and femininity, as elaborated in the second part of this chapter.

There is ample evidence in our data, including that within our two case studies, that female leaders regularly and skilfully draw on and combine elements of masculine and feminine speech styles in their everyday workplace interactions, thereby getting their work done while also doing gender. These local practices of doing gender are reflections and intricate aspects of constructing second-order notions of cultures, as constantly enacted, shaped, challenged and modified by interlocutors throughout an interaction, and they may be in line with or differ from people's assumptions and claims about culture$_1$.

Clearly, claims and generalisations about the alleged link between culture$_1$ and gender need to be treated with caution, because they tend to overlook and ignore the diversity of practices that can be observed in the local context, i.e. in the culture$_2$ context of everyday interactions in actual workplaces. We agree with Ladegaard (2012) and others (e.g. The Women's Foundation 2006) that more research on gender in Hong Kong workplaces is necessary. We would emphasise, however, that in order to produce genuinely new and relevant insights into gender issues, future research needs to move away from claims based on first-order notions of culture and towards (discourse analytic) case studies that capture the dynamics of workplace interactions on the micro-level, linking them to locally negotiated and constructed second-order notions of culture. Thus, instead of making grand claims about the potential impact of 'the Chinese' or 'the Confucian culture' on the behaviour of men and women at work, research should focus on local issues and the ways in which certain practices are gendered and have gendered implications in the specific local context in which they appear. Once more evidence from such research is available, we will be in a better position to combine 'the local' with 'the global', and to link observations of local practices in specific workplaces in Hong Kong to larger-scale gender issues – thereby productively combining first- and second-order notions of culture.

The next chapter deals with another issue where 'the global' and 'the local' come together, namely work–life balance. The topic of work–life balance is often explicitly linked to gender issues – not least because it has been noted that 'in the Asian countries, WLB [work–life balance] seems to be synonymous with gender issues' (Chandra 2012: 1044). We explore this link in more detail in the following chapter.

Notes

1 For example, in 2010 The Women's Foundation Hong Kong launched a monthly column in *The South China Morning Post* and the *Hong Kong Economic Journal* website to raise greater awareness of gender issues.
2 This number is considerably higher even in emerging markets such as the Philippines (23%), Israel (12.5%) and South Africa (14.6%) (Hong Kong Council of Social Service 2012).
3 Example 6.4 is also discussed in Kang & Schnurr (2010).

References

Bourdieu, Pierre (1991). *Language and Symbolic Power* (ed. J. B. Thompson, trans. G. Raymond & M. Adamson). Cambridge: Polity Press. (Original work published 1982.)

Brewis, Joanna (2001). Telling it like it is? Gender, language and organizational theory. In Robert Westwood & Stephen Linstead (eds), *The Language of Organization*. London: SAGE. 47–70.

Butler, Judith (1990). *Gender Trouble. Feminism and the Subversion of Identity.* New York: Routledge.

Cameron, Deborah (2006). Theorising the female voice in public contexts. In Judith Baxter (ed.), *Speaking Out: The Female Voice in Public Contexts*. Basingstoke: Palgrave Macmillan. 3–20.

Cameron, Deborah & Don Kulick (2003). *Language and Sexuality*. Cambridge, UK: Cambridge University Press.

Cappella, Chiara (2015). Leaving Mars and Venus behind. A case study on gendered communication styles in the workplace. Unpublished MSc dissertation. University of Warwick.

Chan, A. (2005). Managing business meetings in different workplace cultures. Unpublished PhD thesis. Wellington, Victoria, New Zealand: University of Wellington.

Chandra, V. (2012) Work–life balance: Eastern and Western perspectives. *The International Journal of Human Resource Management* 23.5: 1040–56.

Chee, Harold & Chris West (2004). *Myths about Doing Business in China.* Basingstoke/ New York: Palgrave Macmillan.

Cheng, Winnie (2003). *Intercultural Conversation.* Amsterdam: Benjamins.

Chow, Irene Hau-Siu (1995). Career aspirations, attitudes and experiences of female managers in Hong Kong. *Women in Management Review* 10.1: 28–32.

Community Business (2015). *Women on Boards Hong Kong.* Hong Kong: Community Business.

Cullen, John (1999). *Multinational Management. A Strategic Approach.* Cincinnati, OH: South-Western Publishing.

De Leon, Corinna T., & Suk-ching Ho (1994). The third identity of modern Chinese women: Women managers in Hong Kong. In Nancy J. Adler & Dafna N. Izraeli (eds), *Competitive Frontiers: Women Managers in a Globe Economy.* Oxford: Blackwell Publishers. 43–56.

Ebrahimi, Bahman P. (1999). Managerial motivation and gender roles: A study of females and males in Hong Kong. *Women in Management Review* 14.2: 44–53.

Fletcher, Joyce K. (2004). The paradox of postheroic leadership: An essay on gender, power, and transformational change. *The Leadership Quarterly* 15.5: 647–61.

Hofstede, Geert (1980) *Culture's Consequences. International Differences in Work-Related Values.* Beverly Hills and London: SAGE.

Holmes, Janet (2006). *Gendered Talk at Work. Constructing Gender Identity through Workplace Discourse.* Oxford: Blackwell.

Holmes, Janet (2000). Women at work: Analysing women's talk in New Zealand workplaces. *Australian Review of Applied Linguistics* 22.2: 1–17.

Holmes, Janet & Stephanie Schnurr (2005). Politeness, humour and gender in the workplace: Negotiating norms and identifying contestation. *Journal of Politeness Research: Language, Behaviour, Culture* 1: 121–49.

Holmes, Janet & Maria Stubbe (2003). *Power and Politeness in the Workplace: A Sociolinguistic Analysis of Talk at Work.* London: Longman.

Hong Kong Council of Social Service (2012). *A Statistical Profile of Women and Girls in Hong Kong.* Hong Kong: The Women's Foundation.

Kang, M. Agnes & Stephanie Schnurr (2010). From high society to workplace reality: An analysis of gendered discourses in media and workplaces in Hong Kong. In Janet Holmes & Meredith Marra (eds), *Femininity, Feminism and Gendered Discourse: A Selected and Edited Collection of Papers from the Fifth International Language and Gender Association Conference (IGALA5).* Cambridge, UK: Cambridge Scholars Publishing. 171–90.

Ladegaard, Hans (2012). Rudeness as a discursive strategy in leadership discourse: Culture, power and gender in a Hong Kong workplace. *Journal of Pragmatics* 44: 1661–79.

Lee, Eliza W. Y. (2003). Individualism and patriarchy: The identity of entrepreneurial women lawyers in Hong Kong. In Eliza W. Y. Lee (ed.), *Gender and Change in Hong Kong: Globalization, Postcolonialism, and Chinese Patriarchy.* Honolulu: University of Hawaii Press. 78–96.

Lee, Francis L. F. (2004). Constructing perfect women: The portrayal of female officials in Hong Kong newspapers. *Media, Culture and Society* 26: 207–25.

Lee, Micky & Anthony Fung (2006). *Media Ideologies of Gender in Hong Kong.* Hong Kong: Hong Kong Institute of Asia-Pacific Studies.

Litosseliti, Lia (2006). *Gender and Language: Theory and Practice*. London: Hodder Arnold.

Mahtani, Shalini (2006). Women leaders in Hong Kong – insights into their workplace experiences. www.communitybusiness.org/images/cb/publications/2005/22women.pdf

Marra, Meredith, Stephanie Schnurr & Janet Holmes (2006). Effective leadership in New Zealand workplaces: Balancing gender and role. In J. Baxter (ed.), *Speaking Out: The Female Voice in Public Contexts*. Basingstoke: Palgrave Macmillan. 240–60.

Mullany, Louise (2007). *Gendered Discourse in the Professional Workplace*. Houndmills: Palgrave.

Mullany, Louise & Lia Litosseliti (2006). Gender and language in the workplace. In Lia Litosseliti (ed.), *Gender and Language: Theory and Practice*. London: Hodder Arnold. 123–47.

Ngo, Hang Yue (2001). Perceptions of gender inequality at work in Hong Kong. *Asian Journal of Women's Studies* 7.1: 111–32.

Pauwels, Anne (2000). Inclusive language is good business: Gender, language and equality in the workplace. In Janet Holmes (ed.), *Gendered Speech in Social Context. Perspectives from Gown and Town*. Auckland: Victoria University Press. 134–51.

Pearson, Veronica & Benjamin K. P. Leung (eds) (1995). *Women in Hong Kong*. Hong Kong: Oxford University Press.

Peck, Jennifer (2000). The cost of corporate culture: Linguistic obstacles to gender equity in Australian business. In Janet Holmes (ed.), *Gendered Speech in Social Context. Perspectives from Gown and Town*. Auckland: Victoria University Press. 211–30.

Saidi, Marya (2015). *Research Report on Gender Stereotypes in the Hong Kong Media: A Scoping Study*. Hong Kong: The Women's Foundation.

Schnurr, Stephanie (2013). *Exploring Professional Communication. Language in Action*. Abingdon: Routledge.

Schnurr, Stephanie (2010). 'Decision made – let's move on'. Negotiating gender and professional identity in Hong Kong workplaces. In Markus Bieswanger, Heiko Motschenbacher & Susanne Mühleisen (eds), *Language in its Socio-cultural Context: New Explorations in Global, Medial and Gendered Uses*. Berlin: Peter Lang. 111–36.

Schnurr, Stephanie & Bernie Mak (2011). Leadership and workplace realities in Hong Kong. Is gender really *not* an issue? *Gender and Language. Special Issue on Gender and Language in the Workplace* 5.2: 337–64.

Selmer, Jan & Corinna de Leon (2003). Culture and management in Hong Kong SAR. In Malcolm Warner (ed.), *Culture and Management in Asia*. London: Routledge Curzon. 48–65.

Sinclair, Amanda (1998). *Doing Leadership Differently. Gender, Power and Sexuality in a Changing Business Culture*. Melbourne: Melbourne University Press.

Sunderland, Jane (2004). *Gendered Discourses*. Basingstoke: Palgrave.

The Women's Foundation (2006). *The Status of Women and Girls in Hong Kong 2006*. Hong Kong: The Women's Foundation.

West, Candace & Don Zimmerman (1987). Doing gender. *Gender and Society* 1.2: 121–51.

Women and Media Concern Group, AAF (1992). Survey on gender consciousness in television advertisements (trans. Chau Yee Shun). In Mass Media Awareness Seminar (1990: Hong Kong), *Mass Media and Women in the 90s*. Hong Kong: Hong Kong Christian Service Communications Centre. 183–7.

Yeung, Agnes, Ruby C. M. Chau, & Sam W. K. Yu (2004). Managing social exclusion: The strategies used by managerial women in Guangzhou and Hong Kong. *International Social Work* 47.4: 503–13.

7 Work–life balance. Juggling different expectations

I think people work too long hours here, you know. It always concerns me whether there's a real balance with life.

(Tobias, expatriate Managing Director of a large telecommunications company)

Introduction

At the end of our follow-up interviews, we routinely asked participants to name three things they would like to change. We deliberately left this question open in order to create some space for them to bring up anything that they consider to be important that may not have been covered in the interview. To our surprise, many of the people we spoke to mentioned issues related to what is often referred to as 'work–life balance', such as long working hours and having to juggle the demands of their family life and their work life. Tobias' quote at the beginning of the chapter is a good example of this. In the interview, he commented that these '*long hours here*' are '*[t]he one thing that I'd like to change but won't be able to*'. These sentiments are reiterated by Neil, the owner of a small IT company, who said: '*Gosh, gosh, things I could change, the expectation of working on weekends, and almost [being] on call twenty four hours a day.*'

In this chapter we explore how in reflecting on issues related to work–life balance, our participants often mobilise discourses of practices and expectations associated with first-order notions of cultures. In contrast to the previous chapters where we observed often remarkable differences between participants' claims and the actual practices displayed in their interactional behaviours, we found considerable overlap and similarities when looking at the ways in which participants talk about work–life balance and the ways these claims are oriented to and enacted in their actual workplace interactions. This does *not*, however, necessarily mean that their actual behaviour is indeed a reflection of first-order culture.

Issues of work–life balance in Hong Kong

Juggling different expectations and finding and maintaining a balance between work and personal life have been identified as important issues by many of the expatriate participants in our corpus. In addition to expressing their wish for change, many commented negatively on what they described as the norm in their workplaces, such as working late (and overtime) on a regular basis and the expectation to be constantly available for work-related activities. These complaints are largely in line with the reputation of Hong Kong's employees, who are known for working long hours at the expense of time spent on their private lives. Although significant improvements in work–life balance have been attested to over the past decades in Hong Kong (Welford 2008), a 2009 survey commissioned by an NGO in Hong Kong showed that employees are working 48.4 hours a week on average, which, according to the survey, 'is 21% higher than the 40 hours recommended by the International Labour Organisation' (Ng & Bernier 2009: 2). In an updated survey a few years later, it was reported that the majority of the employees who participated in this research commented that they felt the work–life balance in Hong Kong has been getting worse over the past ten years (Community Business 2015). The authors argued that their findings reflect 'a widespread perception in the market-place that Hong Kong is deteriorating when it comes to work–life balance' and the blame for this is largely put on the global financial crisis, which has affected business environments worldwide and has caused 'many industries and companies [to] face increased competitive pressures, globalisation, slow economic growth, and focus on regulatory compliance and risk management' (Community Business 2015: 3). It is these macro-level changes, they argue, that consequently have affected the work environment of many companies on the micro-level: due to technological advances, 'a 24x7 "always online" work culture has evolved', which 'put[s] a strain on both employers and employees, resulting in long working hours and erratic work schedules' (Community Business 2015: 3).

Many of these topics were mentioned by our participants in the interviews. In particular, many commented on how difficult they found adjusting to these expectations after having worked in other, often Western, socio-cultural contexts. Many of the people we spoke to explicitly made 'culture' (in its first-order meaning) an issue and linked these expectations to the local situation in Hong Kong, where working hard (as typically measured in the long hours spent at the workplace) is often believed to be one of the reasons for Hong Kong's economic success (e.g. Vernon 2009: 6).

But what exactly is work–life balance? A brief look at the relevant literature shows that there is no consensus in the organisational and management literature on what the concept of work–life balance is (e.g. Reiter 2007; Chandra 2012). Felstead et al. (2002: 56), for example, define work–life balance as 'the relationship between the institutional and cultural times and spaces of work and non-work in societies where income is predominantly generated and distributed through labour markets', and Guest (2002: 263) describes it as 'a perceived balance between work and the rest of life'. However, the concept of 'balance' has been criticised for implying that work is not an integral part of 'life' and for assuming that a division exists between these two spheres of life (e.g. Lewis et al. 2003; Reiter 2007; Eikhof et al. 2007; Guest 2002). We continue using the term work–life balance to reflect that this is what our participants have called the issues described here.

Studies on work–life balance point to three main issues: (1) time management (e.g. long working hours, or working at weekends); (2) the conflict between different roles (i.e. interference between different roles and particular roles overtaking other roles); and (3) care arrangements for dependants (Gregory & Milner 2009; De Cieri & Bardoel 2009). We will address each of these issues by discussing what the participants in our corpus said about them and the link that they perceived to exist between these issues and the notion of culture₁.

Time management

Previous research on work–life balance in Hong Kong has identified the practice of regularly working long hours – often until late in the evening – as a normal occurrence in many workplaces across industries. For example, in a survey conducted in 2008 Welford (2008: 1) found that '62.4% of people regularly work unpaid overtime' and '51.7% of people work late into the evenings'. These practices are brought into sharp relief against evidence that points to the detrimental effects of regularly working long hours. For instance, studies generally indicate that both employees and companies benefit from flexible policies and practices in workplaces that allow employees to find a balance between their professional and personal lives (e.g. Community Business 2015; White et al. 2003; Eikhof et al. 2007; Pryce et al. 2006). Among the tangible benefits of such flexibility, as described in the literature, are improved employee morale, greater commitment to work and performance, reduced absenteeism (Kalliath & Brough 2008; Hill et al. 2001; De Cieri & Bardoel 2009), positive effects on employees' mental health and general well-being, as well as easier integration of women back into their workplaces after maternity leave (Gregory & Milner 2009).

The desire to have more flexibility in managing their own schedules was observed in a recent survey among employees in Hong Kong, which found that '[a]n overwhelming 85.0% of employees stated that being able to manage their work and personal responsibilities according to their own schedule is either quite important or very important to achieving work–life balance' (Community Business 2015: 6). Perhaps not surprisingly in light of the discussions around gender presented in the previous chapter, this was more important for women than for men. This appreciation of flexible working times was also expressed by our interviewees, as Example 7.1 shows.

Example 7.1

Context: The extract comes from an interview with Lily, an expatriate co-owner of a language learning centre. When describing her typical working day, Lily started to talk more generally about working hours.

1 Lily: The norm is, that people think you go to work, you have to work from
2   nine to five, otherwise you're not working hard. That's ridiculous.

3   Who said that? Who ever said that a job has to be nine to five and
4   something that's boring, nobody- nobody ever wrote that down,
5   so why can't a job be the hours you want when you want.

In the interview Lily makes quite a strong plea for flexible working hours and for fitting the job around life, and to work '*the hours you want when you want*' (line 5) rather than being restricted to a fixed and strictly prescribed schedule. Later in the same interview she explicitly ridicules those people who believe that they are expected to work long hours. Imitating them by taking on another voice and the persona of one of these people, she said in a mocking tone of voice: '*Oh no-no-no-no-no, I need to be in the office!*' She continues by problematising such assumptions about expectations and practices by saying that '*Oh-oh-oh, what's the point if I have to stay here till six thirty, (.) twiddling my thumbs. (.) I'm not productive, I'm not doing anything, so why can't I just go an hour early, (when) I'll be much happier?*'. Lily not only questions current practices and expectations, but also challenges the ideal underlying the assumption of what constitutes a 'good' employee.

This sense of working long hours being highly unproductive was also shared by some of the other people we spoke to, as the next two examples illustrate.

Example 7.2

Context: In the interview with Neil, the expatriate owner of an IT company. He is talking about his first job after moving to Asia.

1 Neil: Working Saturdays was a bit of a surprise and a shock, um, I'd never done
2   that before. Um, but didn't really appreciate that much in that nobody
3   really did anything on Saturday, they were required to work on
4   a Saturday but they would just-they would turn up and read the paper
5   and shuffle things around the desk, but nothing seemed to get done!

Like many of the people we have interviewed, Neil, too, brought up the issue of working long hours, which he perceived very negatively. He explicitly describes this practice as highly unproductive: '*nobody really did anything*' (line 3) and '*they would turn up and read the paper and shuffle things around the desk, but nothing seemed to get done!*' (lines 3–5).

However, in spite of this clear demand for more flexible working hours, most of our participants commented on the fact that regularly working long hours is normal practice in their workplaces. For example, when asked about whether he observed any differences in the ways things are done in Hong Kong compared to his previous work experience in the UK, Neil said, '*The, um, working late. People were much more prepared to work for free well into the night, and it was (.), certainly at my first job, people were expected to stay till eight, nine o'clock at night.*' A similar picture emerged in an interview with Susan, the expatriate Head of Department of a large international corporation, who told us that she normally starts working around 7:35 a.m. and, '*on a good day*', tries to finish at 6:00 p.m. or 6:30 p.m. – which, according to her, is only possible when she '*[doesn't] take a lunch break*'. These almost 12-hour working days are normal practice for her: '*This is day in and day out. This is (360) days. I work 7 days a week from last year*' – without receiving any compensation for all these extra hours.

In addition to time management, another aspect in which work–life balance issues are manifested is the struggle that many professionals experience as a result of having to juggle different, and often conflicting, roles.

Conflicting roles

There is considerable evidence in the literature to suggest that in addition to having negative effects on employees' health (e.g. Pryce et al. 2006), a poor work–life balance may also negatively impact the quality time with their family and friends (e.g. Community Business 2015; Cooke & Jing 2009). This seems to be particularly true for women, who are traditionally considered to be the primary care-taker of children and family (cf. Chapter 6), and who may thus face more serious challenges when it comes to juggling and trying to combine the different demands of their professional career and their family responsibilities (Pearson & Leung 1995; Lee 2004; Hong Council of Social Service 2012; Gregory & Milner 2009; Xiao & Cooke 2012; Smithson & Stokoe 2005). In particular, those professions that are 'dominated by values of availability and presenteeism—and increasingly, of geographical mobility' (Gregory & Milner 2009: 7) – have negative effects on women's work–life balance (see also Watts 2009).

These issues were also mentioned by the participants in our study. Some of the women, in particular, described the negative effects of a poor work–life balance on their own life. For example, Susan told us how during her two-week holidays she '*continuously got called back*' and how she '*got two conference calls*'. She felt she could not or should not switch off her mobile phone, as she was expected to be constantly available. During this part of the interview, Susan then requested for our audio-recorder to be switched off (which we did), and she told us about the tremendously negative effects her company's expectations (in terms of working hours and constant availability) have on her private life. She talked about how this has not only strained the relationship with her husband, but how this has eventually led to the couple's decision not to have any children (which she appeared to deeply regret). This decision taken by many women in high-status and often managerial posts to remain childless has been described as their personal strategy to reduce or eliminate their work–life balance problems (e.g. Hakim 2006).

Closely related to this point of having to juggle different, and often opposing, roles is the aspect of making care arrangements for dependants (such as children and elderly family members) in ways that make a work–life balance possible.

Care arrangements for dependants

It has been suggested that new technologies, such as email, Skype call, teleconferencing, etc., are contributing to an increasing blurring and perhaps even merging of the temporal and spatial boundaries that have characterised many workplaces in the past, which – at least theoretically – should enable more employees with caring responsibilities to remain active in the workplace (Perrons 2003). In spite of these developments, however, issues around making care arrangements of dependants remain an important issue for many employees – especially women (e.g. Cooke & Jing 2009; Eikhof et al. 2007; De Cieri & Bardoel 2009; Thein et al. 2010). For example, Sabitha, the founder and CEO of a Hong Kong based NGO, put a lot of emphasis in the interview on explaining how hard she tries to structure her professional commitments around her private life. She told us that especially since her first child was born (who at the time of recording was 3 years old), she had to change her working style considerably and had to re-think her previous approach, which was to '*work as long as it took to get the work done*'. But, as she said very explicitly, since '*I had my son, I made a very conscious decision that I would not accept that in my life.*' This emphasis on her family life does not mean, however, that she works fewer hours now, but rather that she has reorganised her day in a way that enables her to spend some time with her son: she works before he gets up and then again after he is in bed. She explained in great detail the care arrangements that she has put into place, and which largely centre around a domestic live-in helper, and how she remains '*in control*' of her son's diet and daily routine while being at work, for example by deciding on his weekly schedule and diet plan. While these arrangements seem to work for Sabitha in that they enable her to remain professionally active (and highly successful), she does admit that she finds this double-bind very tiring and exhausting.

After having outlined some of the issues related to work–life balance that the participants in our corpus mentioned, in the next sections we explore the potential role of culture$_1$ and culture$_2$ with regard to these issues.

The (perceived) role of culture$_1$

Several of our participants explicitly linked the various issues discussed in the previous section to the notion of culture$_1$. Although there is increasing evidence to indicate that work–life balance is a global phenomenon, the concept itself originates from Western scholarship (Lewis et al. 2007; De Cieri & Bardoel 2009) and thus most research on the topic focuses on EU countries, Canada and the US (Brough et al. 2008; Ngo et al. 2009; Crompton & Lyonette 2005). Research on work–life balance in Asian countries is becoming more popular, however (e.g. Lu et al. 2009; Xiao & Cooke 2012; De Cieri & Bardoel 2009; Coffey et al. 2009; Chandra 2012; Thein et al. 2010).

Previous studies have identified and described considerable differences in the ways in which debates and concerns around work–life balance are held across countries (e.g. Crompton & Lyonette 2005; Coffey et al. 2009; Chandra 2012; Thein et al. 2010; Lewis et al. 2007). Thus, although the same terminology is now widely used, the specific issues that it captures and the measures taken to address them vary considerably (e.g. Brough et al. 2008; Chandra 2012). As Thein et al. (2010: 304) maintain, there exist 'cultural differences in how employees and employers tackle work and family issues'.

Some research suggests that in contexts traditionally described as more collectivist, such as Hong Kong, 'employees tend to expect their companies to take care of their work–family needs and provide more substantive support such as compassionate leave and childcare facilities' (Ngo et al. 2009: 12). The opposite, however, is argued in studies by Lu et al. (2009) and Thein et al. (2010), who have analysed work–life balance issues in China and Hong Kong/Singapore, respectively. Lu et al. (2009: 2) claim that due to the fact that in China, often described as collectivist, 'people tend to have closer ties to extended family members who provide both material and social support for family responsibilities' and the easy and affordable access to domestic help, employees in China may not perceive work–life balance issues to the same extent as employees in other countries. Similar observations were made by Thein et al. (2010), who found that professional women in Hong Kong and Singapore regularly relied on family support and domestic help.

Moreover, Cooke and Jing (2009: 28) argue that among Chinese employees there is a stronger willingness to endure an imbalance and potential conflict between work and life, which the authors interpret as a reflection of 'the traditional Chinese work ethics in which work and career achievement is given primacy over family life or self-enjoyment. Diligence and self-sacrifice, including family's wellbeing, for the public good are praised and glorified'. The authors further claim that these practices and the willingness to accept an imbalance between the spheres of work and life are in line with 'the Chinese collectivist and paternalistic culture in which a workplace plays an important role in providing social bonding activities to develop and maintain a harmonious relationship amongst employees and between the firm and its workforce' (Cooke & Jing 2009).

This link that is supposed to exist between specific practices and alleged characteristics of culture$_1$ was also observed, and heavily criticised, in previous chapters. Thus, rather than repeating our critical stance here (but see Chapter 1 for an overview of our argument), it will suffice to point to the fact that the data that informs much of this previous research relies on self-reporting of participants (via interviews and surveys) and does not take into account actual practice. Before we address this issue in the next two sections, we discuss two examples that support the findings of previous studies. In both examples, participants mobilise culture$_1$ to account for differences in people's practices and expectations. Example 7.3 is taken from the interview with Susan, the expatriate Head of Department in a major international financial corporation, and Example 7.4 comes from an interview with Tobias, the expatriate Managing Director of a large telecommunications company.

Example 7.3[1]

```
 1 Susan:  Every country is different. Each partnership is different. So, you do
 2          have a radically different em working environment. I mean I (would
 3          think of) a beautiful story I have (just to summarise this). I (worked)
 4          with the China team (who were) complaining about one of the
 5          Australians ((xxx)). They're saying, oh you know, he gets to six thirty,
 6          you know, he leaves. And I said oh (did he complete his work)? Yeh-
 7          yeh-, he has completed his work. So why shouldn't he leave? Oh no,
 8          you should stay back, (.) and be with the team, 'cause the rest of the
 9          team is working. That's to do things in China. And I, to me, I find that
10          quite amusing, yeh. Finished his work, and it's done, what you're
11          meant to do? But you shouldn't leave because the people in the team
12          haven't done. So you should be there and you should stay at work. (.)
13          That summarises the difference. In Australia, everyone leaves at
14          whatever time. You finished your work and you just go home. Not
15          here, everyone sticks around. [. . .] So for example, I don't finish
16          work on papers until half past eight, so, so, people have to sit
17          around and wait.
```

In this anecdote Susan recounts how her own ideals and expectations of time management have clashed with the expectations and practices of some Chinese people she worked with some time ago in Australia. She tells us how she experienced the '*working environments*' in China and Australia as '*radically different*' (line 2), and how the members of the Chinese team were surprised to see a member of the Australian team leave once he had finished his work. Imitating the various people involved in this incident by using direct speech to give them a voice, Susan shows how the expectations of the Chinese and the Australian team members have clashed. While the former expect '*you should stay back and be with the team 'cause the rest of the team is working*' (lines 8–9), the latter (with whom Susan sides here) wonder '*why shouldn't he leave?*' (line 7) since he has done all this work.

This anecdote thus shows how Susan perceives these differences in expectations and practices relating to time management to be rooted in expectations and norms that she links to first-order notions of culture. This becomes particularly obvious when she states '*That's to do things in China*' (line 9), which she sets in stark opposition to '*in Australia*' (line 13). These claims are also largely in line with the earlier, essentialist literature, according to which working long hours and staying in the office until the last person has finished work could be seen as an expression of the high collectivism which has been ascribed to 'the Chinese culture' in which cooperation, interdependence and group harmony are particularly valued (Wong et al. 2007: 96; see also Hofstede 1980). In the next example, Tobias reiterates some of the points made by Susan.

Example 7.4

Context: This excerpt occurred about halfway through the interview when the interviewer asked Tobias to tell her about any interesting experiences or cultural shocks. We did not normally ask this question, but it emerged from what Tobias had previously told us about his experiences of working in Asia, which we wanted to follow up with some concrete examples. IR = interviewer

```
 1 IR:      Any interesting experiences, any cultural shocks? ((laughs))
 2 Tobias:  Well, yeah, the first thing that was evident for me, and remember
 3          that I'd been coming to Hong Kong for many years before that, was
 4          coming four times- (or) five- five times a year on business trips, so I
 5          really knew this anyway, but you know the evident thing was that
 6          people seemed to work very long hours, but they didn't really, they
 7          spent most of the day (.) actually not being very productive
 8          working in a way which wa::s being to do with people networking,
 9          making sure people understood, yududuhduhduh and then they sort of
10          came to the realisation around four or five o'clock that they
11          hadn't done any work and then spend the next four hours working,
12          so that's why they didn't leave the office before nine o'clock.
13 IR:      Do you think it applies to both locals and expats? ((laughs))
14 Tobias:  No.
15 IR:      Expatriates or mainly locals?
16 Tobias:  Locals, (.) locals, I mean you know in due course expats may be
17          sucked into it, I guess, because often if you talk to Chinese about
18          expat (.) work behavior, they express some surprise you know he
19          gets in at seven o'clock in the morning and leaves at five, (.) this type
20          of stuff, he gets in at seven and works for three hours before
21          anybody else turns up [..]. So I think whilst these are sweeping
22          generalisations, massive generalisations, there is a different
23          work culture.
```

In this excerpt, Tobias, like Susan, reiterates many of the aspects related to work–life balance that were mentioned by other participants, such as regularly working long hours, and the (perceived) unproductivity of this. He also mobilises culture₁ as an explanation. Not only does he produce this reply to our question about '*cultural shocks*', but he also repeatedly sets up opposing subject positions (see also Chapter 5) for Hong Kong locals (e.g. '*people*', '*they*') and expatriates (which the interviewer then picks up in her follow-up question in lines 13 and 15). Like Susan, Tobias describes a discrepancy between '*local*' and '*expat*' practices (line 16): '*often if you talk to Chinese about expat (.) work behavior, they express some surprise you know he gets in at seven o'clock in the morning and leaves at five, (.) this type of stuff*' (lines 17–20). Although he distances himself from such views as reportedly expressed by his Hong Kong local staff members, he also acknowledges that they are part of the local 'culture' and that he needs to find ways of accepting if not adapting to these different ways of doing things, as he explains later in the interview (not shown here): '*you start to live with it, you're not going to change this enormous culture, that's just what it is*'. Interestingly, towards the end of this excerpt, Tobias acknowledges that these perceptions are '*sweeping generalisations, massive generalisations*' (lines 21 and 22) – but he nevertheless remains adamant that '*there is a different work culture*' between local Hong Kong Chinese and expatriate professionals (line 22).

These largely essentialist assumptions about the role of culture$_1$ in relation to work–life balance issues as reflected in Tobias' and Susan's comments in their interviews, also reflect the line of argument proposed in the literature discussed in the previous section where (perceived) differences regarding various work–life issues were often linked to expectations and practices associated with first-order notions of culture. In the next sections we shift our focus to second-order notions of culture and explore how work–life balance issues are reflected and enacted in everyday workplace interactions.

Interactional evidence of work–life balance issues

We found relatively little interactional evidence of the various work–life balance issues in the conversations that we recorded in the various workplaces. It seems that although participants felt strongly about these topics and made the point of bringing up the issue in the interviews, work–life balance (and the various aspects associated with it) was not a topic that featured prominently in the interactional data that we collected. However, we did find various traces of some of the work–life balance issues discussed in the previous sections, which we describe in this and the next section. Most interactional evidence relates to the issue of time management, as in the following example.

Example 7.5[2]

Context: Email sent from an expatriate Head of Department in one of the universities in Hong Kong to his academic colleagues in the department (bold added).

Subject: air-conditioning wars

Dear all

Please note that there will be no air-conditioning in offices this friday (public holiday) and the summer regime will come into force next week, which means that air-conditioning will only be available for restricted hours (**I think it is going off at 7:00pm**). Last summer after heroic resistance led by Henry 'rage against the machine' Morris we were able to get **exemptions up to 9:00 p.m**. If you wish to make a case, I will forward your request to the air-conditioning czar; please give the dates you will be in HK and a reason, i.e. you are working on a research project.

Thanks
Rich

While there is a lot to say about this email,[3] we concentrate here only on the reference it makes to working hours (highlighted in bold) and the underlying assumptions. In this email, Rich, the Head of Department, informs his staff about the new air-conditioning schedule and the fact that it is going to be turned off '*at 7:00pm*'. It could thus be assumed that the general expectation is that staff will have left work at that point. As the rest of the email shows, however, last year staff members '*were able to get exemptions up to 9:00p.m.*'. The reference to last year's exceptions and Rich's request for staff to let him know if they require extensions of the normal air-conditioning schedule further highlight that he is expecting some of his staff members to want to stay in the office long after the air-conditioning will have been turned off at 7p.m.

Although it could be argued that this expectation to work late (past 7p.m.) could potentially be linked to the specific profession of research active academics, who work long hours in order to conduct research (as Rich suggests in this email), it is noteworthy that we observed this tendency to stay in the office until relatively late at night across the many different workplaces where we collected our data. Moreover, most of our expatriate participants (regardless of their professional affiliation or organisational status) commented on this in the interviews – even in the NGO, where we would not have expected such behaviour.[4]

While these issues are often perceived negatively by our participants and although they often mobilised notions of first-order culture when explaining them, these expectations, which may negatively impact on the time management of many professionals, are normal practice in many workplaces around the world and are a reflection of the technological advances and structural changes that accompany them (e.g. Schnurr 2013). Neil (the expatriate owner of a small IT company), having complained about the situation in his workplace in Hong Kong, reflects on this by saying that '*the expectation of working on weekends, um, and almost [being] on call twenty four hours a day – not sure how much that is an Asian thing or a twenty first century thing*'.

In the next section we look in more detail at how some of these issues of work–life balance mentioned by our participants in the interviews and described in the literature are reflected in the actual workplace interactions that we have recorded.

Actively negotiating work–life balance. A case study

Our analyses in this section provide insights into the ways in which these work–life balance issues are enacted on the micro-level of everyday workplace interactions. We aim to illustrate the importance of the local context for work–life balance and to discuss the role of culture$_2$. We conduct a small case study by analysing in detail a one-to-one interaction that occurred at the large international financial corporation where Susan works. This conversation took place between

Susan, the expatriate Head of Department, and Cheryl, the leader of one of the teams in the same department, about the long hours that Cheryl's team members regularly put into work.

Example 7.6

Context: This is a one-to-one meeting between Susan and Cheryl. Cheryl is a local Hong Kong Chinese and has just taken over the leadership role for the administrative team in the department that Susan is heading. In the conversation Susan mentions Peter, to whom Susan reports. In the first extract Susan compliments Cheryl on the selection of a new team member.

1	Susan:	Nice. You made a very good selection there, she's a lovely girl.
2	Cheryl:	Ye[ah].
3	Susan:	Ye[ah].
4	Cheryl:	And she is- her energy is very good,=
5	Susan:	=isn't it?
6	Cheryl:	[Yeah].
7	Susan:	Ye[ah].
8	Cheryl:	And she's willing to stay very late, and when I ask her, do you
9		need any help or just go home, and it's not our peak season,
10		you can pick (a bit of this) but she's very nice.
11	Susan:	Oo::h, a sweetheart. Ahumm.

After Susan has complimented Cheryl for hiring a '*lovely girl*' (line 1) for her team, it is interesting to observe how Cheryl responds to this. After an initial agreement ('*yeah*' (line 2)), which overlaps with Susan's agreement token (line 3), Cheryl starts listing some of the characteristics that she believes make the newcomer such a valuable asset, namely '*her energy is very good*' (line 4), and – very interesting in the context of our discussion of work–life balance – the fact that '*she's willing to stay late*' (line 8). This acknowledgement that one element of being a good employee is a willingness to work long hours is agreed to by Susan, who immediately after Cheryl's claim overlaps with her by commenting '*Oo::h, a sweetheart. Ahumm.*' (line 12), complimenting the newcomer for her dedication to the team and the company (see also De Cieri & Bardoel 2009).

Cheryl's comments here about her appreciation of her new team member's willingness to work long hours and the ways in which this is linked to perceptions of being a good employee also reflect participants' comments in the interviews. This short exchange eventually leads Susan to discuss issues of long working hours in Cheryl's team. As becomes clear in the next few extracts, in contrast to her acknowledgement of the new team member being a good employee, Susan is concerned about the practice of regularly working long hours displayed by Cheryl's team and would like to change it.

Example 7.7

Context: This extract comes from the same meeting between Susan and Cheryl and occurs a few minutes after the discussion of a new employee as presented in Example 7.6.

```
 1 Susan:    .hh I'm- I'm- still I kno:w that people work: (.) quite long, I know that
 2           people work longer hours, I'm just wondering hmm (.) because over
 3           time it's harder to prove, is there anything that we can do: I'm
 4           thinking, if peop-, if people don't have a programme,=
 5 Cheryl:   Hmm.
 6 Susan:    =(.) because we know they are going to stay past five thirty, °we
 7           know they're probably going to stay till six o'clock°,=
 8 Cheryl:   Hmm.
 9 Susan:    =it's your choice, it's your team, but if people don't have a
10           programme, do you want to start them at nine o'clock?
11 Cheryl:   °Hmmhm° mhm uhmmm, if they do not have a programme you
12           mean (.) uhm wu- wu- wu- whether I feel happy to let them,=
13 Susan:    =start at [nine o'clock]? Because we know they don't leave at five
14           thirty.
15 Cheryl:   hmhmm hmhm
16 Susan:    We know, most people,=
17 Cheryl:   hmhmm hmhm
18 Susan:    =most evenings leave, a quarter to [six, six] o'clock=
19 Cheryl:   [Hmm hmm]
```

((8 turns are omitted))

```
20 Susan:    Maybe we can start at nine o'clock and people can then st- finish
21           their normal=
22 Cheryl:   Hmm.
23 Susan:    =quarter to six- six o'clock, what do you think? Will that work?
24 Cheryl:   I think it's a good idea.
25 Susan:    Yeah.
26 Cheryl:   But I don't know (where) to appro::ach our ((xxx)).
27 Susan:    IF you want me to do that,=
28 Cheryl:   Hmm.
29 Susan:    =I will organise it with Peter.
30 Cheryl:   =Hmhm hmhm
```

In this excerpt Susan explicitly makes work–life balance an issue by discussing ways of cutting down the long working hours regularly undertaken by the members of Cheryl's team. She starts the discussion by stating that '*people work quite long*' (line 1), which is then repeated in slightly different words (lines 1–2). These observations function as starting points here for Susan to open the discussion about whether '*there [is] anything that we can do*' (line 3) to help address this issue. What is particularly interesting here is how Susan through her formulations in these few lines frames (and constructs) the practice of working long hours as an issue that needs to be addressed rather than as a valued practice that demonstrates the commitment of Cheryl's team (as in Example 7.6). In the following lines Susan continues to outline her concern and explicitly refers to team members staying longer than expected (i.e. '*we know they're probably going to stay till six o'clock*' (lines 6 and 7)). Noteworthy here is her repeated use of the inclusive pronoun '*we*', which seems to refer to Cheryl and herself, thereby signalling that they both share these concerns. However, Cheryl's relatively passive role in this exchange (e.g. her frequent production of minimal feedback (lines 5, 8, 11–12, 15, 17, 19 and 22) and asking a clarifying question (lines 11 and 12) rather than a more active participation in the discussion) jeopardises Susan's attempts to involve Cheryl.

In line 9, Susan seems to change her strategy slightly by explicitly emphasising Cheryl's responsibility in this issue, '*it's your choice*', and by directly asking her about her opinion on a very concrete solution (namely to let people start their workday later (lines 9 and 10)). When Cheryl does not immediately provide an answer but rather repeats Susan's suggestion and asks some clarifying questions (lines 11 and 12), Susan seems quite keen to provide an answer as her turn co-completion with Cheryl illustrates (lines 12 and 13). This is followed by some more explanations of the rationale behind Susan's suggestions, which are responded to by minimal feedback from Cheryl (lines 15–22).

After some more discussion (which we have omitted here), Susan then utters a direct question in which she explicitly asks Cheryl for feedback: '*what do you think? Will that work?*' (line 23). Cheryl's reply is positive but sounds reluctant (see the utterance-initial hedge in '*I think it's a good idea*' (line 24)). After having agreed to Susan's suggestion, however, Cheryl mentions the problem of how to put Susan's plan into practice (line 26), which is then solved by Susan who takes over this responsibility by offering to organise a programme that will help implement shorter working hours and talking to Peter (who is a partner in the company and who ultimately oversees Susan's department).

Susan's behaviour in this interaction, in particular her great interest in bringing an end to the long working hours of Cheryl's team, links to and directly addresses some of the issues that Susan (and others) mentioned in the interview (see Example 7.3). It is noteworthy, however, that while in the interview Susan explicitly linked these practices to culture₁ (cf. her reference to '*in China*' and '*in Australia*'), there is no such explicit link here. Rather, she frequently refers to the localised practices of Cheryl's team and negotiates them in the specific context of the company (e.g. by discussing the possibility of implementing a particular programme to organise working hours). Thus, although in this case, some of the claims made by Susan in the interviews seem to coincide with people's actual behaviour, this does not necessarily imply that this behaviour is a reflection of first-order culture. Rather, it could also be a reflection of the expectations and norms of working in this particular company or this particular team, which we would link to the notion of second-order culture. In fact, the next example, which is also taken from the same interaction, supports such an interpretation and highlights the crucial role of '*the firm*' in this discussion around working hours.

Example 7.8

Context: This is a continuation of the same meeting.

```
 1 Susan:    I've just been watching (.) people, and like you say, Margaret works-
 2           or everybody works hard,=
 3 Cheryl:   Hmm, hmm.
 4 Susan:    =and every night, I see people staying back,=
 5           =and at the moment they are giving so much to the firm,=
 6 Cheryl:   Hmm, hmm.
 7 Susan:    =because they are taking part-paid lea:ve.=
 8 Cheryl:   Hmm.
 9 Susan:    They're- they're trying very ha:rd=
10 Cheryl:   Hmm.
11 Susan:    I'm just thinking that, it might help (.) them=
12 Cheryl:   Hmm.
13 Susan:    =to feel more,=
14 Cheryl:   Hmm.
15 Susan:    =ahmm, (.) more okay about this, what do you think?
16 Cheryl:   Hmm. (Maybe, yeah,) is a good idea, because they will think that
17           the firm is s- also support them.
18 Susan:    yeah.
19 Cheryl:   They will have a uhm a bit more comfortable to have uhm to
20           contribute to the firm=
21 Susan:    =[yeahm]
22 Cheryl:   [And more] committed to [the firm]
23 Susan:    [.hhh]
```

In this excerpt the discussion between Susan and Cheryl continues, and Susan further tries to convince Cheryl of the benefits and the necessity to implement a system that would help them organise the work-hours of the staff on Cheryl's team and that would prevent Cheryl's team from having to work late on a regular basis. As in the previous extract, Cheryl's contributions are largely confined to minimal responses (lines 3, 6, 8, 10, 12, 14), and it is only after Susan explicitly asks for her opinion (line 15) that she contributes more actively (albeit merely repeating Susan's previous arguments). This observation that it takes Susan some effort to get Cheryl on board could perhaps be interpreted as an indication that long working hours are indeed the norm in this company.

In this particular extract, which occurs after Example 7.7, Susan mobilises and explicitly orients to the assumption that working long hours is a sign of commitment to the company. She specifically mentions Margaret, one of the team members, before using the more generic, all-inclusive '*everybody*' and '*people*' to emphasise how '*hard*' the team works (lines 1–2, 4). In line 5 she explicitly comments that '*they are giving so much to the firm*'. However, inter- estingly, rather than using this statement to compliment Cheryl's staff on their dedication to the company (as Cheryl does in Example 7.6 in relation to her new team member), Susan uses this for the opposite effect, namely to problema- tise this situation and to initiate a discussion about what can be done to make them feel '*more okay about this*' (lines 13 and 15).

Up to this point Cheryl's contributions to this interaction were limited to minimal feedback, which only changes when Susan directly asks the question '*what do you think?*' (line 15). While Cheryl's response appears positive, it is characterised by several hesitation markers (e.g. lines 16 and 17) and merely repeats Susan's point of view rather than adding anything new. After stating that Susan's suggestion '*is a good idea*' (line 16) in a relatively non-committing way (e.g. note the hedging '*maybe yeah*'), Cheryl repeats Susan's previous argument by stating that with the new programme to help them avoid long working hours '*they will think that the firm is s- also support them*' (lines 16 and 17), which will make her team members '*a bit more comfortable*' (line 19) and ultimately '*more committed to the firm*' (line 22). Susan's regular use of minimal feedback throughout Cheryl's elaborations (lines 18, 21, 23) indicates that she approves of and is content with these responses.

After spending some more time discussing the details of the proposed programme (which will be largely based on sharing responsibilities among the team members and making sure one of them (rather than the entire team) is available at certain (particularly early or late) hours of the day), the deci- sion (made in Example 7.7) for Susan to suggest the introduction of this programme to Peter is repeated and thus ratified (cf. Chapter 3), as shown in Example 7.9.

Example 7.9

Context: This extract comes towards the end of the meeting between Susan and Cheryl.

```
1 Susan:    =Have you managed to take any of your overtime, cause I'm worried
2           for you as well, I mean part of your headache, I know is [because]
3           you're very busy,=
4 Cheryl:   [Hmmhm], hmhm, is o::k:.
5 Susan:    Ye::ah.
6 Cheryl:   I'm fi:ne, [mhh mhh] mhh.
7 Susan:    [Huh OK] .hh uhm, OK. Is there anything else we can do for your
8           staff?
```

This short excerpt is also noteworthy in the context of our discussions of work–life balance, as it makes explicit reference to yet another issue frequently related to this topic: the negative health effects that regularly working long hours may cause (e.g. Brough et al. 2008; Welford 2008; Pryce et al. 2006). This excerpt occurred at the end of the interaction and after Susan and Cheryl had discussed (and agreed on future actions relating to) a possible solution to avoid staff working overtime. While the discussion thus far was about Cheryl's team more generally, at this point in the interaction Susan specifically focuses on Cheryl and enquires about the negative effects this working practice may have on her health. She expresses her concern ('*I'm worried for you*' (lines 1 and 2)) and explicitly links Cheryl's health issues ('*your headache*') – at least partly – to her '*very busy*' work schedule (lines 1–3). This link between an imbalance and various health problems is often discussed in the literature on work–life balance, such 'as a poor diet, insomnia, and increased sickness' (Community Business 2015: 10).

After acknowledging Susan's concern (via minimal feedback), Cheryl rebuffs this by saying that '*is o::k:*' (line 4) and reassuring her superior that '*I'm fi:ne*' (line 6). At this point Susan does not probe any further but rather accepts Cheryl's answer and asks whether there is '*anything else we can do for your staff?*' (lines 7 and 8), thereby opening the floor and giving her the opportunity to bring up other issues. However, since Cheryl does not mention anything else, the interaction closes soon after and the interlocutors leave the room.

Discussion

In this chapter we have looked at work–life balance, a topic that many of our participants have explicitly commented on in their interviews as being particularly problematic and as being a reflection of what they commonly referred to as 'culture' (what we would classify as culture$_1$). This explicit link between various practices and expectations related to work–life balance and first-order notions of culture was not only suggested by our expatriate participants but is also aligned with the literature, and was to some extent reflected in their actual workplace interactions.

In spite of this agreement, we have taken a more critical stance in our discussions and have argued that although there may be some similarities between what our participants say about work–life balance in the interviews and the ways in which work–life balance issues are enacted and oriented to in actual workplace interactions, this does not necessarily mean that a causal relationship between culture$_1$ and culture$_2$ exists. Nor does this imply that the culture$_2$ practices that we have described (based on our observations and analyses of authentic workplace interactions) are indeed a reflection of first-order notions of culture. Quite the opposite: we remain very sceptical about any attempts to establish direct, causal links between first- and second-order notions of culture; and in line with the arguments brought forward in the previous chapters, we distance ourselves from these essentialist, and we believe rather simplistic and unnecessarily limiting, explanations provided by some of the earlier literature in which work–life balance issues are mainly explained with reference to different characteristics of culture$_1$ (e.g. collectivist vs individualist).

Rather than relying on these essentialist, and often stereotypical, classifications of culture$_1$, we believe it is more productive to understand any practices (related to work–life balance or other issues) in the specific context in which they appear and to acknowledge that a diversity of practices exists. As we have previously argued (cf. Chapter 2 and 3), it is crucial to look at more local levels (as captured in our notion of culture$_2$) and to understand observed or perceived practices against this backdrop. For example, there is considerable evidence in the literature that shows that a supportive workplace climate has a positive impact on work–life balance issues (e.g. Ngo et al. 2009). This relevance of local norms and practices was particularly reflected in the interaction between Susan and Cheryl, where concrete issues of work–life balance (e.g. regularly working long hours) were discussed and negotiated. Much of this discussion centred around the localised practices that Cheryl and her team members typically employ in the context of the wider organisation, including organisational expectations (e.g. of what is considered to be a good employee) and organisational needs (e.g. how many team members need to be present outside of normal working hours), as well as the relationship between the organisation and its employees (e.g. to ensure staff commitment).

Thus, while work–life balance, without a doubt, is an issue that affects many employees and employers across different professions and different industries, this does not necessarily mean that these issues are closely related to first-order notions of culture. Rather, work–life balance is a complex phenomenon and, just like gender (as discussed in the previous chapter), it is 'global' and 'local'. It is 'global' in the sense that it affects employees worldwide; and it is at the same time 'local' as the specific ways in which work–life balance is enacted, negotiated and addressed are closely linked to the specific context in which an encounter occurs.

In the next chapter we discuss these issues in more detail together with the insights gained from our discussions in previous chapters.

Notes

1 Shorter versions of Examples 7.3, 7.4 and 7.7 are also discussed in Schnurr & Zayts (2012); and Example 7.5 is also discussed in Schnurr & Rowe (2008) albeit from a very different angle.
2 Spelling is left as in the original.
3 See Schnurr & Rowe (2008) for a discussion of the humour in this and many other emails.
4 Interestingly, similar trends were observed in the survey conducted by Community Business (2015) which found that of all the professional groups surveyed, NGO staff were least satisfied with their current work–life balance situation.

References

Brough, Paula, Jackie Holt, Rosie Bauld, Amanda Biggs & Claire Ryan (2008). The ability of work–life balance policies to influence key social/organisational issues. *Asia Pacific Journal of Human Resources* 46.3: 261–74.
Chandra, V. (2012). Work–life balance: Eastern and Western perspectives. *The International Journal of Human Resource Management* 23.5: 1040–56.

Coffey Betty, Stella E. Anderson, Shuming Zhao, Yongqiang Liu & Jiyuan Zhang (2009). Perspectives on work–family issues in China: The voices of young urban professionals. *Community, Work & Family* 12:2: 197–212.

Community Business (2015). *The State of Work–Life Balance in Hong Kong. Ten Years of Work–Life Balance Research in Review.* Hong Kong: Community Business.

Cooke, Fang Lee & Xingyao Jing (2009). Work–life balance in China: Sources of conflicts and coping strategies. *NHRD Network Journal. Special Issue on Work–Life Balance* 3.2: 18–28.

Crompton, Rosemary & Clare Lyonette (2005). Work–life 'balance' in Europe. *City University GeNet Working Paper* 10: 1–32.

De Cieri, Helen & E. Anne Bardoel (2009) What does 'work–life management' mean in China and Southeast Asia for MNCs? *Community, Work & Family* 12.2: 179–96.

Eikhof, Doris Ruth, Chris Warhurst & Axel Haunschild (2007). Introduction: What work? What life? What balance? *Employee Relations* 29.4: 325–33.

Felstead, Alan, Nick Jewson, Annie Phizacklea & Sally Walters (2002). Opportunities to work at home in the context of work–life balance. *Human Resource Management Journal* 12.1: 54–76.

Gregory, Abigail & Susan Milner (2009). Editorial: Work–life balance: A matter of choice? *Gender, Work and Organization* 16.1: 1–13.

Guest, David (2002). Perspectives on the study of work–life balance. *Social Science Information* 41: 255–79.

Hakim, Catherine (2006). Women, careers, and work–life preferences. *British Journal of Guidance & Counselling* 34.3: 279–94.

Hill, Jeffrey E., Alan J. Hawkins, Maria Ferris & Michelle Weitzman (2001). Finding an extra day a week: The positive influence of perceived job flexibility on work and family life balance. *Family Relations* 50.1: 49–58.

Hofstede, Geert (1980). *Culture's Consequences. International Differences in Work-Related Values*. Beverly Hills and London: SAGE.

Hong Kong Council of Social Service (2012). *A Statistical Profile of Women and Girls in Hong Kong*. Hong Kong: The Women's Foundation.

Kalliath, Thomas & Paula Brough (2008). Work–life balance: A review of the meaning of the balance construct. *Journal of Management and Organization* 14: 323–7.

Lee, Francis L. F. (2004). Constructing perfect women: The portrayal of female officials in Hong Kong newspapers. *Media, Culture and Society* 26: 207–25.

Lewis, Suzan, Richenda Gambles & Rhona Rapoport (2007). The constraints of a 'work–life balance' approach: An international perspective. *The International Journal of Human Resource Management* 18.3: 360–73.

Lewis, Suzan, Rhona Rapoport & Richenda Gambles (2003). Reflections on the integration of paid work and the rest of life. *Journal of Managerial Psychology* 18: 824–41.

Lu, Jia-Fang, Oi-Ling Siu, Paul Spector & Kan Shi (2009). Antecedents and outcomes of a fourfold taxonomy of work–family balance in Chinese employed parents. *Journal of Occupational Health Psychology* 14.2: 182–92.

Ng, Winnie & S. Bernier (2009). *The State of Work–Life Balance in Hong Kong*. Hong Kong: Community Business.

Ngo, Hang-Yue, Sharon Foley & Raymond Loi (2009). Family friendly work practices, organizational climate, and firm performance: A study of multinational corporations in Hong Kong. *Journal of Organizational Behavior* 30: 1–15.

Pearson, Veronica & Benjamin K. P. Leung (eds) (1995). *Women in Hong Kong*. Hong Kong: Oxford University Press.

Perrons, Diane (2003). The New Economy and the work–life balance: Conceptual explorations and a case study of new media. *Gender, Work and Organization* 10.1: 65–93.

Pryce, Joanna, Karen Albertsen & Karina Nielson (2006). Evaluation of an open-rota system in a Danish psychiatric hospital: A mechanism for improving job satisfaction and work–life balance. *Journal of Nursing Management* 14: 282–8.

Reiter, Natalie (2007). Work–life balance: What DO you mean? The ethical ideology underpinning appropriate application. *Journal of Applied Behavioral Science* 43: 273–94.

Schnurr, Stephanie (2013). *Exploring Professional Communication. Language in Action.* Abingdon: Routledge.

Schnurr, Stephanie & Charley Rowe (2008). The 'dark side' of humour. Analysing subversive humour in workplace emails. *Lodz Papers in Pragmatics. Special Issue on Humour* 4.1: 109–30.

Schnurr, Stephanie & Olga Zayts (2012). 'You have to be adaptable, obviously.' Constructing cultural identities in multicultural workplaces in Hong Kong. *Pragmatics* 22.2: 279–99.

Smithson, Janet & Elizabeth H. Stokoe (2005). Discourses of work–life balance: Negotiating 'genderblind' terms in organizations. *Gender, Work and Organization* 12.2: 147–68.

Thein, Htwe Htwe, Siobhan Austen, Janice Currie & Erica Lewin (2010). The impact of cultural context on the perception of work/family balance by professional women in Singapore and Hong Kong. *International Journal of Cross Cultural Management* 10.3: 303–20.

Vernon, Kate (2009). *Work–Life Balance: The Guide.* Hong Kong: Community Business.

Watts, Jacqueline H. (2009). 'Allowed into a man's world' meanings of work–life balance: Perspectives of women civil engineers as 'minority' workers in construction. *Gender, Work and Organization,* 16.1: 37–57.

Welford, Richard (2008). *Work–Life Balance in Hong Kong: Survey Results.* Hong Kong: The University of Hong Kong and CSR Asia.

White, Michael, Stephen Hill, Patrick McGovern, Colin Mills & Deborah Smeaton (2003). 'High-performance' management practices, working hours and work–life balance. *British Journal of Industrial Relations* 41.2: 175–95.

Wong, Jonny, Philco Wong & Li Heng (2007). An investigation of leadership styles and relationship cultures of Chinese and expatriate managers in multinational companies in Hong Kong. *Construction Management and Economics* 25: 95–106.

Xiao, Yuchun & Fang Lee Cooke (2012). Work–life balance in China? Social policy, employer strategy and individual coping mechanisms. *Asia Pacific Journal of Human Resources* 50: 6–22.

8 Understanding language and 'culture' at work. Taking stock and looking ahead

I erm also think that it's a bit more than just the culture.
(Tobias, expatriate Managing Director of a large
telecommunications company)

Introduction

This chapter brings to together the theoretical and analytical insights gained in our analyses of the various aspects of professional communication and first- and second-order notions of culture discussed in the previous chapters. It continues our discussion about the role of language and the different orders of 'culture' at work that we started in Chapter 1. We summarise and highlight the various benefits of approaching this intricate relationship by looking back at the previous chapters where we applied the conceptual distinction between culture$_1$ and culture$_2$ to our corpus of workplace discourse collected in a range of workplaces in Hong Kong. The chapter ends with a view ahead, spelling out some implications for future research on language and first- and second-order culture – both conceptually and methodologically.

Taking stock

The motivation to write this book and the starting point of our argument was the analytical and conceptual dilemma that we (and other researchers with an interest in workplace discourse and what is commonly referred to as 'culture') faced when working with authentic data collected in a wide range of different so-called 'multicultural' workplaces. On the one hand, the theme of culture (in its first-order meaning) was made very explicit in the interviews with our participants, who claimed that it played a crucial role in their professional interactions as it reportedly influences almost every aspect of their professional lives. But on the other hand, we were struck by how little evidence of this perceived influence we could actually find in the authentic workplace interactions that we recorded. We took this discrepancy between participants' own perceptions and sense-making mechanisms and our analytical and theoretical approaches as the starting point to propose a new way of analysing 'culture' at work. Our main suggestion was to make a conceptual distinction between different orders of what is commonly referred to as 'culture'. Drawing on insights gained from politeness research, where a similar debate about different notions of politeness has engaged academics over the past few decades, we proposed to differentiate between first-order culture (or culture$_1$) and second-order culture (or culture$_2$). While culture$_1$ captures lay people's understandings and perceptions and typically refers to a relatively abstract and static entity that often equates with nation states, culture$_2$ is a more dynamic conceptualisation based on observed practices, and functions as an analytical concept that enables researchers to make sense of participants' actual (interactional) behaviour.

This conceptual distinction between first- and second-order culture was then applied to several aspects of workplace discourse, including face and politeness, decision making, leadership, identity construction, gender and work–life balance. The decision to focus on these aspects of professional communication was largely motivated by the comments made by our participants in the interviews, and they capture those topics where participants felt that (first-order) culture had a particularly strong influence on their everyday workplace interaction. We have used these themes as entry points into our academic analyses of second-order culture and have focused on exploring the often resulting discrepancies – with the aim of finding ways of engaging in a productive dialogue between participants' and analysts' (often opposing) perspectives.

While Chapters 2–4 largely focused on illustrating this discrepancy between culture$_1$ and culture$_2$ with regard to the topics of face and politeness, decision making and leadership, Chapters 5–7 suggested concrete ways of combining first- and second-order notions of culture when analysing issues of identity, gender and work–life balance. One of the insights that strongly emerged from the analyses in all chapters was that any analytical approach that exclusively focuses on first-order notions of culture (as reflected, for example, in the quotes of some of our participants at the beginning of many chapters) is too limiting and runs the danger of stereotyping. Such a focus by no means captures the complexities of actual workplace interactions. For example, there is a wide variety of ways in which interlocutors negotiate face and politeness issues (Chapter 2), make decisions (Chapter 3), do leadership (Chapter 4), construct and negotiate their various identities (Chapter 5) and orient to gender norms and expectations on different levels (Chapter 6). Thus, an exclusive focus on culture$_1$ is unnecessarily restrictive and often does not move beyond lay people's perceptions and expectations (which themselves are often informed by stereotypes). Such an approach overlooks and largely ignores the diversity and complexity of actual interactional practice in situ.

Inquiries which are purely based on second-order notions of culture and which, as a consequence, do not incorporate and often ignore participants' views and interpretations are equally limiting. Although such an approach may succeed in capturing the complexities of actual workplace practices, it is quite likely that insights gained from research exclusively focusing on how culture$_2$ is constructed, enacted and negotiated on the micro-level of an interaction are of very little or no relevance to lay people. In fact, they may even perceive such an endeavour as problematic and disturbing since it does not incorporate their own perspective. This dilemma is of course further intensified by the use of the same terminology (i.e. 'culture') among researchers and lay people to refer to ultimately different (even if perhaps related) phenomena (Piller 2011; Baumann 1996; Hua 2014). But if we, as researchers, are interested in taking up real-life issues and if we want our research to have meaningful implications and applications outside of academia, we cannot ignore the perspective of those who have participated in our research.

In what follows, we briefly summarise and reflect on the relevance (and possible pitfalls) of researching culture$_1$ and culture$_2$ before discussing in more detail some of the ways in which these two notions of culture may be productively brought together and combined in academic inquiry.

Culture$_1$: More than a subsidiary aspect of 'culture' at work

Throughout this book we have provided evidence to support our arguments that first-order notions of culture – whether in the form of participants' perceptions or more generally held views and expectations – are an important aspect of 'culture' at work and should thus find consideration in academic inquiry. We have also established that culture$_1$ is a complex concept, and that it is defined in vastly different ways within the field. These first-order notions of culture may be reflected, constructed and negotiated by different sources and on different levels; they not only come to the fore in participants' accounts of their workplace experiences (as in Chapters 3, 5 and 7), but are also reflected (and reiterated) in the popular media (as in Chapters 2 and 6).

While we maintain that the notion of culture$_1$ is an important aspect of any attempt to better understand the complexities of language and 'culture' at work, we found this concept particularly useful with regard to the topic of identity construction (Chapter 5). In this chapter we showed that interlocutors' own views and self-perceptions constitute an important aspect of how they portray themselves – often in relation to their colleagues and clients from different socio-cultural backgrounds by mobilising perceived differences regarding culture$_1$. Our analyses and discussions in this chapter in particular highlighted some of the benefits of considering claims about first-order notions of culture in academic inquiry, as they are a crucial aspect of participants' meaning making of their everyday workplace encounters.

However, as we have argued throughout, over-relying or exclusively focusing on these first-order notions of culture runs the danger of stereotyping and unnecessarily (over)simplifying a rather complex picture (see also Cheng 2003; Scollon & Scollon 2001; Sarangi 1994a,b; Hartog 2006). As Holliday (2013: 4) maintains, participants' accounts are cultural products themselves, and 'what we choose to say and project may not actually represent how things are, but rather our dreams and aspirations about how we would like them to be, or the spin we place upon them to create the impact we wish to have on others'. This was particularly true with regard to issues of face and politeness (Chapter 2), decision making (Chapter 3) and leadership (Chapter 4), where our analyses provided ample evidence of interactional behaviour that contrasts and challenges the generalising (and often stereotypical) claims of our participants about their perceived behaviour. Rather than taking culture$_1$ accounts at face value and treating them as particularly authentic or authoritative, it is important to acknowledge that these claims are themselves primarily constructions of culture$_1$ and are thus necessarily subjective, interpretative and variable. Culture$_1$ is merely one part of a very complex picture, and culture$_2$ is another part of that picture.

These claims about culture$_1$, however, may provide useful entry points for identifying issues or topics that are of particular relevance to participants. And, as we have demonstrated in the previous chapters, in some instances participants' views are in line with observations of actual practice, while at other times they are at odds with them. For example, while there was some evidence in our corpus of behaviours that reinforce participants' culture$_1$ claims,[1] it is also crucial to acknowledge counter-evidence and to include those examples where participants' actual behaviour does not confirm their claims.[2] But, as we have emphasised in Chapter 7, even in those cases where claims about culture$_1$ and observations about culture$_2$ coincide with each other, this does not necessarily mean that a causal nexus exists between these two notions of culture, and that culture$_2$ practices are indeed a reflection of first-order notions of culture as our participants have often suggested.

Thus, although it may at times be tempting and perhaps even pervasive to exclusively draw on first-order notions of culture, such an approach, which purely focuses on culture$_1$, is analytically unproductive, because it does not generate new insights but rather (re-)produces and reinforces stereotypes. This thin line between culture$_1$ claims and stereotypes was particularly obvious in Chapters 4 and 6, where we explored the topics of leadership and gender. Chapter 4 has shown that in spite of the usefulness of incorporating statements about first-order culture into an analytic inquiry of leadership, exclusively focusing on participants' claims and general assumptions about culture$_1$ is too limiting and runs the danger of stereotyping (see also Schnurr et al. fc). Similar reservations apply to investigations of gender and its relation to first-order notions of culture. As we have demonstrated in Chapter 6, claims and generalisations about the perceived link between culture$_1$ and gender need to be treated with caution, as they tend to overlook the diversity of practices that can be observed on the local level. Clearly, there are almost endless ways in which interlocutors orient and respond to global gender norms and expectations, and there are equally many ways in which people do leadership – as individuals and/or as teams. It is thus important to move beyond an exclusive focus on first-order notions of culture and to pay more attention to localised practices and the specific context in which an interaction takes place – as captured in the notion of culture$_2$.

Culture₂: From general claims to more concrete and localised practices

Our discussions of various aspects of professional communication have identified several aspects of culture$_2$ that are particularly relevant for understanding participants' interactional practices: i) the specific norms, values and practices that are constantly developed, negotiated and shaped among the members of specific localised communities of practice (CofPs); ii) the different kinds of workplaces and professional industries in which participants interact; and iii) the specific interactional context in which an encounter takes place. Although there is clearly some overlap between these different aspects, we briefly discuss each of them in turn here.

We have argued throughout that the CofP is one of the most useful concepts for understanding participants' interactional practices, as it provides a framework for analysing actual (rather than perceived) behaviour in the local context in which it takes place. Rather than looking for grand explanations and making generalising claims (as is typical for culture$_1$ enactments), the CofP framework takes as a starting point the localised practices that have developed and are regularly enacted (and shaped) by its members. These practices that have emerged among the members of a specific group are much more dynamic and fluid than those (stereotypically) assigned to first-order culture, and an emphasis is put on acknowledging that the practices that characterise a particular CofP are actively shaped and constantly negotiated among members and thus regularly change (e.g. Holmes et al. 2007). Culture$_2$ practices are thus of a very different type than the relatively stable and static attributes often associated with culture$_1$.

These localised practices that are normative in a specific CofP are particularly useful for understanding the enormous variety of interactional behaviours that we observed across workplaces and working teams – for example, how members of different workplaces and different teams orient to and negotiate each other's face needs (Chapter 2) when refusing or disagreeing with each other. Some of these interactional norms developed in specific CofPs are in line with and reinforce general perceptions and assumptions associated with first-order notions of culture (e.g. the relatively unilateral decision making in Sabitha's team described in Chapter 3), while others challenge and reject them in favour of more localised ones (e.g. the sharing of leadership responsibilities among the team of geneticists described in Chapter 4). It is precisely these localised norms, practices and assumptions that have developed (and are constantly developing) in specific CofPs against which members' interactional behaviour has to be analysed and interpreted. Only then can we explain, for example, why Sabitha's relatively direct and potentially face-threatening way of giving directives to her subordinates is not perceived as such by them but is rather considered appropriate and normative behaviour (Chapter 2); or why the highly collaborative decision making style typically displayed by the team of geneticists (discussed in Chapters 3 and 4) is particularly effective in this professional context even though it challenges rather essentialist claims about expected decision making in the (allegedly) high power distance context of Hong Kong.

The second aspect of culture$_2$ that is of particular importance for analysing interlocutors' interactional behaviour is the professional context in which an encounter takes place. Throughout the various chapters we have looked at examples from a range of different professional contexts and different workplaces – including hospitals, an NGO, an IT consulting company, a large multinational financial corporation, several language learning centres and a District Council. One of the advantages of this eclectic mix, as we have argued in Chapter 1, is that it provides insights into the discursive and behavioural practices across different teams, workplaces and professional sectors without being too restrictive or limiting. Indeed, as our various examples have illustrated, there is an impressive diversity in the practices displayed by members of different professions, different workplaces and different teams. This was evident in our discussions in Chapter 6, where we looked at the ways in which global assumptions about the gender order and the roles of men and women are reflected in or challenged by interlocutors' actual behaviour, which in turn is a reflection (and at the same time construction) of the climate or characteristics of a specific workplace. Conducting case studies of two successful women managers of different language learning centres in Hong Kong, we observed remarkable differences in the ways in which these women get things done and make decisions in the specific professional context in which they act. We have argued that rather than explaining these practices with reference to culture$_1$, they need to be understood in the context of the specific workplace in which they occurred and as a response to the specific norms that characterise each particular context.

The third aspect of culture$_2$ is the importance of the specific local interactional context in which an encounter takes place. For example, in Chapter 5 we argued that although it is often claimed that interlocutors' identities are located in the wider socio-cultural context in which an interaction takes place (e.g. Kidd & Teagle 2002), the local context and the localised practices and expectations associated with particular roles to which interlocutors orient are important. The examples presented in Chapter 5 demonstrated how interlocutors set up and negotiate specific subject positions for themselves and each other throughout an interaction. These subject positions, which are created and negotiated on the very local level of an interaction, may shift throughout the encounter and the interactional behaviours displayed by interlocutors often challenge stereotypes and claims about culture$_1$. Rather, the specific activity type involved in an interaction, and the interactional rights and obligations associated with them, have an impact on the identities and roles that are available to interlocutors. Thus, the specific identities and roles that are mobilised, oriented to and constantly negotiated throughout an interaction are closely related to the specific context in which an interaction takes place and to specific activity types, which, in turn, form an integral part of culture$_2$.

In our analyses we have shown that it is very important to acknowledge the more local and emergent nature of these practices and norms as reflected in the notion of culture$_2$, rather than limiting analyses to often stereotypical culture$_1$ claims. The three aspects of culture$_2$ all have an impact on participants' interactional behaviours. However, these aspects do not form distinct and easily measurable entities but instead interact with, overlap and feed into each other in complex ways. Thus, explaining any kinds of observed behaviour by trying to relate it to relatively abstract and static first-order notions of culture is fraught with challenges and does not capture the complex and diverse behaviours that can be found in a specific interactional context. In the next section we address this point and discuss in more detail how first- and second-order notions of culture can productively be brought together in an analysis.

Bringing culture$_1$ and culture$_2$ together

We argued that rather than exclusively focusing on either first- or second-order notions of culture, it is analytically more productive to combine the two. In Chapters 5–7, we provided concrete suggestions on how this might be accomplished. We do not want to claim, however, that the analytical practices and processes that we have employed here are exhaustive; clearly, other ways of analysing and combining culture$_1$ and culture$_2$ are possible and should be explored by future research.

In the Introduction we formulated several questions about conceptualising and approaching these different notions of culture. We asked: What exactly is the relationship between first-order and second-order culture? How can we usefully draw on this distinction in our research? And how can we utilise it in meaningful ways so that it enables us to move forward with our research agenda in intercultural communication? We will now return to these questions and answer each of them in the light of the insights gained in the previous chapters.

Regarding the first question about the relationship between culture$_1$ and culture$_2$, we have shown that both constitute an integral part of what is commonly referred to as 'culture', and both are important for an understanding of 'what is going on' in the workplace context. Each order of culture is distinct in the kinds of insights it provides and in the analytical values it generates. While first-order culture captures participants' own interpretations and perceptions of their workplace realities, second-order notions of culture are analytical concepts that assist researchers in developing a better understanding of observed practices. It is important to reiterate that both culture$_1$ and culture$_2$ are important for academic inquiry, since they both produce (sometimes different but nevertheless) complementary insights into workplace realities. We believe that neither one should take precedence over the other, and both should be considered in any attempt to understand 'what is going on'. While both notions are clearly relevant, the question arises of whether culture$_1$ and culture$_2$ are indeed distinct analytical categories or whether they influence, and perhaps sometimes overlap with and feed off, each other in complex ways. Although we are not able to answer this question comprehensively here, we will briefly discuss some of the insights gained from our analyses in the previous chapters in relation to this important issue.

In Chapters 2–4, our analyses and discussions established that often a discrepancy exists between first-order culture (as reflected, for example, in the claims made by our participants) and second-order culture (as reflected in our in-depth analyses of actual workplace interactions). These differences seem to point to the different nature of each of these concepts and suggest that they are quite distinct in the sense that they capture and refer to fundamentally different phenomena (i.e. perceptions versus actual practice). However, this assumption was to some extent challenged by our findings in Chapter 7, where we observed a considerable overlap between participants' claims about work–life balance and their actual practices. In spite of these overlaps, we argue that we need to be careful with assuming that a causal nexus exists between culture$_1$ and culture$_2$. Nevertheless, these observations indicate some kind of relationship between the two concepts, which, in this specific case at least, seem to be connected and perhaps reciprocally influential.

Questions around the nature of first- and second-order meanings and the relationship among them, as well as the most productive ways of incorporating and combining both in analytic inquiry, are also part of an ongoing debate that politeness researchers are currently engaging in (e.g. the contributions in Kienpointner 1999 and Kadar & Roe 2012; Haugh 2012; Terkourafi 2011). Although it would go too far here to reproduce this debate, it seems that some of the challenges politeness researchers are facing are similar to the ones that research on intercultural and cross-cultural communication is dealing with, such as the necessity to 'carefully deconstruct' 'the first–second order distinction [. . .]' in regards to both its epistemological and ontological loci', and to avoid 'treating the first–second order distinction as a simplistic dichotomy' and instead explore ways of combining both (Haugh 2012: 114). There are clearly many overlaps between current thinking in politeness research and the analytical framework for understanding 'culture' we have proposed here, and we hope that our elaborations will contribute to initiating a dialogue between the two fields of inquiry. Such cross-fertilisation of ideas and approaches has the strong potential to assist researchers in both areas to not only theorise about first- and second-order notions (of either concept) and their mutual relationship, but also to develop means for operationalising the ways in which these concepts may inform and advance academic inquiry.

Coming back to the second question about how we can usefully draw on the distinction between first- and second-order notions of culture in our research, our analyses demonstrated the necessity of taking a critical stance towards first-order notions of culture and moving away from an exclusive focus on it, while at the same time refraining from discarding instantiations of culture$_1$ as merely stereotypical. However, at the same time, rather than only making relatively localised observations about specific discursive practices by individuals in a particular workplace or CofP, we need to find ways of combining both and of linking participants' claims and perceptions of first-order culture to locally negotiated and constructed second-order culture in order to generate genuinely new and relevant insights into the fascinating but incredibly complex relationship between language and 'culture' at work. Only then can we capture the dynamics of language and 'culture' in workplace interactions.

Drawing on politeness research, one possible way of moving forwards may be to 'orient [. . .] towards the interactional achievement' (Haugh 2007: 304) of first-order culture and to explore how underlying assumptions about what exactly is or makes up a particular 'culture' may inform and may be enacted in participants' (interactional) behaviour. Such an approach, however, involves close cooperation between participants and researchers, and also implies a critical re-thinking of the role of the analyst (see also Haugh 2013). A similar approach, which relies less on participants' cooperation, is proposed by Terkourafi (2011: 163). Transferring her suggestions about 'politeness' to our issue with 'culture', this would entail starting with an examination of 'canonical understandings' of culture$_1$ – for example by referring to 'didactic and/or prescriptive works from different parts of the world and from antiquity to this day' (Terkourafi 2011: 163). The culture$_1$ identified through such an exercise could then be used to develop a theory of culture$_2$ that incorporates core elements of culture$_1$. Another possibility mentioned in the Introduction is to focus on the struggle over first-order notions of culture and to explore the ways in which lay people utilise the term 'culture' to make sense of their everyday workplace experiences (see also Moon 2010; and Watts 2003 for a similar argument about politeness). Based on the insights gained in the previous chapters we would add to this suggestion that it is crucially important to incorporate second-order culture to an analysis of these struggles. Thus, one possible way forward might be to complement an analysis of lay people's struggles over the term (and its implications on their practices) with an analysis of their actual practices, similar to what we have done in this book.

Regarding the closely related third question, then, of how we can utilise this distinction between first- and second-order culture in meaningful ways so that it enables us to move forward with our research agenda in intercultural and cross-cultural communication, we have identified and described several benefits of bringing together and combining them. First, such an approach facilitates identifying and overcoming the discrepancy that often exists between participants' reflections on and perceptions of the role of 'culture' on their workplace performance, and the actual practices displayed by them. Second, such endeavours remind us of the limitations of exclusively relying on participants' views which produce a relatively static, one-sided and hence rather limited and one-dimensional picture of what is commonly referred to as 'culture' at work that simply cannot capture the diversity and complexity of actual practice. Third, making a distinction between first- and second-order notions of culture provides useful analytical tools and processes to challenge some of the prevailing assumptions about 'culture' in a specific local context. This is not only useful when trying to understand relatively localised discursive practices (such as decision making, disagreeing and refusing), but can also help generating new insights into more global phenomena, such as gender, leadership and work–life balance, and the ways in which 'the global' and 'the local' are intertwined with each other. Thus, both first- and second-order notions of culture should be considered in an academic inquiry about language and 'culture' at work, and we believe that neither of them is more central or more important in such an endeavour.

Looking ahead

We hope that our analyses and arguments have illustrated that culture$_1$ and culture$_2$ are useful analytical concepts, and we hope that they will be picked up and further developed by future research. This distinction is important and links to the crucial question of 'what "culture" are we (as analysts or lay people) actually researching and contemplating?'. We believe that the research and the ideas presented here help address these questions and have several implications for future research – both conceptually and methodologically.

Conceptually, we have proposed one possible way of addressing the analytical dilemma of researching language and 'culture' at work. Drawing on our corpus of workplace discourse collected in a range of different workplaces in Hong Kong, we demonstrated the necessity of distinguishing between different orders of culture to address this dilemma, and we invite future research to test those propositions and to apply this distinction to other data in different contexts. Such an endeavour is also likely to generate further insights into the complex relationship between the two, thereby continuing the discussion we have started here.

This conceptual distinction also has some methodological consequences. For example, different kinds of data are more likely to provide insights into the different orders of culture. Interviews and popular texts (in the form of self-help, advice books or media texts (both written and spoken)) proved useful in our research to illustrate first-order notions of culture, while recorded authentic workplace interactions (supplemented by participant observation) were an excellent source for gaining insights into the ways in which second-order notions of culture are enacted and negotiated. The methodological choices associated with each type of data, of course, crucially depend on the focus of inquiry.

While we advocate more awareness in terms of what kinds of data provide insights into the different orders of 'culture', we do not want to suggest that this is an 'either–or question'. On the contrary, as our own analyses showed, much can be gained by combining different types of data – such as interviews, interactional recordings, observations and written documents. In fact, we propose that future research on language and 'culture' should draw on various data sources in order to combine first- and second-order investigations – for example, by more systematically considering and incorporating participants' views as reflected in their interviews.

Thus, rather than exclusively focusing on either culture$_1$ or culture$_2$, one potentially very interesting and rewarding avenue for future research could be to further explore the dilemma between participants' and analysts' understanding of 'culture' at work and to focus on this analytical struggle. It may well be that by exploring this struggle at the interface between first- and second-order culture we will learn more about the relationship between the two and the ways in which they impact on, contribute to and feed off each other. Aiming to explore how 'culture' (in both its first- and second-order meanings) is enacted and oriented to by interlocutors has the potential to further our understanding of the complexities of language and 'culture' at work.

Notes

1 This was particularly the case of asking for advice and being expected to be told what to do (Chapter 2), some instances of unilateral decision making (Chapter 3) and autocratic leadership (Chapter 4).
2 This was shown with regard to refusing or disagreeing with one's superiors (Chapter 2), engaging in collaborative decision making (Chapter 3) and sharing leadership responsibilities (Chapter 4).

References

Baumann, Gerd (1996). *Contesting Culture. Discourses of Identity in Multi-Ethnic London.* Cambridge, UK: Cambridge University Press.

Cheng, Winnie (2003). *Intercultural Conversation.* Amsterdam: Benjamins.

Hartog, Jennifer (2006). Beyond 'misunderstandings' and 'cultural stereotypes'. Analysing intercultural communication. In Kristin Bühring & Jan ten Thije (eds), *Beyond Misunderstanding. Linguistic Analyses of Intercultural Communication.* Amsterdam: Benjamins. 175–88.

Haugh, Michael (2013). Im/politeness, social practice and the participation order. *Journal of Pragmatics* 58: 52–72.

Haugh, Michael (2012). Epilogue: The first–second order distinction in face and politeness research. Chinese 'face' and im/politeness. An introduction. *Journal of Politeness Research* 8.1: 111–34.

Haugh, Michael (2007). The discursive challenge to politeness research: An interactional alternative. *Journal of Politeness Research* 3.2: 95–317.

Holliday, Adrian (2013). *Understanding Intercultural Communication. Negotiating a Grammar of Culture.* Abingdon: Routledge.

Holmes, Janet, Stephanie Schnurr & Meredith Marra (2007). Leadership and communication: Discursive evidence of a workplace culture change. *Discourse and Communication* 1.4: 433–51.

Hua, Zhu (2014). *Exploring Intercultural Communication. Language in Action.* Abingdon: Routledge.

Kadar, Daniel & Keith Roe (2012). Chinese 'face' and im/politeness. An introduction. *Journal of Politeness Research* 8.1: 1–10.

Kidd, Warren & Alison Teagle (2002). *Culture and Identity.* Houndmills: Palgrave.

Kienpointner, Manfred (ed.) (1999). *Pragmatics. Special Issue on Ideologies of Politeness* 9.1.

Moon, Dreama (2010). Critical reflections on culture and critical intercultural communication. In Thomas Nakayama & Rona Tamiko Halualani (eds), *The Handbook of Critical Intercultural Communication.* Oxford: Blackwell. 34–52.

Piller, Ingrid (2011). *Intercultural Communication. A Critical Introduction.* Edinburgh: Edinburgh University Press.

Sarangi, Srikant (1994b). Accounting for mismatches in intercultural selection interviews. *Multilingua* 13.1/2: 163–94.

Sarangi, Srikant (1994a). Intercultural or not? Beyond celebration of cultural differences in miscommunication analysis. *Pragmatics* 4.3: 409–27.

Schnurr, Stephanie, Angela Chan, Joelle Loew & Olga Zayts (fc). Leadership and culture: When stereotypes meet actual workplace practice. To appear in Cornelia Ilie & Stephanie Schnurr (eds), *Challenging Leadership Stereotypes through Discourse: Power, Management and Gender.* Delhi: Springer.

Scollon, Ron & Suzanne Wong Scollon (2001) *Intercultural Communication. A Discourse Approach.* Malden, MA: Blackwell.

Terkourafi, Marina (2011). From politeness$_1$ to politeness$_2$. Tracking norms of im/politeness across time and space. *Journal of Politeness Research* 7: 159–85.

Watts, Richard (2003). *Politeness*. Cambridge, UK: Cambridge University Press.

Transcription conventions

[. . .]	parts omitted from transcript
–	unfinished or broken-off word or utterance
?	rising intonation
.	a stopping fall in tone
,	continuing intonation (like when enumerating things)
!	an animated and emphatic tone
(.)	just noticeable pause
(0.2)	measurable pause; the number inside the brackets indicates the duration of the pause in seconds
::	prolongation of sound
((xxx))	transcriber's comments
(love)	not entirely audible speech; the words inside the brackets represent the transcriber's best guess
(xxx)	inaudible speech
=	latching-on of two utterances without a pause
<u>love</u>	word spoken with emphasis
↑↓	a shift into a higher or a lower pitch in the utterance-part immediately following the arrow
p(h)etty	laughter particles that occur within speech
[	the beginning of an overlapping word or utterance
]	the end of an overlapping word or utterance
° °	a word or an utterance said much quieter than the surrounding utterance
HUGE	especially loud sounds in relation to the surrounding talk
??	unknown speaker
.h	inhalation

Index